HANS-WERNER GENSICHEN

translated by
Herbert J. A. Bouman

We Condemn

How Luther and 16th-Century Lutheranism

Condemned False Doctrine

CONCORDIA PUBLISHING HOUSE • SAINT LOUIS

Original title: *Damnamus*

Copyright 1955 by Lutherisches Verlagshaus

Herbert Renner, Berlin-Grunewald

for the German edition

Copyright 1967 by Concordia Publishing House, St. Louis, Missouri

for the English edition

Translator: Herbert J. A. Bouman

Library of Congress Catalog Card No. 67-17792

Concordia Publishing House, St. Louis, Missouri

Concordia Publishing House Ltd., London, E. C. 1

MANUFACTURED IN THE UNITED STATES OF AMERICA

Preface to the English Edition

To issue in translation, but otherwise unchanged, a book first published a decade ago is a venture fraught with manifold risks. During this time scholarly research has not remained static. This is true both with reference to the historical antecedents of the subject matter and also with reference to the main chapters of the book. Quite apart from other circumstances, the fact that the author's teaching field has meanwhile become something very much different from church history and the history of dogma may serve at least in part to explain why the author found it impossible to subject the book to a needed revision. Yet the gracious and generally favorable reception accorded the study in its original German version has given the author the courage to permit the publication of an English edition in unaltered form.

For a better understanding of the book's purpose the reader is asked to bear two things in mind.

1. This strictly historical study has no intention of prejudging the dogmatic consideration that must be given to the questions concerning doctrinal and ecclesiastical fellowship. Undoubtedly these reflections in the history of theology demand an application as a matter of principle. However, this study cannot itself make this application, if only because this task will be relevant in ever new ways whenever it confronts a new situation, in the sense of the distinction which Ernst Sommerlath formulated between the "identity" of the church and her message and the "variability" which results from the church's openness for the changing historical scene. "Both, the church's identity with itself and its variability, connected with each other and related to each other, constitute the true continuity of the church without which its catholicity cannot be maintained" ("Die Ka-

tholizitaet der Kirche," in *Stat crux dum volvitur orbis. Fest-schrift fuer H. Lilje,* ed. G. Hoffmann and K. H. Rengstorf. Berlin: Lutherisches Verlagshaus, 1959, pp. 148 – 158).

2. As regards the theological and historical content of this book, the author is grateful to Hermann Sasse for his suggestions *(Lutherische Blaetter,* IX, 53 [1957], 46 – 51) and would like to call attention to at least two necessary supplementary items.

Werner Elert's important work *Eucharist and Church Fellowship in the First Four Centuries,* which appeared too late to be utilized by the author, should by all means be consulted for the historical background of the problem of condemnations in the early church. Elert's book not only contains important historical materials to supplement the author's study, but also demonstrates that significant parallels existed between the events of the fourth century and those of the sixteenth.

The author's investigation was thematically limited to the Lutheran churches of the 16th century. However, this horizon will be considerably enlarged if, as Sasse properly suggests, the history of the rejection of false teaching within the Reformed churches is included, in addition to a treatment of the Anabaptists and Antitrinitarians as well as the intra-Reformed controversies of a later date, especially in Holland and in England.

The author may be permitted to conclude these remarks for the English edition with the closing sentence of the Preface to the German edition: "As negative as the title may sound and the subject may appear to be, it was and is the purpose of this study to make a modest positive contribution to a better understanding among churches by means of this investigation of a controversial historical question."

Heidelberg, September 1965   Hans-Werner Gensichen

Contents

Preface to the English Edition   iii

Introduction   vii

Part I: The Antecedents   1

    Chapter 1. The Anathemas in the Bible and in the Ancient Church   3

    Chapter 2. Main Lines of Development in the Middle Ages   15

    Chapter 3. Luther's Roman Trial as an Example of the Attack on Heretics in the Late Middle Ages   23

Part II: Luther   29

    Chapter 4. The Antithesis Against the Roman Verdict   31

    Chapter 5. Doctrine – Pure Doctrine – False Doctrine   43

    Chapter 6. The Church of the Pure Doctrine   55

    Chapter 7. Significance, Authority, and Limits of Rejection   61

Part III: The Period of the Augsburg Confession (1530 – 1565)   81

    Chapter 8. The Condemnations in the Augsburg Confession   83

    Chapter 9. Luther, Melanchthon, and the Swiss   109

    Chapter 10. Condemnation as Practiced by the Gnesio-Lutherans   123

Part IV: The Era of Concord (1565 – 1583)   153

    Chapter 11. The Controversy About Condemnations and the Preliminaries to the Formula of Concord   155

    Chapter 12. The Controversy over Condemnations in Strasbourg   175

    Chapter 13. The Formula of Concord and the *Damnamus*   189

Introduction

Any experience with, or consideration of, the theological and ecclesiastical problems involved in interdenominational relations must necessarily lead to reflection in two opposite directions: on the one hand, to that which binds the denominations together and, on the other hand, to that which separates them. We may find the accents to be quite unevenly distributed. A time in which the desire for church union is strong will consider the question concerning the factors which the churches have in common and which bind them together more important than concern about the divisive factors. An era of denominational self-sufficiency will pay more attention to erecting and defending barriers than to finding means of dialog and approach among churches. It will not be possible, of course, to place one side of the issue into the foreground without injury to the other. Such a procedure would do harm to the whole matter under discussion. Both honesty and objective consideration are endangered where the required double movement is cut short in favor of one of the two points of view. This is no less true for the interdenominational dialog. Both the experiences of centuries in the Lutheran-Reformed debate and the results of ecumenical endeavors to date have made it sufficiently clear that every serious disruption of the balance between these points of view has undeniably put the value of the interchange in doubt. Where for the sake of an ideal of unity men think they can bypass or delete the reality of divisive factors the results are generally no less unsatisfactory than in places where a scrupulous insistence on denominational peculiarities blurs the vision for what churches have in common.

Under such circumstances it would seem that the condemnatory judgments in the Lutheran Symbols, especially those directed against the Reformed, must give rise to the gravest misgivings. Does this not clearly represent a state of affairs that paralyzes a proper consideration of interdenominational relations and that brings the dialog to a dead end? Does this not clearly and seriously upset the desired balance affecting the method of discussion in the direction of making the divisive factors absolute? Does not the fact of denominational division here lead to conclusions so radical that the possibility of a dialog becomes altogether illusory? How is it possible to engage in an honest discussion if one side begins by solemnly condemning the other side? And if, in answer to such questions, attention would be called to the fact that, after all, there has been an ongoing Lutheran-Reformed dialog, it could still be asserted in rebuttal that the Lutherans have not been completely faithful to the battle line drawn by the Lutheran Confessions.

If these misgivings are justified, it would be not only desirable but prerequisite for the interdenominational dialog of our day to be freed from the burden of those condemnations. Please note: Where this request is made today, it is not at all motivated by a falsely applied concept of tolerance as in the Enlightenment, which intentionally does away with every distinction between true and false doctrine and no longer dares to be sure of the thesis because it is afraid of the antithesis. Rather, this gives voice to the deep-seated concern that the specific rejections of Reformed teachings, as expressed in a part of the Lutheran Symbols, are no longer applicable to the confessional status of our time, so that their intensely serious verdict seems to be spoken into a vacuum. Is it perhaps possible that a repetition of these condemnations in our time will erect "church divisive" barriers in areas where only "theological" differences exist, or where, to quote Karl Barth, "the opposition of the earlier confessions of two churches has been made obsolete by a new and common confession and has become a mere difference in theological thinking"? [1] Consequently, is it possible that for the sake of a "pet theological theory that has run into a blind alley" we should deny church fellowship to those who are in truth our brethren? [2]

Certainly we must give these questions the most serious consideration. Even if the claim were made that since the con-

fessional discussions of the Reformation age the situation of the
theological dialog has not changed decisively in its essential
points, we should have to ask all the more emphatically whether
those marks of cleavage were not unjustly established already
then and are therefore not all the more in need of removal. In
any case we shall achieve clear results only if the doctrinal issues
are themselves carefully examined. Unless we are badly mistaken, the disposition of this problem is still a long way off, and
its solution dare not be prejudiced by premature decisions.

Without, however, becoming guilty of a premature judgment, we may certainly be permitted to consider the problem
of pronouncing condemnations from another point of view, and
indeed it may even be necessary to do so. Before the question
regarding the significance and validity of the individual doctrinal antitheses is decided and before the attempt is made to
understand if and under what circumstances it is still possible
to reaffirm the *Damnamus* of the Lutheran Symbols, another
question should be considered. It will be necessary to ask what,
exactly, these confessions meant with their words of condemnation, for what purpose they were spoken, and how they were
understood and received. Without clarifying this historical question it will not be possible to provide a clean-cut decision regarding the present-day evaluation of condemnatory judgments.

The fact that the *Damnamus* has become a part of the Lutheran Symbols lends it a special dignity and isolates it from the
countless number of private theological opinions. It may not be
set aside as a disagreeable or irrelevant appendix. But this does
not mean that it calls for blind acceptance, as if it were an unalterable and timelessly valid decision. Thus we are not some-
how released from the obligation carefully to isolate the meaning
of these condemnations within the framework of the conditions
of their own time, of their relation to what precedes and what
follows them, and last but not least, of their controversial character. Like the confession itself, the *Damnamus* stands beneath
the double aspect which is described at the beginning and at
the end of the Formula of Concord and which serves as the over-
arching span of the whole and holds it together: It is a witness
in the presence of God, a confession for present and future generations, yes, in view of the judgment seat of Christ, and yet also,
in sober awareness of their time-bound character, the confes-

sional statements are "witnesses and expositions of the faith, setting forth how at various times the Holy Scriptures were understood in the church of God by contemporaries with reference to controverted articles, and how contrary teachings were rejected and condemned." [3]

It is this latter aspect with which a historical study must primarily concern itself. Without disrupting its connection with the first aspect, we may still allot to it due consideration, also in view of the problem connected with the condemnations. That is to say: A historical study cannot decide the question whether and to what extent the condemnations in the Lutheran Symbols can still become an "event" for us in such a way that we shall be bound by them in the presence of God and for all time. The study can only lead us up to that decisive question, but that much it can and should accomplish. It may have the confidence that nothing was in vain in the multi-layered and complicated history of the condemnations, including the often truly distasteful controversies that raged because of them. The historical approach surely may not offer this history as a collection of models for wrong and right conduct with respect to the problem of rejecting opposing doctrine. It may hope, however, that all those battles and decisions have some relevance for the questions and answers of the present—just because they are concerned for the one truth of the Gospel, in spite of all human inadequacy and folly, and because even in these battles the connection with the history of the church as the body of Christ was never completely broken.

Notes to Introduction

[1] *Church Dogmatics*, trans. G. T. Thomson, Harold Knight (New York: Charles Scribner's Sons, 1956), Vol. I, Part 2, p. 632.

[2] Hans Joachim Iwand, "Lutherische Kirche?" *Evangelische Theologie*, 1947, p. 388.

[3] Solid Declaration XII, 40; Epitome, Comprehensive Summary, 8. All quotations from the Lutheran Symbols are cited according to *The Book of Concord, The Confessions of the Evangelical Lutheran Church*, trans. and ed. by Theodore G. Tappert, in collaboration with Jaroslav Pelikan, Robert H. Fischer, Arthur C. Piepkorn (Philadelphia: Muhlenberg Press, 1959).

Part 1

The Antecedents

Chapter 1

The Anathemas in the Bible and in the Ancient Church

The rejection of false doctrines and false teachers is manifestly one of the points in which the Reformation has preserved a certain continuity with the pre-Reformation church. The *Damnamus* of the Lutheran Symbols clearly echoes the *Damnamus* or other rejection formulas by means of which the church had for centuries delimited itself against heresies. That this echo was not unintentional is evident already from a fleeting glance at, for example, the condemnations in the Augsburg Confession. Also the condemnatory judgments pronounced against the Reformed are apparently, according to their form and position in the confession, only a special case to begin with, in a long line of antitheses that must be traced back to the Middle Ages and to the ancient church. This does indeed presuppose that this continuity cannot be an unbroken one, since it, too, has received its normative principle from the new era brought about by Luther. Here, too, it is Luther's stature and work that form the connecting link with the old only by means of a decisive break. For a correct understanding of the Lutheran *Damnamus* attention must therefore be paid both to the points of contact and to the gaps between Luther's new approach and the heritage of pre-Reformation times.

At the same time it must not be overlooked that the condemnatory judgments of Luther and the Lutheran Church are always accompanied by references to Bible passages, so that also for the *Damnamus* the support of the Scriptures and the practice of the first church is claimed. This is not the place to investigate the validity of this claim in individual cases or to present a comprehensive study of the attack on false doctrine in the earliest days of Christianity. Still, one might be tempted to proceed from the New Testament anathema as the model for the condemnations of the church in later times and draw a continuous line to the Lutheran Church. Such a procedure would soon demonstrate, however, that the anathema does not automatically furnish a sort of common denominator for the whole practice of condemnations from the Jewish synagog down to Lutheranism or even to the canon law of today. The Reformation anathema follows lines of development different from that of the past, though absorbing some of its essential features. Similarly, the Reformation anathema becomes the fountainhead of equally divergent currents in the future, which appropriate it and yet largely reshape its meaning.

The religio-historical context into which the Biblical anathema belongs is without question that of blessing and cursing.[1] But already in the Old Testament this framework is broken through. In the extra-Biblical world the curse is a "word of consecration," which "requires no gods nor spirits to execute it"[2] and hence accomplishes in itself what it says, but this typically magical feature was already overcome in ancient Israel, at least as far as the "cherem," or "curse," is concerned, which comes into consideration as the prototype of the anathema.[3] Here it is not man who by his decree "evokes" constructive or destructive results, blessing or curse. Rather, the formula of excommunication merely confirms that a matter or a person has come irrevocably under God's sentence. Thus the "banning" in the Old Testament is an explicit and conscious surrender to God's disposal, especially to His wrath. The Septuagint uses other terms beside anathema to translate the Hebrew original. One such word is "destruction" ($\dot{\alpha}\pi\dot{\omega}\lambda\epsilon\iota\alpha$).[4] This suggests an additional feature by which the Biblical "ban" is distinguished from extra-Biblical usage. The latter, as shown by the Greek curse-tablets of Megara, aims at partial damage to the person concerned, while the former deals with the possibility that God's punitive action will become effective in its comprehensive destructive force.

Not until postexilic Judaism was the ban established in its religious and social setting in a way that became so significant for later times. The synagog or its representatives assume the authority to fix the boundaries of synagog fellowship by excommunication. The traditional formulas show that occasionally the thought of a magical operation of the curse may also be involved, but it never becomes decisively significant.[5] The consciousness that the action is taken by God's command and for His sake remains decisive. One who violates God's honor by transgressing His law or by dishonoring His ambassadors has become subject to His punishment. For that very reason he can no longer be regarded as a full-fledged member of the synagog. For an evaluation of the New Testament anathema it is significant that at this point a twofold development begins. One who has been placed under the ban is not yet outside the synagog like the heretics, who are entirely excluded [6] and for whom there is no participation in eternal life but only the damnation of hell. Three times a day the Jew prayed, "Let no hope be given the apostates . . . and may the heretics *(Minim)* perish in a moment." [7] On the contrary, one who has been placed under the ban, simple or intensified, is by no means to be excommunicated from the synagog, but every effort is to be made to keep him and to lead him back to the *Torah.* In this way the ban obtains a "medicinal" sense. The punitive character is modified by the aim at improvement. The Old Testament surrender to God's judicial wrath, which removed the culprit from all human intervention, has become a means of communal discipline within the synagog.[8] For centuries both lines of development run parallel in Judaism. Not until the beginning of the ninth century is there a combination of exclusion from the synagog and of the intensified ban.[9]

It is evident that against this background the New Testament anathema [10] is seen to be bound up with, yet also to break through, the traditional framework. Neither ascribes any magical effect to the banning formula; in fact, Jesus forbids cursing as an invasion of God's prerogative. Neither in the Old nor in the New Testament is it a man or a community of men who make the disposal, but the matter is turned over to God. For both periods the anathema reveals the profound cleavage between God and man, a cleavage that is bound to have its consequences also for human fellowships. But all of this takes place under basically changed presuppositions. "From its Old Testament roots the Biblical anathema grows out of the conviction of the pious man that he is obligated to separate himself from the impious man for the preservation of God's honor according to the measure of the revelation of His will in the Law. Hence the anathema presupposes the finality of the Torah-piety. By revealing God as the Father of mercies Jesus rejected this kind of anathema." [11] Jesus Himself stepped into the breach between God and man. It is now no longer a matter of God's rightful judgment asserting itself, but of His grace.

Precisely for this reason the anathema has not been abolished in the New Testament fellowship. It becomes the mark of separation that is in force when the saving fellowship with God is sought in some other place than in the fellowship with Christ and His body, in other words, when the finality of Christ's redemptive act is knowingly and intentionally attacked within the community. The manner in which the New Testament speaks of the anathema [12] shows that it involves an extreme case, something that should not be possible in Christ's community at all. Occasionally the matter itself is spoken of without using the term "anathema" [13] — perhaps to avoid any impression of resorting to a curse that works by magic, or of taking disciplinary measures that might be placed on a level with the ban executed within the synagog.[14] For where the anathema becomes operative the means of pastoral guidance and discipline have been exhausted. It is at this point that the New Testament anathema goes beyond the application of the ban in the synagog, while it might still be compared with the act of exclusion from the synagog (although the term "cherem," which corresponds to "anathema," is not used). The New Testament anathema is exclusively "a protective device, not a disciplinary measure." [15] It is a protective measure which may be necessary for the sake of the community if its foundation has been attacked. It declares that the culprit has placed himself outside the fellowship of the body of Christ (Tit. 3:10f.). The fact that the community can be in the position of giving expression to this state of affairs is nothing else than the final consequence of an uncompromising faith in the one Lord—of that faith which the Lord Himself creates in His community and which He must now also expect of His disciples. Thus also in the New Testament thesis and antithesis are inseparable.

It belongs to the nature of the "extreme case" pictured above that it by no means applies to all situations in which schisms (αἱρέσεις) upset and disturb the community, and certainly not in cases where one of its members falls prey to "works of the flesh" and repudiates his calling by disobedience in life and activity. The situation in Corinth, for example, that Paul had in view when he wrote his first letter to that church, is clearly characterized by certain cleavages, but Paul does not feel driven to such drastic polemics as against the Galatian false teachers. The distinction between errors that threaten the foundation of the church and going astray in less weighty matters, in general the distinction between false teaching and mistaken belief, between heresy and erroneous opinion, so important later on, is in any case suggested already in the New Testament[16] and is to be presupposed for an understanding of the anathema. It is true, the anathema in its essence leaves no room for a distinction between persons and things, a matter that created problems for the 16th century and later. This is so because the anathema is not to be regarded as a human action in which the scope of its validity could be limited, but its purpose is to place the whole man before the face of God. In this connection the New Testament knows just as little about a conflict between truth and love. "Truth ($\dot{\alpha}\lambda\dot{\eta}\vartheta\epsilon\iota\alpha$) is possessed only in the circuit of the divine love ($\dot{\alpha}\gamma\dot{\alpha}\pi\eta$), and love only in the $\dot{\alpha}\lambda\dot{\eta}\vartheta\epsilon\iota\alpha$ of the divine truth of the saving revelation."[17] The anathema, too, has its place in the area of "doing the truth" and therefore does not violate the boundaries set by the law of love.

In view of the fact that the New Testament anathema is so closely linked with the truth and the reality of the revelation of Christ and receives its justification and its dimensions from this revelation alone, the question would naturally arise in the course of the church's emergence concerning the norm and decisive court which were available for such a verdict. It will hardly do to speak quite so confidently, as is done in Roman Catholic circles,[18] of the "principle of authority promoted by Paul" and of the "doctrine that has been handed down from the beginning" as of the weapons that have been effective in primitive Christianity and up to the present for the fight against heretics. The oldest history of the church shows how fluid the boundaries could be between "orthodoxy" and heresy.[19] We must, of course, beware of relativizing too freely. False doctrine in primitive Christianity is surely not only what was subsequently labeled as such by the victorious party in the controversies of the first centuries. The contrast between false doctrine and orthodoxy already permeates the New Testament itself. Certainly rival groups engaged in church politics and fighting for control have left their traces and thus blur the original picture. But it is equally certain that the "doctrine" the heretics attacked did not come into being and maintain itself merely by virtue of the law of the victor. Regardless of how the Pauline authorship of the Pastoral Epistles is viewed, what they call "sound doctrine" was in essence present and known already in the oldest Christian communities, even where they were not aware of any immediate threat from false doctrines. The early development of confessional formulas, which are certainly not rooted only in the attempt to combat heresy,[20] shows that faith has an urge to find expression and formulation in words, without necessarily falling prey to becoming frozen in doctrinal formulas. Also the use of the term ἀλήθεια ("truth") in Paul's epistles (e. g., 2 Thess. 2:10ff.; Gal. 5:7; 2 Cor. 6:7; 13:8; etc.) grants insight into this quite self-evident linking of the reality of the new life experienced by faith with its expression in the new doctrine, which must then also be fenced off from other doctrines and must for that very reason press for a normative, authoritative formulation.[21] To do justice to the further development of the church's war on false doctrine it will be necessary not to underestimate all this and not to overemphasize unnecessarily the cleavage between the alleged "elasticity of the Pauline spirit," his "tolerance . . . which regards hardly anyone as a heretic," [22] and the subsequent belligerent orthodoxy. It must, indeed, not be overlooked that the later development departs in decisive aspects from the apostolic age.

It will not be necessary to pursue in detail the factual shaping of doctrinal development in the ancient church. As regards the demarcation over against false doctrine, it was determined in later periods principally by three closely related trends which did not become fully effective until the Middle Ages but which are noticeable already in the ancient church. These trends are: the objectivization of doctrine, the institutionalizing of the church in conjunction with an increasing centralization of all church power in the Roman bishop, and the progressive legalism of the church, particularly in punitive procedures.

Not exclusively, yet to a very large degree, it is just this fight against heresy that gives impetus to the development in this threefold direction. In the first place, by an incontestable inner necessity and propriety the Scriptural canon is established, which is to safeguard the witness of the apostolic age in its uniqueness over against the arbitrariness of current opinion. Next to the canon there arises the *regula fidei*, the "norm of truth," as a summation of the total New Testament witness. However, already the Apologists tend to domesticate the faith in the soil of ideological discussion. The faith loses its offensive character and becomes accessible to natural thought processes. For this reason the canon and the creed are associated in increasing measure not only with the living witness of the reality of Christ, but also with a legalistically manipulated doctrinal norm that could be controlled by reason. Next to the emergence of a questionable ethic of works this doctrinal legalism is the price the developing church has to pay for the demolition of heresy.

Corresponding to the development of a norm of doctrine is that of the church's teaching authority, which is in charge of the norm. The trend toward the creation of tangible guarantees reaches its goal in the establishment of the apostolic succession, which enables Rome particularly to guarantee its claims of primacy. Only where the historically unbroken line of bishops proves continuity with the apostolic age can the norm of doctrine be managed properly and heresy be defined as such. Since both doctrinal supremacy and the chief disciplinary authority belong to the monarchical episcopate, a mere rebellion against the episcopal guardians of the apostolic tradition is enough to evoke the punishment of the church. Cyprian calls disobedience to the priest of God *(sacerdos Dei)*, the judge in Christ's place, the source of all heresy and all schismatic inclinations.[23] How this claim could be exploited by a Roman bishop already a half century earlier is shown by the procedure of Victor, who expelled the churches of Asia Minor from the common unity as heterodox, merely because of a dispute about the calendar.[24] It is true, this did not happen without protest; yet a precedent had been established.

Finally, as regards the beginnings of legalistic procedures, it was above all the orderly heresy trial invented by the jurist

Tertullian in his *Praescriptio* that paved the way for later developments. On the basis of the apostolic character of the church Tertullian, as the church's attorney, filed the legal objection *(praescriptio)* and thus put on the heretics the burden of proof for their claim to be the church—a maneuver that left only two possibilities for the outcome of the proceedings: Either the heretic must recant and acknowledge the priority of the church's claims, or he must become subject to the anathema.

It is inevitable that under all these circumstances the anathema should change its nature. It is still to be regarded as the mark of that separation from Christ and His church which results from contradiction to Christ. Yet the authority of the episcopate presumes to supersede the claims of Christ, the church's norm of doctrine tends to displace the witness of Christ's lordship, and the altered application of the anathema makes this shift manifest. At first the awareness continues that the anathema should be applied only in the most extreme cases. Since the fourth century, however, the scope of application is occasionally broadened so as to include the area of church discipline. In 313, at the Synod of Elvira, it is possible to anathematize those who post lampoons on church doors or bring them into the church [25]—a provision that was incorporated into canon law.[26] Later, at the second Synod of Tours (567), the anathema is pronounced also against such as lay hands on church property.[27] In view of such decisions it must indeed be said that the church had gone back beyond the Pauline use of the anathema to the practice of the synagog,[28] so that here the anathema obtains a disciplinary significance and tone to which it had not been confined in the New Testament. Nevertheless, many dogmatic decisions of the next centuries show that the anathema continued to be understood primarily as the expression of a judgment and a separation made in central concerns of the faith. Chief among these is the Council of Nicaea (325), where the orthodox creed is supplemented by an enumeration of heretical statements whose proponents are anathematized by the catholic and apostolic church.[29] A synod held at Laodicea sometime between 343 and 381 pronounces the anathema against Judaizers,[30] while at the second Ecumenical Council (Constantinople, 381) the anathema is summarily applied to "every heresy."[31] And since the teachings of dead heretics continued to have an influence, it was inevitable that also dead heretics should be anathematized, as was done in the case of Origen, who was condemned as a heretic by Theophilus of Alexandria nearly 200 years after his death, and again at the Synod of Constantinople in 543.[32] This, too, proves that during this period the anathema was by no means established primarily as a course of action in church discipline.

There is no uniformity in the form of the verdict. It may be directed against individual heretical statements, precisely defined, or it may strike the teaching of a heretic as a whole in the manner of a comprehensive condemnation *(damnatio in globo)*, perhaps as in the condemnation of Nestorius by Cyril at the Synod of Ephesus in 431. A formula "concerning the Trinity and the Incarnation" *(de trinitate et incarnatione)*, originating in a Roman synod of 379 or 380, expresses the delimitation against errors in different ways. The anathema is pronounced eight times, fourteen times the false teacher is judged to be a heretic *(haereticus est)*, and in one case the verdict is: "he does not believe correctly" *(non recte sentit)*.[33] This seems already to prepare the way for the later distinctions in the theological verdicts; yet there are no means of achieving a clear-cut isolation of the individual pronouncements.

The significance of the verdict derives from the fact that the organized church as the supreme court of doctrine is at the same time understood as the bearer of Christ's globe-circling lordship. In its decision the church draws from the fact of the heresy the self-evident conclusion stated at the beginning of the sixth century in the formula *Clemens Trinitas* (probably of Gallic origin) with respect to the heretic: "He must be adjudged a profane man and one alienated from the catholic and apostolic church." [34] The consequences of this state of affairs concern the eternal fate of the heretic. Gelasius I in 495 explains the anathema as equivalent to placing the seal on eternal damnation.[35] Three centuries later the Synod of Meaux (845) would in all due form define the anathema as the "damnation of eternal death" *(aeternae mortis damnatio)*.[36] Much as this formula as such still reveals a proximity to the New Testament anathema, it is equally certain that the total development had definitively separated itself from the primitive church. The ancient and the medieval church merge at the point where—in the language of the modern Roman Catholic historian of dogma — the church's tradition, as it were the "exponent" of the "church's store of revelation," appears as the guarantor that "a truth is or is not a part of the treasure of revelation," and where the assets of revelation receive their "normative status through the teaching office of the church," in which both dogmatic norm and dogmatic authority are combined.[37]

Notes to Chapter 1

[1] Cf. Lyder Brun, *Segen und Fluch im Urchristentum* (Oslo, 1932). Skrifter utgilt av det Norske Videnskaps-Akademi i Oslo, 1933.

[2] Gerardus van der Leeuw, *Phaenomenologie der Religion* (Tuebingen, 1933), p. 385; trans. J. E. Turner, *Religion in Essence and Manifestation*, Harper Torchbooks (New York: Harper & Row, 1963), II, 409. Cf. G. Mensching, *Das Heilige Wort* (Bonn, 1937), p. 116.

[3] Brun, pp. 11ff., does not sufficiently clarify this difference between the Old Testament and extra-Biblical religion.

[4] Cf. Joh. Behm, s. v. ἀνάθεμα, in Gerhard Kittel, *Theologisches Woerterbuch zum Neuen Testament* (TWNT), I, 356.

[5] Strack-Billerbeck, *Kommentar zum Neuen Testament aus Talmud und Midrasch*, IV, 1 (Munich, 1928), pp. 302, 327.

[6] Ibid., pp. 329ff.

[7] Ibid., p. 331.

[8] Cf. Brun, pp. 107f.

[9] Strack-Billerbeck, p. 331.

[10] For the individual passages see G. Heinrici, in *Realencyklopaedie fuer protestantische Theologie und Kirche* (RE), 3d ed., I, 493 – 495; K. Hofmann in *Reallexikon fuer Antike und Christentum*, I, Col. 427ff.; J. Behm, pp. 356f.

[11] Karl H. Rengstorf, unpublished lecture, 1947.

[12] Mark 14:71; Acts 23:12, 21; Gal. 1:8f.; 1 Cor. 12:3; 16:22; Rom. 9:3.

[13] Luke 22:60 (but see Mark 14:71; Matt. 26:74!); John 6:70; 1 John 4:3.

[14] Rengstorf.

[15] Heinrici, p. 495.

[16] Cf. H.-D. Wendland, "Die Einheit der Kirche und die Idee der Toleranz," *Luthertum*, 1939, pp. 42f.

[17] Ibid., p. 44.

[18] J. Brosch, *Das Wesen der Haeresie* (Bonn, 1936), p. 97.

[19] Cf. W. Bauer, *Rechtglaeubigkeit und Ketzerei im aeltesten Christentum* (Tuebingen, 1934).

[20] Cf. Hermann Doerries, *Das Bekenntnis in der Geschichte der Kirche*, 2d ed. (Goettingen, 1947), pp. 8ff. Especially also the entire investigation by Wilhelm Maurer, *Bekenntnis und Sakrament*, Part I: *Ueber die treibenden Kraefte in der Bekenntnisentwickelung der abendlaendischen Kirche bis zum Ausgang des Mittelalters.* (Berlin, 1939).

[21] Rudolf Bultmann, ἀλήθεια, in Kittel, TWNT, I, 244f.

[22] Bauer, p. 236.

[23] C. Mirbt, *Quellen zur Geschichte des Papsttums und des roemischen Katholizismus*, 4th ed. (Tuebingen, 1924), 29, 27ff.

[24] Ibid., 11, 18.

[25] Canon LII: "If people are discovered to have posted lampoons on the church, they are anathematized" (Mansi, *Collectio conciliorum*, II, 311).

[26] *Decretum Gratiani*, V., 1, 3.

[27] F. Kober, *Der Kirchenbann nach den Grundsaetzen des canonischen Rechts* (Tuebingen, 1857), pp. 37f.

[28] Heinrici, p. 495.

[29] τούτους ἀναθεματίζει ἡ ἀποστολικὴ καὶ καθολικὴ ἐκκλησία (Denzinger-Bannwart, *Enchiridion Symbolorum*, Vol. 27 [Freiburg, 1951], No. 54).

[30] Canon 29: εἰ δὲ εὑρεθεῖεν ἰουδαισταί, ἔστωσαν ἀνάθεμα παρὰ χριστῷ — "If Judaists are discovered, let them be anathema from Christ" (Mansi, II, 570).

[31] Denzinger, No. 85: ἀναθεματισθῆναι πᾶσαν αἵρεσιν.

[32] Kober, p. 92; C. J. v. Hefele, *Conciliengeschichte*, II, 790ff.

[33] Denzinger, Nos. 58—82.

[34] Denzinger, No. 18: *Profanus et alienus ab Ecclesia catholica atque apostolica iudicandus*.

[35] *Decretale de recipiendis et non recipiendis libris*, Denzinger, No. 166.

[36] Canon 56 (Mansi, XIV, 832).

[37] Brosch, pp. 113, 115.

Chapter 2

Main Lines of Development in the Middle Ages

In the Middle Ages that threefold development is consolidated and completed, the beginnings of which were already discernible as background for the ancient church's war on heresy. The church is conscious of being the bearer of the redeeming office of Christ and therefore claims the exclusive right to establish new truths of the faith. The church's dogmas, symbols, and dogmatic decisions constitute the true doctrine to which every one is obligated. At the same time the dogmatic authority is tied with finality to the priestly office. In the bifurcation of the church's power into the "power of order" and the "power of jurisdiction" the dogmatic power is coupled with the latter. For the first, the Roman bishop's claim to represent the pinnacle of church power received only limited recognition in the ancient church. In the Middle Ages, however, this comprehensive claim to primacy was dogmatized. Thomas Aquinas quite definitely ascribes "immediate jurisdiction over all Christians" to the pope, a jurisdiction that includes the supreme authority over doctrine and over decisions in matters of faith. The pope determines "what belongs to the faith" (quae fidei sunt). It is necessary for salvation to submit to his judgment. Even councils are subjected to this claim, for they can be convoked only by papal authority, and their decisions require papal confirmation. Since the church as a whole is inerrant, and since the pope as the representative of the church's unity acts in behalf of "the church's judgment," his verdicts "concerning faith and morals," pronounced in solemn definition, are inerrant also. It is true that even in the Middle Ages this claim is not accepted without opposition and that it does not attain dogmatic finality until the First Vatican Council. Yet the claim must necessarily be made again and again as "authority for the highest jurisdiction to apply legal compulsion." [38] It is particularly in the church's procedure against false doctrine that a continuous demonstration is given that the infallibility of the decision made by the dogmatic authority implicitly has definite legal consequences.

The growing legalization of the church, which began to develop already in the ancient church, thus flows into a primacy of canonical thinking that today even Roman Catholic writers have pictured and criticized as the most distinctive feature of the whole development in the church of the Middle Ages.[39] What the Roman Catholic teacher of canon law demonstrates from the relationship of "order and jurisdiction," of jurisdiction and teaching office, as well as the relationship of canon law to individual doctrinal decisions, must become apparent also in dealing with false doctrine: The "legal categories rest on the whole domain of the realization of what is Christian," "what is Christian is gathered up in legal forms," the church puts on a "legal armor." [40] The fact that the teaching office functions as a species of jurisdictional power is only one aspect of this "process of making the jurisdictional autonomous." [41] This aspect is indeed fraught with grave consequences and will in a special measure provoke Luther's opposition. It rests on the axiom that the church must not only proclaim the truth but must also compel its acceptance and punish every refusal to acknowledge it.[42] In this way the teaching office has become primarily a dogmatic *force*, and jurisdiction is ranked above proclamation.

Against this background the medieval war on heretics was developed. The era of the great ecumenical decisions in doctrine is essentially past, but the need for guaranteeing the "deposit of faith" remains active and leads to ever more careful extension of the church's punitive authority. Three related steps in the procedure against false doctrine may be distinguished. The first and oldest step is that of applying the church's punitive measures and censures to one who has been convicted of conscious rejection of a church dogma. Here indeed there is contact with the development in the ancient church. But it is significant that now also the anathema is included in this step of the censures. While it originally designated expulsion from the church, it is now more and more understood as a judicial verdict which is to effect the expulsion. The mark of separation over Christ and for Christ's sake has become a tool of the church's punitive power. The practice in the church of the Middle Ages shows that in the application of the anathema it is not the New Testament concept that prevails, but rather that of the synagog, that is, church discipline.[43]

First of all, the relation between the anathema and excommunication, which is the most important censure, experiences some fluctuation. A decision of Pope John VIII, which was also taken up into canon law, regards excommunication as separation from the "brotherly fellowship," while the anathema is regarded as separation from the "body of Christ, which is the church." [44] The latter is therefore regarded as the more comprehensive exclusion in contrast to the "lesser ban of the church," which bars only from the Eucharist and the other sacraments.[45] Since Gregory IX, however, excommunication definitely has the force of the greater ban.[46] Since the anathema in its essence simply could not be made to signify less, the difference was sought entirely in the form, that is, while excommunication is pronounced by a simple judicial verdict of the church, the use of definite solemn formulas must be preserved in the imposition of the anathema.[47] In this sense the *Pontificale Romanum* finally specifies: "Excommunication is threefold, namely, minor, major, and anathema," the latter being defined as the "solemn excommunication for more serious guilt." [48] It is possible that the addition of *maranatha*, taken over from 1 Cor. 16:22, provides a further intensification.

Thus the anathema has received its final and fixed place in the framework of the church's punitive jurisdiction. It has become a means of church discipline, one "censure" among others, though the most severe of all. A special character of doctrinal discipline still clings to it, inasmuch as it is applied above all to heretics. Yet the general punitive sense always predominates. Quite logically, the anathema is no longer applied to the dead — if only because in that case the improving, "medicinal" purpose which should characterize the ban would lose its significance. It is not forgotten that the anathema is basically intended only to express something that is already finished. However, while this circumstance originally served to avoid representing the anathema as merely a continuation of the Jewish ban, it now shares in the juridical fixation and establishment of the application of the ban. This is taken into account in the special form of the *excommunicatio latae sententiae* ("a verdict already rendered"), which declares in contrast to the *excommunicatio ferendae sententiae* ("a verdict still to be rendered") that the punishment of heretics is in effect at once with the transgression *(ipso facto)*, that is to say, without requiring a specific judicial verdict. The canonists put it in this way: "Excommunication sticks to heresy as leprosy to the leper and as a shadow to a man." [49] To be summoned before the court and dealt with on the basis of the evidence, procedures which are normally the precondition for imposing excommunication, are not required in this case. It is true, Augustine had called attention to the rule drawn from Ecclus. 11:7, "Before you have investigated, do not judge. Know first and then pass judgment." [50] Yet Augustine could also be quoted in support of the claim that evidence as required by a court of law is superfluous the moment the infraction is proved to be "notorious," that is, the moment it should be and is recognized "by all" as an infraction.[51]

The next step in the procedure is the punishment of the heretic by the arm of the secular power. It was simply a matter of proceeding farther along the lines already indicated in the ancient church. Since the end of the fourth century heresy was regarded in the statutes of the Roman empire as a public crime, and hence it is to be avenged not only by ecclesiastical but also by civil penalties. The legal enactments of the Merovingian and Carolingian periods are still quite cautious in this matter, but since the 11th century the old imperial legal practice is reinstated in full measure.

More important than the step of civil intervention is the third stage, which is not developed until the late Middle Ages and is then used as a special preliminary to supplement and introduce the other two customary parts of the procedure. Here, in the area of *theological* judgments, the teaching office of the church receives a special field of activity. For the first, there is room only for the theologians of the universities in their activity of rendering opinions, but in the general scheme it cannot be removed from the jurisdictional sphere, which encompasses the total power of the church. More and more it must become necessary to label heresy as such by a special decree of the church and to distinguish it from less important aberrations. Formerly it was customary to point to the condemnation of the 28 statements of Master Eckhart as the first instance of this kind of theological judgment.[52] Recently, however, it has been demonstrated that the oldest document of this nature antedates the one mentioned by 60 years.[53] This is the answer which Albertus Magnus, 1270, gave to the statements made by Aegidius of Lessines, although it is more of a philosophical than a theological opinion.[54] Pope John XXII establishes the connection between the church's teaching office and the activity of the theologians in furnishing opinions. Henceforth theological examiners are appointed for each individual case for the purpose of providing theological criteria. These examiners are instructed to label the controverted teachings according to the degree of their divergence from the dogma of the church. In 1326, for example, 51 articles from William of Occam's *Commentary on Sentences* were examined, where an extensively integrated scale of judgments is already apparent: "Heretical; false: (a) simply false, (b) false in philosophy and theology, (c) falseness, not against faith or good morals; ridiculous; ill-sounding." [55] The commission charged with investigating the 28 statements of Master Eckhart, 1329, arrives at a fourfold classification under the general judgment of "condemnation and disapproval" *(damnamus et reprobamus):* 17 statements are labeled heretical, the remaining 11 are rejected as either "under the suspicion of heresy, or imprudent, or ill-sounding." [56] The same procedure is applied at Constance against the teachings of Wiclif and Huss. The following judgments are listed: "Notoriously heretical, erroneous, imprudent and seditious, offensive to pious ears," [57] although it is not indicated in connection with the individual statements which is which. This form of review is later called "general condemnation" *(condemnatio in globo).*[58] A century later Luther's teachings are subjected to the verdict of the church's censors.

By the introduction of the theological critiques the church took note of the progressive distinctions in the theological development. It might seem that in this way a counterweight had been provided for the penal fixing of the anathema, so that alongside church discipline the evaluation and judgment of new teachings in the original sense of the anathema would also have an independent place. However, the "spread of juridical thought patterns in the church"[59] has already progressed too far. Also the theological opinions, having arisen in the universities, are at once drawn into the sphere of action of the jurisdictional teaching authority and constitute nothing more than the first step in the penally oriented procedure against heretics. Beyond this the practice of rendering theological opinions proves that the formalizing of the church's doctrine became as dominant as its inseparable association with the church's judicial function. Since faith has become a matter of obedience to the prescriptions of the church, doctrinal discipline can have no other task than to establish divergences from these prescriptions and to punish them in accordance with the church's punitive authority. Both norm and authority for separating pure doctrine from false are united in one teaching office which regards and exercises its power primarily as the power to impose penalties.

From this it is clear that the Reformation could not simply adopt either the anathema reduced to excommunication or the *Damnamus* of the theological censures frozen in jurisdictional ways. The new approach granted Luther here, too, with reference to the distinction of true and false doctrine is only one aspect of his total "reformatory approach" and can be properly evaluated only from that perspective. At the same time the personal experience of the heretic through all three stages of the church's heresy trial retains its own importance for the proper understanding of the break with medieval tradition. In addition, the legal proceedings against Luther provide another comprehensive survey of the three steps of the procedure and the effect of those three trends which were determinative from the days of the ancient church until the late Middle Ages for the development of the church's teaching office and its attack on false doctrine.

Notes to Chapter 2

[38] P. Hinschius, *System des katholischen Kirchenrechts*, IV, (Berlin, 1888), 435.

[39] Joseph Klein, *Grundlegung und Grenzen des kanonischen Rechts* (Tuebingen, 1947), pp. 12, 16. W. Maurer presents a particularly penetrating

investigation of the secularization of canon law in the section, "Bekenntnis und Ketzerrecht," of his book mentioned above in footnote 20 (pp. 60ff.).

[40] Klein, pp. 10, 12.

[41] Ibid., p. 16.

[42] Cf. G. Schneemann, *Die kirchliche Lehrgewalt* (Freiburg, 1868), pp. 39f., 202f. J. B. Saegmueller, *Lehrbuch des katholischen Kirchenrechts*, I/1, 4th ed. (Freiburg, 1925), 32f.

[43] Heinrici, p. 495. A special investigation would be required to determine to what extent extraneous conceptions of a curse are influential. In the case of *Maranatha* there certainly was such influence, as is shown by the use of this formula in medieval endowment and gift deeds (cf. Du Cange, V, p. 258).

[44] "You know that Hengiltrude, the wife of Boso, was repeatedly struck not only by excommunication, which separates from the fraternal fellowship, but also by the anathema, which cuts off from the very body of Christ (which is the church)." Gratian comments: "Thence we are given to understand that those who have been anathematized must be viewed as not simply separated in every way from the fraternal fellowship but from the body of Christ (which is the church)." *(Decr. Greg.,* III, 4, 12; Friedberg, I, 514)

[45] Kober, p. 38.

[46] *Decr. Greg.,* V, 39, 59 (Friedberg, II, 912).

[47] Explained in *Decr. Greg.,* XI, 3, 106 (Friedberg, I, 674).

[48] Cf. also the definition given by Du Cange, s. v. (I, p. 329): ". . . Anathema, properly speaking, signifies among church writers the excommunication imposed by a bishop or by a council, not, however, as though it were a separation from fellowship, but as that which is decreed with the curse and malediction."

[49] Kober, p. 95.

[50] "If then the Holy Spirit wished a person to be neither berated nor arrested unless he were given a hearing, how much more criminal is it for people to be not only berated or arrested but even condemned, who in their absence could not be questioned at all about their crimes?" *(Epist.* XLIII, c. 3, n. 11; Migne, SL, 33, 165).

[51] "When anyone's crime is so well known that it appears as execrable to all, and that it has no defenders at all or not such as could produce a schism, let the severity of the punishment not sleep, in which the more thorough is the correction of the evil, the more diligent is the preservation of love" *(Contra epist. Parmen.,* Lib. III, c. 2; Migne, SL, 43, 92; incompletely cited by Kober, p. 162).

[52] As recently as B. Bartmann, *Lehrbuch der Dogmatik,* I (8th ed., Freiburg, 1932), 42.

[53] J. Koch, "Philosophische und theologische Irrtumslisten von 1270 – 1329" *(Melanges Mandonnet,* II [Paris, 1930], 305ff).

[54] Ibid., pp. 316ff.

[55] Ibid., pp. 322f.

[56] Denzinger, Nos. 501 – 529.

[57] Denzinger, No. 661.

[58] Cf. M. J. Scheeben, Article on "Censuren" in Wetzer-Welte, *Kirchenlexikon,* 2d ed., II (Freiburg, 1883), Cols. 2091ff. Franz Diekamp, *Katholische Dogmatik,* I, 3d – 5th ed. (Munich, 1921), 61ff.

[59] Klein, p. 12.

Chapter 3

Luther's Roman Trial as an Example of the Attack on Heretics in the Late Middle Ages

The official proceedings against Luther [60] began when Marius de Perusco, the official prosecutor at the papal court, proposed legal action to the pope in June 1518. Thereupon the pope commissioned Sylvester Prierias, "master of the sacred palace" and expert adviser on questions of doctrine and heresy, to prepare a theological opinion. The pope also asked the "confidential auditor" *(auditor camerae)* to conduct the preliminary judicial investigation, while reserving the rendition of the verdict to himself. Prierias did not go to too much trouble in the matter. Within three days he had prepared his Dialog, in which he proceeded from the Thomistic point of view, discussed Luther's Ninety-five Theses quite superficially, and distributed his criticisms. "Stupid and ridiculous," "falseness," "rashness," "error," "heretical doctrine" — these are the labels with which he tagged Luther's statements.[61] Luther received the document together with the official summons which was drawn up by the confidential auditor and in which on the basis of a suspicion of heresy Luther was threatened with the ban and, if necessary, assorted other punitive measures, in case he would not appear at Rome within sixty days.[62]

Meanwhile the cardinal legate Cajetan forwarded further charges against Luther to the papal court, material that rested on falsifications circulated by the Dominicans but did not fail to make an impression in Rome, especially since the emperor, too, requested immediate action against the heretic. On the basis of this material, which exposed Luther not only as a critic of indulgences but also as one who denied the power of the papal ban, the case appeared to be a notorious one that should make a quick and radical conclusion of the action possible. Accord-

ingly, Cajetan received authorization to initiate summary proceedings, which above all included Luther's arrest. Political
considerations involving Luther's elector did, indeed, prevent
this step. But since Luther did not recant when Cajetan conducted a hearing in Augsburg, Cajetan now demanded the extra-
dition of the heretic, which Frederick the Wise refused to grant.
Nor did the mission of the vain and pompous Miltitz accomplish
this or anything else. It only succeeded in postponing the entire
matter for a whole year, so that the proceedings against Luther
were not resumed until the beginning of 1520.

To demonstrate the damnableness of Luther's teaching,
new evidence was now available in the form of opinions drafted
by universities, a procedure that again followed customary
methods of censorship. The theologians of Cologne, in their
opinion given at the end of August 1519, explicitly aimed at "applying a verdict of disapproval on doctrinal grounds." Using an
edition of Luther's works that appeared in Basel in 1519, they
stated that these writings were full of "offensive, erroneous, and
heretical matters" and therefore "injurious to the community
of the faithful." [63] The faculty of Louvain followed suit in No-
vember. [64] In Luther's writings they had discovered a mass of
"assertions that were false, offensive, heretical, and smacking
of heresy," plus "propositions that were suspect and dangerous," as well as an assortment of "absurd and erroneous statements." The conclusion was: "It is our opinion that the book
itself, as well as all and sundry treatises of his, in which these or
some of these are contained, must be condemned, and therefore
on doctrinal grounds we condemn the book and the treatises as
harmful to the community of the faithful, as opposed to true and
sound doctrine, and we judge that they must be removed from
circulation and burned with fire, and their author must be compelled to revoke and repudiate the above." [65] This is a classic
example of what Roman Catholic dogmatics calls a "judgment
by opinion and consultation" to distinguish it from the *censura
judicialis*, the "judicial or authoritative" judgment. [66]

These judgments were important also because they served
as working documents for the papal commission called together
at the beginning of February 1520 for the purpose of condemning
Luther. The commission, which consisted of the cardinals
Cajetan and Accolti and was assisted by leading representatives

of the mendicant orders, simply voted on the statements of Luther that were treated in the opinions of the universities — a procedure so obviously inadequate that in the same month Cajetan made provision for adding a number of theologians. The verdict of this enlarged commission was essentially different: Only a fraction of Luther's theses were said to be heretical and therefore damnable; the others received the epithet "offensive" or other less severe criticisms. For the rest, it was recommended not to condemn Luther's teachings explicitly but to reject them in a "special papal decree" *(extravagans)* without mentioning Luther's name. It is true, this sensible trend did not prevail. Under the influence and with the participation of Eck a third commission set to work entrusted with the task of formulating the bull threatening excommunication. The commission leaned on 41 articles which Eck had compiled and which in turn were based on the Louvain opinion, to which in all probability the commission had access. At Eck's insistence it was decided to condemn Luther's statements "summarily" *(in globo)*. In several consistories Cajetan still pleaded that instead of a blanket condemnation it should be determined point by point which statements would have to be labeled heretical and which deserved a less severe criticism. It was Cajetan, too, who had advised representatives of the Cologne and Louvain faculties to be cautious, even before their opinions had been formulated. Regarding Luther's statements Cajetan said, "They might be errors, but they are not heresies." [67] Yet Cajetan could make no headway with Eck.

There was one other conflict that disturbed unanimity in these final deliberations preceding the publication of the bull, and that was the old tension between curialists and conciliarists.[68] Especially the Spanish cardinal Carvajal objected to the open circumvention of conciliar authority (to which Luther had explicitly appealed). Guided by the same concern, the theologians of Louvain — in contrast to Eck's 41 articles — had quietly ignored Luther's statements against the authority of the pope. Since, however, an appeal to a council had been placed under the penalty of heresy by the constitutions of Pius II and Julius II, the curialists under Accolti's leadership retained the upper hand.

The canonical proceedings were no longer influenced by

the fact that in the spring of 1520 the Sorbonne faculty, which had been asked together with the Erfurt faculty to serve as umpire in the Leipzig debate, had meanwhile also entered the arena with a condemnation of 104 statements of Luther. Yet also this critique, like the rest, would be helpful to Luther in clarifying his judgment on this type of *Damnamus*.

On June 15, 1520, *Exsurge Domine,* the papal bull threatening excommunication, was drawn up. With explicit reference to the opinions of Cologne and Louvain the bull drew the final conclusions. After a listing of the objectionable statements, the verdict of rejection was given: "We condemn, disapprove, and reject altogether all and sundry articles or errors as indicated, respectively, either as heretical or scandalous, or false, or offensive to pious ears, or seductive to simple minds, and as opposing catholic truth." [69] This is the customary form for a blanket condemnation, as already indicated by the word "respectively." The criticisms demonstrated the customary gradations that were only made more precise later on. "Heresy," otherwise confined to the immediate contradiction of a catholic divine truth, an acknowledged revealed dogma, and "error"— contradicting a conclusion drawn from the catholic dogma—are here seen to coalesce; "false," too, belongs in this category. The second group comprises sentences that "are reprehensible because of special reference to God, to the saints, and to the church" and are therefore deemed "offensive to pious ears or scandalous." [70] Perhaps this last term should be assigned to a third group, where all "statements connected with moral danger" belong.[71]

Finally, the papal bull described Luther as "notoriously suspect concerning the faith, yea, truly heretical," and applied these terms also to his supporters.[72] This corresponds to the usual procedure against heresy without notoriety, as fixed by Innocent III at the Fourth Lateran Council.[73] Luther had done nothing to purge himself of the suspicion of heresy, nor had he obeyed the citation to the papal court, and thus he was already regarded as a heretic banned by "excommunication in a verdict already rendered" *(excommunicatio latae sententiae),* exactly like everyone else who had been under the ban for one year without applying for absolution.[74] The fact that the bull did not now impose the ultimate anathema, as the theologians wished, but at the request of the canonists extended the time for revocation by another 60 days was not an "outburst of Christian compassion," as the bull claimed, but simply a juridical formality in itself expendable, which could favor an intensification of the punitive measures after the period of grace had expired.[75]

On Jan. 3, 1521, the bull *Decet Romanum Pontificem* brought the entire proceeding to a conclusion by a definitive ban of Luther and his supporters. On Maundy Thursday, 1521, Luther and his sympathizers appeared for the first time on the roster of heretics in the bull *Coena Domini*, that collection of excommunications solemnly read by the pope since the 13th century, preferably on Maundy Thursday. The measures against Luther could have been executed immediately after the expiration of the period of grace, i. e., Nov. 21, 1520, and the emperor and the estates were also ready to carry out the ban. First, however, they wanted to make sure that Luther was actually the author of the condemned writings and that he refused to recant. Both points were verified at Worms.

Notes to Chapter 3

[60] The following presentation is based on the investigations and/or presentations of Karl Mueller, "Luthers roemischer Prozess," ZKG, 24 (1903), 46ff.; Paul Kalkoff, "Zu Luthers roemischem Prozess," ZKG, 25 (1904), 90ff., 273ff., 399ff., 503ff.; ZKG, 31 (1910), 48ff., 368ff.; ZKG, 32 (1911), 1ff., 199ff., 408ff., 573ff.; ZKG, 33 (1912), 1ff.; "The bull 'Exsurge,'" ZKG, 35 (1914), 166ff.; ZKG, 37 (1918), 89ff.; *Forschungen zu Luthers roemischem Prozess* (Rome, 1905), "Kleine Nachtraege zu Luthers roemischem Prozess," ZKG, 44 (1925), 213ff.; and Heinrich Boehmer, *Der junge Luther*, 4th ed. (Stuttgart, 1951), trans., John W. Doberstein and Theo. G. Tappert, *Road to Reformation* (Philadelphia: Muhlenberg Press, 1946).

[61] Erlangen edition of Luther's works (hereafter cited as EA), *Opera varii argumenti*, I, 341ff.

[62] Mueller, pp. 60ff.

[63] Weimar edition of Luther's works (hereafter cited as WA), 6, 178ff.

[64] Their opinion was, however, not published until February 1520, and then without faculty authorization (Kalkoff, ZKG, 25, p. 106).

[65] WA 6, 175ff.; 178, 7.

[66] Cf. Scheeben, Col. 2098.

[67] Kalkoff, ZKG, 25, p. 115. Luther himself had written to Spalatin, Aug. 28, 1518: "I shall never be a heretic. I may err in the course of a debate" (WA *Briefe*, 1, 190, 21).

[68] Ibid., pp. 109, 120ff.

[69] Denzinger, No. 781. Complete text of the bull: *Magnum Bullarium Romanum*, I, (Lyons, 1692), pp. 614–618; also (with Hutten's marginal notes) in EA, *Op. var. arg.*, 4, 261–304.

[70] F. Hettinger, *Lehrbuch der Fundamental-Theologie*, 2d. ed. (Freiburg: 1888), pp. 777ff.

[71] Scheeben, Col. 2097.

[72] *Bullarium Romanum*, pp. 616ff.; EA, *Op. var. arg.*, 4, 290, 295.

[73] "Those, however, who might be found to be noteworthy by suspicion alone should be struck with the sword of anathema, unless by a proper purging they demonstrated their own innocence according to the consideration of the suspicion and the quality of the person, and they should be avoided by all until they have made worthy amends, so that if they would persist in their excommunication for a year, they would thenceforth be condemned as heretics" (*Decr. Greg. IX.*, V, 7, 13; Friedberg, II, 787f.). — Note also the decision of Alexander IV: "Since stubbornness, especially in a matter of faith, adds a strong presumption to the suspicion; if one suspected of heresy, summoned by you to give an account of the faith, has been bound by you with the chain of excommunication because he failed to make an appearance or obstinately stayed away, let him be thenceforth condemned as a heretic, as if he had held out a whole year in an unyielding state of mind" (*Liber sextus*, V, 2, 7; Friedberg, II, 1071).

[74] Documentation in Kober, pp. 437ff.

[75] Boehmer, p. 288; Mueller, pp. 80f.

Part 2

Luther

Chapter 4

The Antithesis Against the Roman Verdict

In the opening stages of his trial Luther, in a letter to Spalatin, calmly and confidently discounted the fear that the anathema might strike him. He surely would not have to start a war against papal decrees and the traditions of men. "The wrath of the decretals neither binds nor harms when the mercy of Christ is held fast." [1] Even when the outcome of the trial changed the situation, Luther's confidence remained unshaken. However, it was now necessary for Luther to respond. He neither could nor would avoid coming to grips with the papal authority in teaching and punishing. Around the turn of the year 1521–22, while he was at the Wartburg, Luther found the leisure to prepare an edition of the Maundy Thursday bull, annotated with pointed comments in which above all he unsparingly settled the score with the financial aspects of the papal excommunication practice. [2] Hence it was not yet the ban itself that Luther attacked but rather the abuse connected with it. Luther was provoked to express strong objections, not because the pope imposed the ban at all, but because he applied it as a coercive device for safeguarding and increasing his income. "St. Paul did indeed execrate false teachers, Gal. 1, but he did it for the sake of the Gospel, to uphold God's honor. But where he is attacked in matters pertaining to himself, he constantly pronounces blessing." [3] Herewith Luther was already going beyond his first objection and entering upon what is basic. In general, both before and after his trial, Luther did not consider his criticism of the financial abuse of the ban as essential as some of his contemporaries did. [4] While in his Open Letter to the Christian Nobility he deplored the application of the ban exclusively "for the sake of temporal possessions," [5] and while in the regulations for the Leisnig Common Chest he mentioned "the horrible abuse of the ban, so that it scarcely does more than torment the people for the sake of the property of priests and monks," [6] this was not the chief issue. As late as 1530 Luther could accuse the pope of applying the ban only when his own arbitrary decrees were disregarded, "when it concerns the dear penny and the tonsure," and of permitting the loosing key to become rusty for the sake of his money and his power.[7] But in Luther's first utterance on this theme, in his sermon of March 14, 1518, which caused such a stir and nearly subjected him to summary proceedings, this point of view faded into the background and was replaced by the question concerning the proper essence of the ban.[8]

Luther, too, insisted that the church's ban means excommunication, exclusion from the fellowship of the faithful, but only to the extent that this fellowship manifests itself in the organized, visible church. The ban cannot exclude from the true, spiritual treasures of the church if the spiritual excommunication through sin and spiritual death has not already preceded. To that extent the ban merely confirms a state of affairs that has already been created on another level. The ban becomes the sign by which the banned person is to recognize that through sin he has already separated himself from the true fellowship of the faithful. The church, however, is concerned about rescuing the sinner from the devil and bringing him back to God, and this is to be done by the ban, correctly understood. For this reason Luther wanted to see the "medicinal," amending significance of the ban restored, and he pronounced his woes upon all who changed this "maternal chastisement" into an instrument of a tyrannical and arbitrary vindictiveness, or the medicine into poison. Let them consider that it could be more dangerous to excommunicate than to be excommunicated. "To prescribe many laws is to set many snares for poor souls," [9] – and it can easily happen that people are only banned out of the church when they should be banned into the church.

It was this fundamental conviction that generated the angry scorn with which Luther annotated the Maundy Thursday bull: "To curse and to slaughter souls" – that seems evidently to constitute for the pope the chief content of the apostolic office. By means of his anathemas he aims at casting the alleged heretics into the abyss of hell, "he burns their bodies to ashes, he curses their names, destroys their honor, and robs them of their property." He can do nothing else than "exclusively, only, nakedly condemn, ban, execrate, curse, rave." [10] It is true, also "Scripture curses what acts contrary to the Gospel." But Scripture is concerned about "amendment of souls," whereas the pope "exclusively curses body and soul, property and honor, friend and companion. His aim is not betterment but simply destruction." [11]

This remained Luther's position throughout. He had no desire to combat or abolish the ban as such but rather that jurisdictional overrefinement and intensification that confronted him everywhere in the church's punitive practice of his time and that he experienced in his own person. Incidentally, he condemned this practice also because it invaded functions of the secular government. "Let kings and emperors reestablish the worldly ban," but in the church such methods have no place.[12] We refer to one more utterance of Luther. Immediately after the presentation of the Augsburg Confession he sums up once more what properly belongs to the ban: We "must deal with certain public sins, committed by persons who are known." Furthermore, "such sins are supposed to have been reproved first in a brotherly manner and finally established as sins by the whole community. Therefore the bulls and papal bans that read, 'We excommunicate at once after sentence has been passed (ipso facto lata sententia), though only after three admonitions' and 'out of the fullness of our power,' we call in our language an execrable ban (ein Scheissbann). I call it a devil's ban and not God's ban, contrary to Christ's command, when people are sacrilegiously cursed with the ban before they have been convicted in the presence of the assembled community." [13] Luther's attack on the papal absolutist pretensions and the canon law created the presuppositions for the possibility of letting the ban become again the expression of fraternal church discipline in the sense of the New Testament. The subsequent fortunes of this new approach in the churches of the Reformation cannot be detailed here.

We must now enter more fully into Luther's treatment of the condemnatory practice in the narrow sense, that is, the specific doctrinal discipline. Luther's critique concerned itself first of all with the theological opinions basic for his condemnation. In view of the consistently superficial and formalistic way in which these criticisms were composed, they surely offered enough opportunity for manifold strictures. They were, above all, unfounded or at least not sufficiently proved. This is the first weighty objection that crops up again and again in connection with individual criticisms, often expressed in different ways. In his answer to the *Dialogus* of Prierias [14] Luther held that the latter had rendered his verdict as a faithful disciple of his master, Thomas Aquinas, and he had done this "without Scripture, without the fathers, without the canons, and finally, without any reasons at all." Luther accused the Cologne and Louvain theologians, too, that they "have 'we condemn' instead of 'we approve' in their mouth and nothing else." As long as they can say *"Damnamus,"* they feel no obligation to prove their assertions.[15] The "jackasses at Paris" do not know any better. It is nothing but shameless presumption for them to put their operations on a level with the doctrinal discipline practiced by the apostles and councils. "For the apostles did not assert or do anything without good reason. . . . But if it is proper that everyone may condemn the other person without having to furnish basis, justification, and cause for such action, very well, then I and everyone else have the same privilege. What a fine game we can play with this!" [16] The gentlemen in Rome who passed judgment on Luther's teaching must suffer the same reproach: If they press the elector to compel Luther to recant, they are doing this "without any known cause, which also they themselves do not mention by a word." [17] Shortly thereafter, in his "offer," in which he appealed to the protection of the emperor,[18] Luther declared that no revocations could be expected of him as long as they had not refuted him by means of "reasonable arguments based on the Sacred Scriptures." In this situation the suggestion of Erasmus of an impartial court of arbitration to examine his teaching could impress Luther as worth considering.[19] In this connection it is impressive to note how Luther kept the issue itself in view, without being distracted by the confusing mass of political considerations that crisscrossed and overlapped each other at this climax of his trial in Rome as well as in Germany. This means that just at this stage he insisted on adequate documentation for his condemnation. We must clearly understand that in fact "in the whole process of this trial . . . the authority that claimed for itself the ultimate and exclusive decision in matters of doctrine never offered the accused one word of proof in support of this unconditional rejection of his position." [20] Reference to the opinions of Prierias and of the faculties did not alter this fact. Among the opponents none other than Eck was distressed by this difficulty. Occasionally he expressed the wish that Luther's errors be refuted on the basis of the Scriptures, the fathers, and the councils, and that learned theologians furnish the proof for the pope's decision [21] — an insight which, alas, occurred to Eck too late.

In his rejoinder to the bull *Exsurge*, Luther once more laid special stress on this point. He thought that the "Antichrist," who issued the bull, had in his unfounded condemnation proved himself to be a docile pupil of the Cologne and Louvain condemners. If the matter were actually that simple, if everything could be accomplished simply by saying, "I condemn," then one could just as well believe the Turk or approve of all kinds of heretics, simply because they, too, were experts in the use of this weapon! In this context Luther was particularly critical of the blanket condemnation *(damnatio in globo)*, in which he saw nothing but a manifestation of the condemner's bad conscience. Incisively he pinpointed the weakest aspect of the judgments in general. If people no longer know the fundamental difference between true and untrue, between Christian and heretical, a distinction which alone comes into play in doctrinal decisions, the whole structure of the remaining graded censures collapses. If, for example, a certain statement is not labeled heretical, it makes no sense to tag it "offensive" or "scandalous." Such transitions and nuances only serve to blur the sharp contours of true and false doctrine.[22] Luther did not, of course, mean to say that no distinction should be made between heresies which must be condemned as "injurious doctrines" and the error which clings unavoidably to the human form of church and theology.[23] His one concern was that the essential distinction between true and false doctrine be kept clearly in view, something he could not presuppose with regard to the theologians of the papal court. For that reason Cajetan's opinion, which tried to uncover errors rather than heresies in Luther's writings, would probably have been of dubious value to him.

Thus Luther's first objection progressed to a second, which penetrates even more deeply into the essence of condemnation. He questioned in principle the authority of the originators of the condemnation. Already the faculties were charged with uncertainty in this matter. They vacillate, they are not sure whether they should pose simply as condemners of doctrine *(doctrinales damnatores)*, who merely offer opinions, or actually as authentic condemners *(autentici damnatores)*, whose verdict has binding force.[24] Their aim is clear enough. They wish "that only they in the world had the power to condemn, to establish, and to do as they please, over against friend or foe." [25]

The question concerning authority becomes really acute where the pope and his power are at issue. In the course of his trial Luther had by repeated appeals made it plain enough that he wanted his case decided by a council and not by the pope. For the time being, he thought and acted in this point no differently than the conciliarists at the end of the Middle Ages, whose influence made itself felt all the way up to the circle of Luther's judges. Erasmus, too, in his evaluation of the bull *Exsurge* had at once made use of the fact that the conciliar authority had been improperly disregarded.[26] The council continued to be regarded as the bearer of the supreme doctrinal authority, and in theory this remained unchanged until the First Vatican Council. In practice, however, the trend toward ranking the pope's authority above that of a council was in evidence already in the Middle Ages. Luther, on the contrary, was convinced all along of the priority of conciliar authority and expressed this view as late as 1539 in his book "Of the Councils and the Church." To be sure, since his Leipzig debate with Eck he believed that even councils were by no means inerrant. To do justice to its task a council must therefore, in his opinion, observe two rules: The council dare not regard its mandate as the arbitrary establishment of new articles of faith but should rather "suppress and condemn new articles of faith." And this must be done, according to the second rule, "in conformity with the Scriptures and the ancient faith," as was done in Nicaea against Arius, in Ephesus against Nestorius, and in Chalcedon against Eutyches.[27]

It was this latter aspect which provided the decisive impetus for Luther's rebellion against the manner in which the pope manipulated the teaching office. The pope subordinated the norm of the Scriptures, the authority of the divine Word, to his own plenary power. The humanist, Crotus Rubeanus, put his finger on it when he reported to Luther regarding the situation at Rome, in a letter of Oct. 16, 1519: "The decisive verdict rests with the Roman See, not with the Scriptures." [28] There, in fact, lay the decisive contrast, and Luther never tired of setting against the pope and his sentence the Scriptures and nothing but the Scriptures. Luther regarded Scripture as "in itself completely certain, clear, open, its own interpreter, testing, judging, and clarifying all things," and in no need of being supplemented by human authority.[29] And even though from the beginning Luther was sure of the primacy of Scripture, the realization that he was free to question the very principle of papal authority did not suddenly fall into his lap. He acquired this liberty in a long and difficult struggle, whose individual stages cannot be detailed here.

Luther received decisive support for his view when he studied canon law in preparation for the Leipzig debate. In connection with this study, as he wrote to Spalatin on March 13, 1519, the question occurred to Luther, for the moment to be whispered only into Spalatin's ear, whether the pope is himself the Antichrist or his apostle. "So wretchedly is Christ (that is, the truth) corrupted and crucified by him (the pope) in his decrees." [30] During that same period of preparation for the debate with Eck Luther jotted down his thoughts concerning the papal primacy and came to the conclusion that one could speak of a papal primacy only on the basis of certain decretals in canon law, but not on the basis of the Holy Scriptures.[31] Thus already at this early date the battle lines were becoming clear for Luther before his own trial entered its decisive stage. On the one side are Christ and the Scriptures; on the other side stands the pope with his antichristian, antiscriptural claims to power, for which he forges his chief tool in canon law. Canon law is charged with nothing less than that Christ Himself is being crucified in it. This is certainly a drastic, yet in Luther's view entirely appropriate, way of expressing that jurisdictional infiltration of the teaching office that developed so disastrously in the medieval practice of condemnation.

The outcome of his trial, the personal experiences which

Luther had with the church's condemnation and excommunication procedures, made him fully aware of these relationships. In his address "To the Christian Nobility" he pronounced an annihilating verdict on canon law: It would be well "altogether to eradicate canon law from the first letter to the last, especially the decretals. There is enough written in the Bible for us, how we should conduct ourselves in all things." [32] Luther regarded the decretals as the chief support of that wall of human authority with which the papacy fortified itself against the primacy of Scripture. "This is why there are so many heretical and unchristian, even unnatural statutes in canon law." [33] By the act of book burning on Dec. 10, 1520, Luther publicly drew the conclusion from this insight. As early as the beginning of July he had mentioned in a letter to Spalatin that he planned to throw into the fire or at least publicly condemn all of papal law, this "hydra of heresies." [34] Therefore it was not so much the burning of the bull of excommunication as it was the burning of canon law that constituted the "real event of the day"—for both Luther himself and his contemporaries. It was not without reason that in addition to canon law he also threw the *Summa Angelica* of Angelo de Chiavasso into the fire—because he knew that in this work the "purely juridical treatment of ethical and religious questions perhaps reached their peak," and that "pastoral care was handled entirely as a branch of the spiritual jurisdiction." [35]

It is significant that in his vindication of the "judgment by fire outside the Elster gate" Luther ignored the burning of the bull altogether and interpreted his deed as an attack on the real essence of canon law. Whoever does not agree should see for himself "what poisonous and frightful doctrines are contained in holy canon law," and that its only purpose was to buttress and bolster the unspiritual absolutist pretensions of the pope.[36] What little good may perhaps be discovered here and there in the decretals exists only to promote this goal.[37] Luther was also fully aware that he had taken an important step beyond all late medieval anticurialism. It is true that Wyclif and Hus had declared the decretals to be apocryphal, but it remained for him to prove them to be "impious and opposed to Christ, emitted solely by the spirit of Satan," and for that reason he had confidently thrown them into the fire.[38] Nearly two decades later he stated that he would like to burn them again.[39]

In this manner the way was open for separating the power of jurisdiction from the teaching office *(magisterium)*. Two weeks after the book burning, in a Christmas sermon, Luther characterized the Roman understanding of the teaching authority as tyranny and depraved doctrine. He was not ready to deny the pope his teaching office altogether. Yet the pope himself debased the office by using it to exercise his coercive rule over consciences — whereas Christ rules "in no other way than by faith" — and by the fact that he and his associates "suppress the Christ and Christian teaching." [40] In so doing the papal teaching office has forfeited the claim to recognition. As long as this office refused to be judged by the Scriptures but rather lorded it over the Word of God and itself established articles of faith, and above all presented the visible Roman church as the one true church of Christ and made submission to the former the condition for membership in the latter, so long the pope was and remained for Luther "neither Pope nor Christian" but the "Antichrist." [41] At the beginning of 1520 Luther thought that, apart from this claim to be the authority in matters of faith, the pope might be permitted to remain and would have to be endured in patience.[42] The decisive renunciation had been made, however, a renunciation that found expression in Luther's casting the verdict of condemnation back upon its author.

In the document already mentioned concerning papal authority, which Luther wrote in March 1519 in preparation for the Leipzig Debate, a degree of reserve is still in evidence at this point. Luther made the claim that he could dispute the papal primacy not only from the Scriptures but also on the basis of certain references in canon law, and then he added, "Therefore let them condemn me as much as they like. I have here a rule that condemns the Roman pontiff for being called the universal pontiff, yet I have never pronounced condemnation on this claim." [43] Secretly he was already convinced that none but the Antichrist himself stood behind the pope and his power, and it evidently afforded him a measure of satisfaction to find this suspicion confirmed even in a canon of the ecclesiastical law. Yet he was not ready to pronounce his "I condemn" on the pope in public. The German version of his rejoinder to the bull *Exsurge* provides insight into the considerations that led him to exercise such caution. He expressly rejected the thought that

he desired to "arouse the laity to rise above the clergy" [44] —
surely not out of respect for the arrogated sanctity of the clergy
but because it might be difficult for him to interfere so drasti-
cally in the ordered structure of the church.

Luther's readiness in the depth of his heart to take the
final steps is indicated already in the letter to Spalatin of July 10,
1520, in which he expressed himself regarding the burning of his
books, "Let them condemn and burn my things; I'll do the same
for them." [45] Especially to be considered here is the Latin edition of his answer to the bull, published even before the more
cautious German version, but not intended for the general lay
public. It is here that Luther repaid the pope in kind and with
all firmness returned his *Damnamus* to him: "Let us then fire
that folly of the Antichrist back into his mouth, and let us judge
and condemn him by his own words. . . . I herewith cast the
condemnation back upon those people themselves." [46] In sar-
castic imitation of the solemn papal style, Luther opposed the
bull with his own personal "I curse and execrate." [47] But this
was surely not intended to weaken in the least the supremely
serious intent of the formulas of condemnation. That there can
be no doubt about this is clear from the way in which Luther
underscored his *Damnamus* at another place: "If you persist in
that madness of yours, we condemn you and together with that
bull and all decretals of Satan we consign you to the destruction
of the flesh, so that your spirit may be set free together with you
in the day of the Lord. In the name of Him whom you are persecuting, Jesus Christ our Lord. Amen." The conclusion of this
essay points in the same direction: "Just as they excommunicate
me in the interests of their own sacrilegious heresy, so I in turn
excommunicate in the interests of the holy truth of God. Christ
the Judge will see which of the two excommunications counts
with Him. Amen." [48] Apparently Luther wanted to say — and it
does seem strange — that he would like to turn back upon the
originator not only the sentence of condemnation but also the
anathema.

We must be careful not to draw too far-reaching conclusions from this extreme provocation. Luther's own understanding of the ban did not in principle permit him to combat the pope
with the pope's own weapons, since Luther himself had acknowledged them to be questionable. His concern was not with

the form of the verdict but with its meaning, with the principle, the authority. In any case, he was sure that henceforth the pope must be numbered with the heretics.[49] His basis for this revolutionary reversal of the tradition and practice of the doctrinal hierarchy demonstrates the significance of this shift: "I too shall use my power by which in Baptism through the mercy of God I was made a son of God and a joint heir with Christ, founded upon a solid rock which fears neither the gates of hell nor heaven nor earth."[50] Against the whole powerful machinery for deployment of the papal forces Luther had nothing to draw up except the authority of the baptized child of God, the simple certainty of faith which is yet superior to all hierarchical pretensions. Only on the basis of this profound approach is it possible to understand the fact and the manner in which the extreme concentration of the negative was for Luther linked with the most decisive and certain positive, that both indeed conditioned and demanded each other, and that the one was inconceivable without the other.

Notes to Chapter 4

[1] Jan. 14, 1519. WA *Briefe*, 1, 302, 54.

[2] "*Bulla coenae domini*, that is, Concerning the Gluttonous Supper of the Most Holy Lord, the Pope, Done into German by Martin Luther, 1522," WA 8, 691ff.

[3] Ibid., 705, 14.

[4] Cf. Boehmer, p. 187.

[5] WA 6, 445, 20 (1520); cf. *An Open Letter to the Christian Nobility*, Holman (Philadelphia Ed.), Philadelphia: Muhlenberg Press, 1943, II, 126.

[6] WA 12, 15, 19 (1523). Cf. Preface to an Ordinance of a Common Chest, Holman, IV, 97f.

[7] WA 30 II, 493, 37; 474f. *(Von den Schluesseln)*; cf. American ed., 40, 335.

[8] *Sermo de virtute excommunicationis*, 1518, WA 1, 634ff. German version, in part more sharply worded, *Ein Sermon von dem Bann*, 1520, WA 6, 63ff. Cf. *A Treatise Concerning the Ban*, Holman, II, 40ff.

[9] WA 6, 74, 35; Holman, II, 53.

[10] WA 8, 694, 25; 695, 26; 704, 32.

[11] WA 8, 706, 10.

[12] WA 47, 289, 34 (comment on Matt. 18:18, from *Matthew 18—24, Expounded in Sermons*. Copy by Aurifaber, 1537—1540).

[13] WA 30 II, 502, 5 *(Von den Schluesseln)*. Cf. *The Keys*, American ed., 40, 370f. [For the translation "community" *(Gemeine)* see Large Catechism, Eighth Commandment, par. 280.—Trans.]

[14] WA 1, 647, 32 *(Reply to the Dialog of Sylvester Prierias Concerning the Power of the Pope, 1518)*.

[15] WA 6, 189, 41; 188, 13 *(Doctrinal Condemnation of the Books of Martin*

Luther Prepared by Some of Our Teachers at Louvain and Cologne. The Lutheran Reply to the Same Condemnation, 1520).

[16] WA 8, 291, 21, 26 *(An Opinion of the Paris Theologians Concerning the Teaching of Doctor Luther. A Counteropinion of Doctor Luther, 1521).* Luther undertook a thoroughgoing balancing of accounts with the Paris and Louvain theologians shortly before his death, but he did not complete it (WA 54, 447ff.).

[17] WA *Briefe,* 2, 135, 34 (Luther's letter to Spalatin, July 9, 1520, which was meant to furnish "material for the Elector's answers" to communications from Rome, Kalkoff, ZKG, 25, 457).

[18] WA 6, 483, 6 *(Erbieten. Oblatio sive protestatio, 1520).*

[19] Kalkoff, pp. 457, 552.

[20] Ibid., p. 567.

[21] Ibid, p. 572f.

[22] WA 6, 599, 2; 601, 8 *(Adversus execrabilem Antichristi bullam.* Cf. also the German version: *Wider die Bulle des Endchrists,* 1520, WA 6, 617ff.).

[23] WA 6, 618, 10.

[24] WA 6, 184, 1.

[25] WA 8, 293, 13.

[26] Kalkoff, ZKG, 25, 120ff.

[27] WA 50, 607, 7; cf. 7, 134, 15.

[28] WA *Briefe,* 1, 543, 87.

[29] WA 7, 97, 23 *(Assertion of All the Articles of Martin Luther Condemned in the Latest Bull of Leo X, 1520).*

[30] WA *Briefe,* 1, 359, 29.

[31] WA 2, 185ff. *(Luther's Resolution on His Thirteenth Proposition Regarding the Power of the Pope, 1519).*

[32] WA 6, 459, 2; cf. also K. Koehler, *Luther und die Juristen* (Gotha, 1873), pp. 31ff.; R. Sohm, *Kirchenrecht,* I (Leipzig, 1892), 460ff.

[33] WA 6, 411, 12.

[34] WA *Briefe,* 2, 137, 28.

[35] Boehmer, pp. 299ff.

[36] WA 7, 164, 11 *(Why the Books of the Pope and His Disciples Were Burned by Dr. Martin Luther, 1520).* Cf. American ed., 31, 384.

[37] WA 7, 180, 14.

[38] WA 7, 136, 9 *(Assertion of All the Articles, etc.).*

[39] WA 47, 293, 22.

[40] WA 9, 522, 17 *(Sermon on Luke 2:1ff.,* Dec. 25, 1520).

[41] WA 6, 322, 18 and 21 *(Concerning the Papacy at Rome).* Holman, I, 391f.

[42] WA 6, 322, 19; 321, 36. Holman, I, 391.

[43] WA 2, 201, 3.

[44] WA 6, 621, 27.

[45] WA *Briefe,* 2, 137, 27.

[46] WA 6, 602, 15; 611, 37.

[47] WA 6, 598, 10.

[48] WA 6, 604, 34; 612, 21.

[49] "You Romans are the heretics and godless schismatics, for you presume upon your own fictions and fly in the face of the clear Scriptures of God" (WA 6, 505, 23, *Concerning the Babylonian Captivity of the Church,* 1520; Holman, II, 184). "The pope is a heretic to me and I to him, because he is an opponent of Christ and I am the antipope" (WA *Tischreden,* 3, 605, Feb. 11, 1538).

[50] WA 6, 604, 21.

Doctrine – Pure Doctrine – False Doctrine

For the medieval attack on heresy both norm and court of judgment were united in the teaching church. Since the days of Thomas Aquinas heresy was defined as the pride-born decision to contradict the doctrine of the church. A heretic was anyone who obstinately contested a dogmatic truth established by the church and thus consciously and intentionally contradicted the church's teaching authority — "which authority resides principally in the supreme pontiff." [51] In his lectures on Romans Luther indeed criticized the manner in which the church was combating heretics,[52] but he was equally critical of the arrogance of the heretics as manifested in their rebellion against the church's doctrine. Instead of listening to the voice of the church they affirm "the wisdom of their own mind." [53] Here it was still a matter of man's teaching versus the church's teaching, of human private opinion versus the decision of the church. Barely five years later Luther found himself on the side of the heretics and schismatics, and now he, in his turn, discovered pride, man-made doctrine, and heresy on the side of the church and uttered his "I condemn." This raises two questions that we shall attempt to clarify here at least in outline (without being able to give exhaustive treatment to the whole complex of problems regarding doctrine and heresy). The questions are: (1) Where does Luther draw the line between pure doctrine and false doctrine, and by what standard does he now judge, since the church's doctrine has itself been recognized as "depraved doctrine"? (2) Where is the boundary line between church and heresy, and which court is to rule on this matter?

It is not surprising that the young Luther, quite in line with ecclesiastical tradition, could understand doctrine as the sum of things believable *(credibilia)*, the sum total of "what the church believes" and asks the people to believe.[54] The protest against the church, self-styled "teacher of the churches" and "norm of faith," [55] did indeed question the Roman teaching authority but did not yet crowd out the concept of doctrine as defined objectively. Yes, even against Carlstadt and his spiritualism reference was made to the "chief parts of Christian doctrine that everyone must observe and retain above all things." [56] However, although Luther in his early lectures spoke of doctrine in this sense, he also suggested an accent that was to become dominant for the whole concept of doctrine: Teaching is derived from "to teach"; doctrine needs to be proclaimed. The prelates, the ecclesiastical superiors, who must be obeyed in order to be protected by the shield of truth,[57] are not only the guardians and preservers of a clearly circumscribed body of transmitted doctrine, but they are the *proclaimers* of the church's doctrine.[58] This element becomes important also for the correct understanding of theology,[59] just as it belongs to the nature of the Word in any case. It is only in the Word, and that means the preached Word, that Christ wants His power and glory to become "manifest." But this does not indicate that the fundamental hiddenness of His rule is thereby set aside.[60] Thus the taught Word, that is, the preached and heard Word, is rated above the written and read Word. "The living voice teaches" *(viva vox docet)* — this is the most concise way to express this situation, which Luther liked to make clear on the basis of Mal. 2:7.[61] Here the spiritual office is very clearly described as a "teaching office," that is, as the office of proclaiming the external Word. Luther equated the "shepherding" entrusted to the pastor with "teaching," [62] and he never tired of recalling the bishops to this their proper task. Later he also used "teaching" and "preaching" as interchangeable terms.[63] Corresponding to the teaching and preaching on the part of the office is the "listening and learning" on the part of the congregation.[64] Occasionally this association of teaching and learning is restricted to the specific area of instruction, as, for example, in the preface to the Small Catechism.[65] But this was not intended to do away with the basic, comprehensive equation of teaching and proclaiming; for the Catechism, too, was to be *preached*.[66] On the other side, doctrine is not only "learned" in the narrow sense of the word, but it is also confessed.[67] It may be said in summary that in asserting that the Word must be taught Luther safeguarded, particularly against the claims of the Spiritualists, the teaching that God cannot be found "without means."

Here we must proceed at once to the subject matter, the content of doctrine — and thus to the significance of pure doctrine as it revealed itself to Luther, especially in his debate with the Enthusiasts and also in his defense against the Roman attack.[68] The Roman teaching hierarchy with its tendency to shape doctrine according to its discretion by means of "supplements" and "subsidiary doctrines," as well as the Spiritualists with their arbitrary reduction of doctrine, were, in Luther's estimation, classic examples of the dangerous attempt to subject the proclamation of the external Word to their own control and to do violence to the doctrinal content.

But how is the content of pure doctrine (a concept Luther used in manifold variations) determined? The first answer is: By means of the Scriptures, which are "the sole true liege lord and master over all writings and teachings on earth." [69] All doctrine must be "the holy, sure doctrine of the Scriptures." [70] Luther added immediately that "no one will produce for you a doctor of the Holy Scriptures save only the Holy Spirit from heaven." [71] The doctrine of Scripture, as sound doctrine, is exclusively also the true ancient teaching of the church.[72]

This, too, would still leave people in danger of getting stuck in the formal aspects and of permitting the proclamation to congeal into a recitation of dead formulas and so making it subject to human control after all, if pure doctrine were not defined more specifically as the doctrine of the Gospel, or — to say the same thing — "doctrine of faith," [73] Christ "should and must be preached in such a way that faith may be created and preserved for you and for me." [74] This happens only when the article of justification is in the center of the message; for this is "the true teaching whereby a man learns to fear and trust God." [75] To put it another way, "the Law and Christ, or simply, the remission of sins," are "the chief point of all Christian doctrine." [76] "To know the doctrine of Christ" means "to believe in Christ without works." [77] In this sense pure doctrine is "a preaching not only of words but also of experience," [78] a preaching that consoles and confirms consciences. Since the doctrine of Erasmus and of the

Enthusiasts does not accomplish this, it is not correct.[79] Luther
constantly summarized this basic feature of sound doctrine by
saying that it "must be in accordance with faith in Christ," [80] not
simply a faith that regards something as true (Luther called this
"knowledge or taking note" and did not recognize it as genuine
faith), but a faith that puts its trust in God, "takes God at His
Word and is daring for life or death," and alone is "living
faith."[81] Pure doctrine has its place not above or beyond, but
within the analogy of faith.

This principle was perhaps demonstrated already in the
first lectures on the Psalms, where in one passage Luther put
hearing, learning, and being apprehended above seeing, teaching, and apprehending.[82] Precisely the same is intended in
directing the "doctor of the Holy Scriptures" not only to the
Scriptures but also to the Spirit. The correlation of Word,
Spirit, and faith is not disrupted by pure doctrine. "Without the
Spirit of God the Word would not maintain itself. But what the
Spirit imprints on the heart and what creates faith is nothing
else than the content of the Word," [83] that content which constitutes the center and the meaning of pure doctrine.

In this framework of the pure doctrine, determined by the
principle of the analogy of faith, there is room for the normative
authority of *articles* of faith. Justification itself was for Luther
one article of faith among others, the "chief article," it is true,
and this is decisive, as it is demonstrated with particular emphasis in the Smalcald Articles. There are, however, additional
articles, such as the articles of faith in the ancient creeds, as well
as "the objective dogmas of the first four ecumenical councils,
the dogma of original sin and the doctrine of the bodily presence
in the Holy Supper." [84] None of them can be excluded from pure
doctrine, the factual preaching of the Gospel in Luther's sense.
All of them, however, have no independent validity apart from
the "chief article" but must be joined with it. In principle, therefore, the "statement of faith" *(fides quae creditur)* and the "faith
in the heart" *(fides qua creditur)* coalesce. The contact with the
teaching of the ancient church as here presented does not
represent an unbroken traditionalism, but receives its guiding
principle from the rediscovery of justification. "The Ecumenical
Creeds are not simply 'points of contact' for Luther for the
purpose of establishing the proper premises for hitherto un-

known insights. They are for him the anticipation of all his own insights." [85] This does not, of course, solve all the problems connected with Luther's relation to the dogma of the church.[86] But the essential aspect is tersely and correctly stated by Ludwig Ihmels, "Not until now (that is, with Luther) does dogma really become life; but in the process of becoming life it becomes new itself." [87]

Within the pure doctrine, as bracketed by the analogy of faith, there is room also for making distinctions in the concept of faith, as suggested by Luther's distinction of knowledge and assent, on the one hand, and of trust, on the other. It would not conform to his thinking to resolve this tension in a one-sided way, for example, by referring pure doctrine exclusively to the "noetic" side of faith. Over against the Enthusiasts Luther insisted that pure doctrine is concerned with knowledge.[88] But the correlation of mind and doctrine, which describes this situation seemingly on a purely intellectual level, is at once enlarged by the inclusion of conscience [89] and thus leads back into the full depth of Christian existence.[90] Also the manner in which Luther occasionally drew believing and learning very closely together indicates that faith as understanding must by no means be isolated from faith as trust.[91] It is true, as he put it at an early stage of his theological development, faith precedes knowledge.[92] This not only assures "trusting faith" that primacy which Luther accorded it later too, but it also gives expression to what matters above all, namely, that both faith and understanding, trust and knowledge are bestowed and created by the Spirit of God and are not the work of man. The act of "learning" drops out of the context of the justifying activity of God in Christ as little as dogma and doctrine. "The doctrinaire aspect that can attach itself to 'pure doctrine' is foreign to Luther's thought. Doctrine embraces the Gospel within itself, and this is a power that lays hold of the entire life, produces faith, love, and works, and unites the Christians in an internal and external fellowship." [93]

Under such circumstances, how can pure doctrine be distinguished from false doctrine? First of all, false doctrine is found wherever doctrine has disappeared, that is, where people think they can get along without the preaching of the external Word. If God really wished to replace this fundamental order by a new one, He would not do it without special signs and wonders, of which, however, there is no indication among the despisers of the external Word.[94] Carlstadt proves himself to be a false teacher in that he ranks the oral Word of the Gospel below the operation of the Spirit,[95] yes, in that he "desires to nullify God's external Word." [96] But in so doing he loses both the external Word and the Spirit. Where doctrine is no longer content to be proclamation of the external Word of God, nothing remains but "parson talk" (Pfaffenrede), the preacher can no longer be sure of his commission, and the congregation is plunged into doubt.[97]

False doctrine is further qualified as such by its content. The Roman "doctrine of men" is not to be condemned simply because it is doctrine preached by men, but because it is "contrary to the Gospel and the Scriptures." [98] "Scripture and God's Word" are the "sure rule" according to which doctrinal decisions must be made.[99] This Word of God, however, is the Gospel of the sinner's justification through Christ. The apostles proceeded so vehemently against the false teachers because, contrary to this Gospel, the false teachers thought of saving themselves in a Jewish manner by their own efforts.[100] One who turns the Gospel into a law and substitutes a doctrine of works for justification knows and hears neither Christ nor the Father — this, then, is "touchstone, straightedge, plumb, and balance" for separating pure doctrine from false doctrine.[101] It is only in this perspective that the Roman teaching is shown to be fully a negation of "God's pure doctrine" [102] and becomes subject to the anathema of Gal. 1:8f.[103] The same is true of the Enthusiasts. They, too, "nowhere teach how to get rid of sins, how to obtain a good conscience, and how to gain a peaceful, joyous heart toward God." [104] Again the analogy-of-faith principle appears: "Those teachers who teach what agrees with the faith in Christ we will honor and keep. But he who does not teach in conformity with the faith, him we will neither hear nor see." [105] Thus Luther comes to a definition of heresy: "Not to believe rightly, this creates heretics";[106] or still more clearly: The "quarrel and all heresy begins" in connection with the article of justification, that is, at this point that Christ's work "applies to me and you" and "that all that is in me and all that I might do is in vain." This is true even though other articles of faith may remain unchallenged.[107]

Luther seemed to be forsaking this principle when he looked at the history of dogmatic development, for he derived all heresy from a denial of the "chief article concerning Jesus Christ," as fixed in the ancient creeds of the church.[108] Yet he remained entirely consistent, because Christology and justification are completely interdependent.[109] The "chief article" of Jesus Christ coincides with the article of justification. Where this one "chief article" is attacked, where the "ring" of the analogy of faith, which encircles the pure doctrine, is damaged, there is false teaching. In this connection Luther used the metaphor of the ring several times. In his commentary on Galatians, 1531, he says, "The doctrine must be a round and golden ring without a crack," which means, "If I deny God in one article, I deny Him in all of them." [110] In his last polemic against the Swiss this thought was broadly developed and supplemented by the picture of the bell which loses its tone altogether as soon as it is damaged at any one place.[111] Hence the conclusion: "Believe everything whole and simple or believe nothing. The Holy Spirit does not permit Himself to be parted or divided, so that He should allow one part to be taught or believed truly and the other part falsely." [112] But does not this negate the primacy of faith in justification? Does not this mean that false doctrine, after all, consists in violating a body of doctrine conceived in formal terms and composed of a list of doctrines? Luther himself furnished examples to refute this interpretation. Arius "lost all articles of faith because he denied Christ, the true God of the creed," and only for this reason, because of this central error, "no article of faith is of any use to him." [113] It was the same with Macedonius and Nestorius, with the pope and his belief in man's own righteousness, with the sacramental teaching of the Swiss, whose remarks about spiritual eating are nothing more than "fig leaves," which cannot cover up the irreparable break in the ring of pure doctrine, the offence against the "chief article." [114] At the end of his life Luther felt that this required vigilance rather than magnanimity. "All heretics are of this kind that they begin by attacking only one article and then proceed to deny them all." [115] This was not intended to do away with a legitimate distinction between error and heresy (see below), between peripheral and central articles, but experience taught Luther that an innocent error is frequently only a pretext for and a prelude to an attack on the foundation.[116]

If, then, the criterion of pure and false doctrine remains anchored entirely in the article of justification, the yardstick of morality, of the pure life, is eliminated. "Doctrine and life must be distinguished" — Luther could not stress this point enough. Untiringly he advanced it against Emser and Duke Henry the Younger of Brunswick-Wolfenbuettel, against Carlstadt and other Enthusiasts who wanted to break away from the Word and lead people to their own works.[117] "The doctrine is not ours, the life is ours . . . Of the doctrine I cannot yield anything, of the life, everything." [118] "The life may be unclean, sinful, and frail, but the doctrine must be pure, holy, clean, and constant . . . Because the doctrine is God's Word and God's truth itself, whereas the life is partly our activity. Therefore the doctrine must remain entirely pure." [119] Naturally this was not intended to separate doctrine and life altogether. Only the proper sequence dare not be inverted. Pure doctrine can and must be held in esteem by *living* according to it, and that means "according to the faith." [120] However, a yardstick for evaluating doctrine cannot be derived from life.

Hence here, too, we must say: "The Word, the Word must do it." [121] The Word itself, when preached rightly, has the power to separate. "The living Word is the guardian of both doctrine and knowledge. It instructs the ignorant, it corrects the erring, it *condemns* the corrupters." [122] This is no place for the kind of tranquillity Erasmus longed for. The Word "must stir things up wherever it goes. If it does not, something is wrong." [123] No church can be built but that the devil will erect his chapel next door. It is "always certain . . . , where the Word of God flourishes, false doctrine, too, will grow, for the devil cannot bear the thought of permitting God's Word to remain clean and pure." [124] It is a life principle of the church that its message is proclaimed only in constantly renewed counteraction, in necessary antithesis to devil, sin, and death. For the church's word is the Word concerning Christ, and "Christ is represented as the One who has conquered and still conquers death, sin, and devil." [125] Just because this "polarity of proclamation" (G. Jacob), which operates in the opposition between pure doctrine and false doctrine, is inherent in the Word, a number of questions might be asked. Why bother about "judging doctrine," why combat false doctrine, if the Word itself already exercises this critical function? In view of Luther's conjunction of pure doctrine and analogy of faith, might it not be conceded that such judging is already in conflict with the principle of the hiddenness of the Word that creates faith? Luther did not evade these questions regarding the meaning and limits of condemnation. It is true, his answer was quite unequivocal, as will be shown later. The community has not only the right but the duty to "judge all doctrine" and protect its teaching from "contamination," "keep it pure," and in general "conserve" it.[126]

Attention must be called at least briefly to one other historical-critical question. Is this insistence on purity of doctrine after all not merely an expression of the much-cited "doctrinairism" of the "old" Luther that can be properly understood only in contrast to the "young" Luther's theology of the cross (theologia crucis)? Unquestionably the later period furnishes more and stronger evidence for this. Unquestionably the attack on the Enthusiasts first made the emphasis on pure doctrine as the correct preaching of the external Word thoroughly urgent and necessary. At first Luther's concern was to renounce and separate himself from the false church of the pope. Only later was he forced to face the question of how to deal with the false teachers in his own ranks. It has also been pointed out that the aging Luther's intensified experience of assaults by the demonic powers produced for him a "sealing off of the poles." As the power of Satan was now experienced in a more massive way, so likewise was the "concreteness of the incarnate God," where the embattled conscience sought and found comfort.[127] Whether in this way Luther's later efforts in behalf of pure doctrine can be adequately motivated cannot be determined here. But surely even this would not yet provide a true antithesis to the earlier theology of the cross. The chief characteristic of God's revelation as a revelation under concealment, on the contrary, would not yet be negated.[128] Likewise Luther's concept of pure doctrine in its decisive feature proved to be not an orientation to concrete norms and precepts but a correlation with justification by faith.

Notes to Chapter 5

[51] *Summa Theologica*, 2, 2, 11, 1 and 2.

[52] Ficker, II, 261, 3; 298, 14.

[53] Zech. 13: "And it shall come to pass, that when any shall yet prophesy, then his father and his mother that begat him (that is, the bishop and the church) shall say unto him, 'Thou shalt not live' (that is, thou shalt be anathematized and excommunicated), 'for thou hast spoken lies in the name of the Lord. . . .' This is the most powerful spear by which the heretics are pierced" (ibid., 248, 7). Cf. ibid., 88, 7; also K. Holl, *Gesammelte Aufsaetze zur Kirchengeschichte*, I, *Luther*, 6th ed. (Tuebingen, 1932), p. 309, n. 1. Documentation from the Lectures on the Psalter, ibid., p. 303, n. 7.

[54] *Lectures on Romans*, Ficker, II, 86.

[55] WA 12, 188, 23.

[56] WA 18, 65, 6 (*Against the Heavenly Prophets*, 1525). American ed., 40, 82.

[57] WA 4, 76, 25.

[58] *Lectures on Romans*, Ficker, II, 88, 10. Cf. Holl, pp. 308ff.

[59] "Sacred theology, though it is doctrine divinely inspired, does not shrink from being treated in letters and words" (WA 6, 29, 5).

[60] "So hidden is the glory and power of Christ's kingdom that unless it were made manifest to the hearer through the preached word it could not be recognized, since to the eyes it appears very much like the opposite, such as disgrace, weakness, lowliness, and extreme despondency in all believers" (WA 4, 450, 39. *Lectures on the Psalter*, 1513/16).

[61] "Reading is not as profitable as hearing. The living voice teaches, admonishes, defends, and withstands the spirit of error. And the written Word of God does not slow down Satan at all, but he takes flight at the speaking of the Word. For this enters the hearts and reclaims the erring" (WA 13, 686, 9. *Lectures on Malachi*, 1526); cf. 6, 564, 18.

[62] "To pasture means to give the doctrine by which the soul lives, namely faith and the Gospel" (WA 7, 417, 9, on John 21:15ff. *Basis and Cause of All Articles*, 1521).

[63] E. g., WA 37, 115, 14 and 18.

[64] WA 18, 124, 13.

[65] WA 30 I, 264ff.

[66] WA *Tischreden*, 4, 434, 10; 6, 181, 28.

[67] "If the confessed doctrine remains, we can do our opponents no greater damage" (WA 28, 290, 5. *Sermon on John 18:19ff.*, Jan. 16, 1529).

[68] On the problem of Luther's views on pure doctrine cf. W. Walther, *Das Erbe der Reformation*, IV: *Luthers Kirche* (Leipzig, 1917), pp. 49ff.; R. Seeberg, *Lehrbuch der Dogmengeschichte*, IV/1, 4th ed. (Leipzig, 1933), pp. 374ff.; H. J. Iwand, *Rechtfertigungslehre und Christusglaube* (Leipzig, 1930), pp. 4f.; K. Thieme, *Die Augsburgische Konfession und Luthers Katechismen* (Giessen, 1930), pp. 231ff.; H. Obendiek, *Der Teufel bei Martin Luther* (Berlin, 1931), pp. 135ff.; H. Preuss, *Martin Luther*, II, *Der Prophet* (Guetersloh, 1933), pp. 192f.; G. Moldaenke, *Schriftverstaendnis und Schriftdeutung im Zeitalter der Reformation*, I: *Matthias Flacius Illyricus* (Stuttgart, 1936), p. 370, n. 17.

[69] WA 7, 317, 7.

[70] WA 6, 460, 26.

[71] Ibid., 460, 30.

[72] WA 27, 511, 8.

[73] WA 18, 118, 5; cf. ibid., 63, 24: *Doctrine of Faith and of a Good Conscience*.

[74] WA 7, 29, 13 (*The Freedom of a Christian*, 1520).

75 WA 7, 445, 24.

76 WA 27, 365, 3; 378, 9.

77 WA 29, 481, 7 and 17 (Sermon on Matt. 7:15ff., July 18, 1529). Cf. 36, 507, 2: "The Gospel does not speak of my work, but of Christ's, who died, etc. These are not my works, but Christ's, which He did Himself. How are they acquired? Through faith, as he says about the Corinthians. This is true doctrine and faith. In the Gospel (these are) the chief articles, and through them you stand and are saved" (Sermon on 1 Cor. 15:1ff., Aug. 11, 1532).

78 WA 45, 599, 5; cf. 36, 506, 6: "I, by the grace of God, am able to preach about faith, because I have Scripture on my side and then also experience. If you would ask all the sectaries, they would be forced to confess that they had not had the experience."

79 WA 26, 52, 21 (Lectures on First Timothy, 1528).

80 WA 30 III, 375, 16; cf. 51, 132, 10.

81 WA 7, 215, 4. 11. 14 (A Short Form of the Ten Commandments, A Short Form of the Creed, etc., 1520). Cf. 16, 232, 11.

82 "In holy and divine matters it is more necessary to hear than to see, to believe than to understand, to be embraced than to embrace, to be grasped than to grasp, to learn than to teach, to be a disciple than to be a doctor or one's own master" (WA 4, 95, 1, Lectures on the Psalter, 1513/16). Quoted by E. Seeberg, Luthers Theologie, I (Goettingen, 1929), 209, n. 72.

83 L. Ihmels, Das Dogma in der Predigt Luthers (Leipzig, 1912), p. 21. Cf. H. Bornkamm, Das Wort Gottes bei Luther (Munich, 1933), pp. 9ff.

84 K. Thieme, p. 232.

85 F. Kattenbusch, Luther und die oecumenischen Symbole (Giessen, 1883), p. 16.

86 In addition to Kattenbusch see also O. Ritschl, Dogmengeschichte des Protestantismus, I (Leipzig, 1908), 268ff.; Thieme, pp. 129ff.; cf. H. Bornkamm's critique ("Die Literatur des Augustana-Gedaechtnisjahres," ZKG, 50 [1931], 212f.).

87 Ihmels, p. 60.

88 "The mind, that is, judgment concerning things . . . is a cognitive power in man which receives doctrine" (WA 25, 39, 13). "Christian doctrine must be frequently taught, because it is seated in understanding, the chief thing among Christians, that they may increase in the knowledge of Jesus" (ibid., 73, 3).

89 Treated in detail in WA 25, 39, 14ff. Also: "All doctrine shapes the conscience" (26, 69, 20), and on the other hand: "All doctrine comes from the conscience" (ibid., 69, 14). Cf. 16, 76, 1.

90 Cf. G. Jacob, Der Gewissensbegriff in der Theologie Luthers (Tuebingen, 1929), pp. 44f., where, however, the passages cited here are not considered.

91 "You must believe and learn that when you hear the Word from the mouth of Christ you may add that it is not man's word but assuredly God's Word, and then you are a pupil of God and of the Lord Jesus Christ, and you believe correctly, and God the Father will then instruct you inwardly" (WA 33, 144, 11, Week-day Sermons on John 6 – 8, Feb. 4, 1531).

92 "Knowledge comes only from faith that is there before" (WA 4, 289, 15). "Because God appeared in human form, He can be perceived by the senses only as man: therefore understanding is necessary and faith supplies it" (ibid., 94, 32; cf. E. Seeberg, p. 208).

93 R. Seeberg, p. 377.

94 WA 18, 97, 1; 27, 510, 4.

95 WA 18, 136, 11.

96 WA 18, 204, 23.

97 WA Tischreden, 6, 253, 10.

[98] WA 10 II, 91, 21.

[99] WA 52, 838, 21; cf. 48, 215, 18.

[100] WA 8, 667, 28.

[101] WA 46, 8f.; 9, 10.

[102] WA 10 II, 106, 17.

[103] WA 2, 462, 29.

[104] WA 18, 213, 30.

[105] WA 30 III, 375, 15.

[106] WA 6, 294, 30; cf. 2, 462, 23: "He is a heretic . . . who sins against the word of faith."

[107] WA 37, 46, 1—4 ("Sermon on the Second Article, April 16/17, 1533"). Cf. Iwand, p. 7, n. 1.

[108] WA 50, 266, 33; 267, 14 ("The Three Symbols, 1538"). American ed., 34, 207.

[109] Cf. the entire book by Iwand, mentioned above.

[110] WA 40, II, 47, 3; 48, 6.

[111] WA 54, 159, 1 ("Short Confession Concerning the Holy Sacrament, 1544").

[112] Ibid., 158, 28.

[113] WA 54, 159, 24.

[114] Ibid., 160, 33.

[115] Ibid., 158, 36.

[116] "A small error in the beginning is a very large one in the end" (WA 40 II, 46, 4).

[117] WA 18, 116, 14.

[118] WA 40 II, 46, 6.

[119] WA 30 III, 343, 24; cf. 7, 278, 36; 13, 688, 13; 18, 112, 9 and 114ff.; 20, 293, 13; 23, 29, 18; 24, 606, 33; 32, 510, 18; 33, 371, 30; 37, 669, 17; 51, 516, 32; 517, 19; WA *Tischreden*, 1, 294, 19; 295, 3.

[120] WA 32, 216, 7.

[121] WA 18, 117, 3.

[122] WA 13, 686, 13.

[123] WA *Tischreden*, 6, 157, 18.

[124] WA 23, 573, 22 ("Commentary on Zechariah, 1527"); cf. 17 I, 448, 7; 28, 289, 5; 33, 365, 10.

[125] G. Jacob, p. 37.

[126] WA 48, 215, 20; 51, 521, 19; 40 II, 51, 1; 25, 47, 21; 30 II, 539, 23.

[127] G. Jacob, pp. 3, 38f.

[128] This is admitted also by Jacob (ibid., p. 3).

Chapter 6

The Church of the Pure Doctrine

Luther's line of demarcation between pure and false doctrine is validated and confirmed by his understanding of the church. Pure doctrine always remains bracketed with the analogy of faith and can never be defined and delimited without reference to justifying faith. In the same way the church in its innermost essence dare not be identified with any specific empirical mode of appearance—neither the salvation-dispensing institution of Roman Catholicism nor the Spirit-community of the Enthusiasts. "To be asked to believe what we see bodily," [129] in other words, to remove the fundamental hiddenness of the church and to substitute sight for faith—this was for Luther the basic error of the Roman view of the church, a view which recurs with a new twist among the Enthusiasts in their ideal of a pure community. Luther, on the contrary, saw the church essentially as "a community or assembly of the saints in faith" [130] and as such "something very much hidden . . . so that no one can know it or see it. It must be grasped and believed exclusively on the basis of Baptism, Sacrament, and Word." [131] This "faith-oriented concept of the hidden church" [132] which alone does justice to the New Testament reality of the church as the body of Christ [133] undoubtedly retained, as we now know, the chief accent in Luther's understanding of the church. This is true even in the light of certain shifts in emphasis which were possible for him within this fundamental view. Hence also the unity of the church can only be a unity in faith and arising from faith. "Those who have a true faith know that everything depends on faith, in this they are of one mind. Therefore they do not part company and become disunited because of any external station, manner of life, or work." [134]

It is, to be sure, no less clear that the invisibility of the church, understood in this way, does not justify letting the church in Luther's sense evaporate into an unreal illusion like a Platonic state. Since the church is the body of Christ, it, too, is "in the flesh" *(involuta in carne)*, and yet it is not flesh. It is in the world, and yet it is not the world.[135] The church is visible — yet not by virtue of the pure life of its members, nor by virtue of their faith, since this is removed from external observation. But the church is visible through the preached Word or, according to Rom. 10:10, on the basis of confession, as Luther expressed these thoughts in the disputation of 1542, referred to earlier, which was so important for his concept of the church. This does not mean, of course, that confession is to be understood as the norm for a "confessional status," but as "the act of making the church's faith explicit in the proclamation of the Word of God." [136] Thus the concepts of church and of doctrine meet at this point. It is the doctrine, the preaching of the Gospel, together with the administration of the sacraments, that assures the empirical recognition of the church — without removing its hiddenness. And it is doctrine in this sense that has its place, though with a different inflection, among the various lists of the church's marks in Luther's writings.[137] As the church is the "creature of the Word" and proceeds from the Word,[138] so in its visible form it can renew itself and grow only through the preaching of the Word.[139]

It should be noted that here, too, orthodoxy as commitment to the church's confessions is not excluded but included, as Luther's estimation of the ancient creeds shows. It, too, helps to make the invisible church perceptible,[140] but the latter's hiddenness is of course not thereby removed in a universally accessible openness to view.[141] Doctrine, as pure doctrine, can only be the message concerning faith, so that precisely from the perspective of the correct understanding of doctrine the primacy of the church's invisibility is always safeguarded, and there can be no cleavage in the invisible-visible church.

Thus while the distinction between the invisibility and the visibility of the church does not signify a separation, it is equally certain, according to Luther, that the true church must be separated from the false church. Here the divisive power which inheres in the Word itself becomes operative. Luther never doubted that there were at all times true Christians also in the papal church and that the true church existed there. But he was equally certain that the majority of the papists did not belong to the "true Christendom," and that this was true of individuals "because of their unbelief and their evil life," [142] or, looking at the Roman Church as such, because it "acts and speaks without Christ's Word and without faith," and thus errs and acts sinfully.[143] This cleavage runs diametrically through the empirical church. With reference to faith the church remains in hiddenness. In the act of separation from false teachers, which is demanded of the church on earth, the church at the same time reaches over into the realm of the perceptible. By separating from the heretics the ancient church showed itself to be the obedient disciple of its Lord and of the Word of God.[144] Quite apart from *what* they teach, heretics cannot be numbered with the true church, already because they teach without a valid call. "Let not the intruder teach." [145] For the church on earth it can actually be a validation of its Gospel preaching to be constantly entrusted with the antithesis to pseudoprophets, and thus it may not count on lasting concord even within its own ranks.[146] What the devil cannot accomplish through the pope and the emperor he now tries to achieve in the inner circle of those who consider themselves in agreement on decisive points.[147] Nothing less is at stake than the antithesis between Christ's church and the devil's church,[148] which corresponds to the opposition between pure doctrine and the devil's doctrine and on its part shares in the tension between the visibility and invisibility of the church. The decision is always made with regard to doctrine: "Where this teaching about Christ is not present nor accepted, there the people of God are not present," [149] even though Baptism and the church's creeds are still unopposed and still used and acknowledged, as Luther adds explicitly. Hypocrites and false Christians may be tolerated in the church; "but when a point of disunity in doctrine is reached, then there must be a separation, and it will become evident who the true Christians are, namely those who have God's Word, pure and straight." [150]

The fact that Luther always traced false teaching back to the devil, and the fact that he called Carlstadt a heathen who has lost Christ [151] was accordingly no hyperbole, but for Luther it was a factual statement of the separation between true church and false church. Luther's position was not always unequivocal on this point. In his first Galatians commentary he asked in connection with Jerome, "How can Paul still call the Galatian groups churches, though they have succumbed to false doctrine and though they lack everything that constitutes the true church?"[152] In 1519 the answer was still tentative. Luther thought that in any case the church on earth would never be perfect and that while the bad members *(mali)* should be corrected and reproved, they would ultimately have to be borne in love and not be renounced. In 1531, with reference to the Enthusiasts, a clearer answer was given: Paul means to say that Satan is active in the midst of the Christian community and that this community is located in the midst of a world full of enmity against God; it will, of course, remain a Christian community only as long as it does not discard Word and Sacrament. It is therefore also proper to say, "The holy church exists among the Enthusiasts, except for those who deny the sacraments and the Word; they are not the church."[153] In the end Luther regarded 1 John 2:19 as the passage that best describes the antithetical relationship between false teachers and the church: "They went out from us, but they were not of us." "They are in the church, but not of the church. Again, they are in numerically, but not rightfully."[154] They will always find a place in the church on earth, yet they do not on that account belong to the true Christendom.

According to Luther, early as well as late, the true church cannot be unequivocally identified with an empirical circle of people. Though it is certain that there are additional marks of the church or of heresy, the doctrine that Luther regarded as the decisive criterion of membership in the true church was and remained the preaching about faith and thus preserved the characteristic of hiddenness even in the area of the empirical church. Without this insight Luther's concept of the church cannot be correctly understood. Hence it must be said: The fact that the true doctrine is present in an empirical fellowship does not yet justify an identification of this fellowship with the true church, although it does permit recognition of the true church within this fellowship.[155] Here, as before, we arrive at a boundary line of the cleavage between true and false church, about which more will have to be said in connection with the limits of condemnation. It was, of course, equally certain for Luther that the negative conclusion may not be drawn in such a way as to suggest that the church as a mixed group must now dispense with every evaluation and rejection of false teachings and teachers.

Notes to Chapter 6

[129] WA 6, 322, 14.

[130] WA 6, 301, 1; cf. ibid., 293, 4.

[131] WA 51, 507, 14 (*Against Hans Worst*, 1541).

[132] Thieme, p. XIII.

[133] Cf. WA 6, 299, 9.

[134] WA 10 I, 1, 132, 14 (*Sermon on Luke 2:15ff.*, 1522).

[135] "The church is a community of such a nature that unless the Holy Spirit would reveal it we could not grasp it, because it is in the flesh and it appears visible, it is in the world and appears in the world, and yet it is not the world, nor is it in the world, and nobody sees it" (WA 39 II, 149, 8; 161, 16. *Disputation*, 1542). Cf. E. Kohlmeyer, "Die Bedeutung der Kirche fuer Luther," ZKG, 1928, p. 478.

[136] W. Walther, p. 33, n. 1.

[137] Cf. M. Doerne, "Gottes Volk und Gottes Wort," Luther-Jahrbuch, 1932, pp. 76ff., where WA 6, 301, 3 should be added. "The preaching of the Gospel in the 'external church' is . . . the external mark of the 'internal church'" (E. Schlink, *Theology of the Lutheran Confessions*, trans. Paul F. Koehneke and Herbert J. A. Bouman, Philadelphia: Fortress Press, 1961, p. 220, n. 19).

[138] WA 2, 430, 6; cf. Doerne, p. 67.

[139] "To teach is to beget, and the church teaches. Through what? Through the ministry of the Word . . . the church should be doing nothing but beget children. And this begetting consists of rightly preaching the Gospel" (WA 40 I, 664, 3 and 8; cf. Iwand, p. 4, n. 1).

[140] Thieme, pp. 237, 243.

[141] Thieme's statement "To determine the purity of doctrine is possible not only for the Spirit and for faith" (p. 243) would seem to be going beyond Luther's view. As Kohlmeyer has shown, the marks of the church are in any case not "conceptual marks" but only "heuristic principle" (p. 500) and therefore must be judged by faith. Luther himself presupposes the Spirit's illumination for the judgment of doctrine (WA 33, 146, 20).

[142] WA 6, 294, 11.

[143] WA 30 III, 342, 28 (*Commentary on the Alleged Imperial Verdict*, 1531).

[144] WA 33, 365, 21.

[145] WA 25, 7, 25; cf. 18, 213, 19.

[146] WA 29, 475, 17; 477, 6; cf. 40 I, 647, 3.

[147] WA 51, 131, 16.

[148] WA 30, II, 321, 12; 29, 476, 16; 38, 545, 24; 51, 477, 25; 512, 19; 518, 35; 530, 27.

[149] WA 33, 627, 25 (*Sermon on John 8:28*, Nov. 25, 1531); cf. 45, 621, 34.

[150] WA 51, 521, 35.

[151] WA 18, 122, 2.

[152] "The apostle gives the name of church to those who were struggling with error not of morals . . . but of faith, and everything that made it possible for them to be called churches was lost" (WA 2, 456, 26).

[153] WA 40 I, 71, 6.

[154] WA 51, 521, 32 et passim. 38, 651, 33.

[155] Cf. Thieme, p. 244; H. Bornkamm, "Die Kirche in der Augustana," *Monatsschrift fuer Pastoraltheologie*, 1930, pp. 192f.

Chapter 7

Significance, Authority, and Limits of Rejection

Luther's rejection of the Roman Antichrist and his judgment on the false teachings in his own camp make it perfectly clear that it is neither possible nor permissible to be indifferent to false doctrine. In practice, however, a multitude of possibilities remain that can hardly be brought into systematic order and yet indicate certain degrees of judgment. It is necessary, first of all, to recognize false doctrine as such and to label it, so that the Christian community will not be deceived by the sheep's clothing of the wolves. Hence there is need of "indication" of false doctrine, and this is one of the duties of the ministry.[156] It is to the community as a whole, however, that Jesus addresses His admonition, "Beware!" "No greater warning" than this can be found in Scripture.[157] It says "that we must surely be on our guard at all times so that such sectarians do not deceive us. We must be armed against them and learn to know them for what they are. By saying, 'beware,' Jesus wants to teach us not to be patient in this matter but to open our eyes, be alert, cautious, and prudent. . . . Here we cannot endure or concede anything, but we must be alert and circumspect and not take our own brother's word for anything, but look with keen, wide-awake eyes exclusively to the Word." [158] The Word itself demands such watchfulness. But it also demands the war on false doctrine, for it is just in this way that the Word demonstrates its power.[159] Luther knew full well that there would not be an unbroken succession of victories. He was skeptical of the "successes" that people might expect. "If we should look at the devil and the false brethren, it would be better if there were no preaching, writing, or action. It would be better just to die quickly and be buried, because they pervert and blaspheme everything anyway." Nevertheless, "we must keep on fighting and suffering." [160]

This, then, is the place for the verdict of rejection in the narrower sense — that "condemnation" as Luther applied it again and again against false doctrine ever since his defense against the Roman ban. Yet there is no set use of certain concepts discernible, nor is the meaning of the verdict defined in a way to fix its precise limits. It is just this that shows what Luther had in mind. He did not want a continuation of the late medieval practice of censures with its whole schematic structure. On the contrary, without having recourse to an application of fixed rules, he wanted simply to determine the error, a decision that would have to be made anew in each case. The conclusions to be drawn for the person of the false teacher really lie beyond this matter and already belong into the domain of church discipline. It is true, the false teachers have already condemned themselves (Tit. 3:11) whether they know it or not. For that very reason the attempt is permissible and desirable to convince them of their error through the power of the truth.[161] For "those are God's children who combine their reproof of evil with long-suffering." [162] But where the brotherly admonition is refused, there is nothing left but to "despise" the false teachers or, according to Matt. 15:14, to "let them alone." [163] Occasionally Luther could say that a false teacher is "apart from Christ and under the devil," [164] and later the "verdict to hell" or the surrender to Satan is mentioned as the ultimate step in the procedure against false teachers.[165] However, the former statement is immediately followed by the counsel, "Pray for him and admonish him, in order to convert him." Luther generally attached much value to brotherly admonition of the erring and practically placed it beside the ministerial office.[166] Judgment on doctrine must indeed be incisive enough: "You must sharpen your teeth and bite whatever is contrary to sound doctrine." At the same time, "You must correct, not castigate." [167] The basic distinction between doctrinal discipline and church discipline, as Luther drew it from the New Testament, should never be removed. In Luther's view, the "apostasy from faith and doctrine," which is a concern of the Pastoral Epistles, is with good reason handled differently by Paul than the case of the incestuous person in Corinth because the latter was not a "sin against the faith." [168]

It is not surprising that there is as yet no consideration of governmental intervention against false teachers in the matter of condemnatory verdicts. It is well known that Luther's views on this point experienced some development.[169] In principle, however, he always clung to the opinion that a distinction must constantly be made between the judgment of doctrine and the governmental penalties against heretics, between the decision to be made on doctrinal grounds and that made on the basis of civil law.[170]

But what is the relationship of the sentence of condemnation to the anathema? Quite clearly Luther had dissociated himself from the formalistic Roman practice of theological censorship. Manifestly he must also repudiate the extravagant claims of the church's penal authority which found expression in the equation of anathema and excommunication in the Middle Ages. Luther in fact broke through this established penal procedure and again saw the anathema primarily as separation from Christ Himself and then, indeed, secondarily also as separation from those who belong to Christ.[171] In the lectures on Romans Luther went so far as to follow the lead of mysticism in making the anathema so spiritual that it is equated with the "resignation to hell," that complete submission to the will of God which dispenses the "perfect saints" from the punishment of purgatory.[172] This view of the anathema was subsequently abandoned. In 1518 Luther gave thought to the etymology of the word anathema without, however, producing new insights into the content of the term.[173] The lectures on Galatians provide a new impetus to ponder the application of the anathema to false teachers. The definition, based on the Old Testament "ban," again goes far beyond the church's penal authority. Anathema signifies a passionate zeal: something cursed, execrated, and completely cut off from the enjoyment of the blessings of God and the association and fellowship with Him.[174] This axiom applies in principle to all false teachers of all time.[175] From this it already follows that Luther was here thinking not of disciplinary measures but rather, in the spirit of the New Testament, of the separation from Christ and His body that the false teacher brings upon himself. In this way anathema and rejection are drawn very closely together, but this is done by leaping over the medieval development of legal procedure. Luther's numerous allusions to Gal. 1:8f. make this abundantly clear.[176] It is true, the anathema retains its specific accent to the extent that it expresses the side of the judgment of condemnation that is turned toward God. The *Damnamus*, on the other hand, wants to be understood primarily as the verdict of the church.

While this verdict is in no sense an ecclesiastical means of punishing false teachers, it is nevertheless very important for the Christian community itself in that thereby false teaching is labeled as such. In view of the false teachers, Luther was occasionally inclined to offer his resignation. As already stated, Luther had few illusions about the possibility of influencing them. All the more he insisted: "For the sake of the pious who want to be saved we must live, preach, write, and do and endure everything." [177] Already in his first lectures on the Psalms Luther had compared the church with a mother hen that covers and "overshadows" her chicks with her wings, that is, with the church's overseers, and she does this by protecting the faithful from the demons by means of the true doctrine.[178] Also later on, in Luther's defense of condemnations, the concern for doubting consciences and for future generations of the Christian community predominated, rather than the thought that possibly some of the false teachers might be brought back to the truth.[179] The welfare of the church is served not only when a "victory" over false teachers has been achieved — a victory that would always remain doubtful — but rather in service to the brethren who are thus alerted to the danger.[180] Hence the chief concern in the rejection of false teaching is the effective self-preservation of the Christian community. Only in this way may we account for the urgency with which Luther impressed upon the church not only the right but also the duty of passing judgment on doctrine.

Basically, according to Luther, the Christian community has only this "single, unconditional obligation . . . to provide free course for the Word." [181] The command to beware of false prophets surely does not imply flight or toleration. A poor Christian indeed who would be satisfied with remaining on the defensive and have no desire to wield the sword of the Spirit himself! [182] "How is it possible to be on guard against the false prophets if we do not take note of their teaching and evaluate and judge the same?" So Luther asks in the monograph written in 1523 specifically to emphasize this responsibility.[183] As Holl has shown, Luther was certain already at an early date that in principle also the individual Christian has the right and the duty to judge doctrine: "The spiritual man is made by faith. He judges all but is himself judged by no one." [184] As a member of the universal priesthood each Christian is "to be concerned for the faith, to understand and defend it, and to condemn all error." [185] Luther found this obligation implied already in the Second Commandment.[186] In principle he wanted no member of the whole "new class of clerics" to be excluded from this obligation.[187] This does indeed require some knowledge of the *doctrina Christi*.[188] Above all it is necessary to rely on the help of the Holy Spirit, whom God has promised to His church and who will give the church's judgments a certainty that transcends all possibilities of empirical demonstration.[189] It is, then, every Christian's right and duty to "separate one teaching from another and say, 'God has said this, He has not said that.' Again, 'this comes from God, that comes from the devil.'" [190] This makes every one a "fine doctor and teacher," [191] who has the authority not by human right but by divine right, to "evaluate and judge all things." [192]

Now, it is true, in the practical application of these principles the ministerial office plays an increasingly more prominent role. Luther knew "that all Christians have the priesthood but not all have its function, even though they all had the ability to teach." [193] Hence the Christian community asks specially qualified or trained preachers and teachers to assume the exercise of its teaching authority. In their commission the act of teaching and of judging doctrine are most intimately linked together.[194] "It behooves . . . a doctor not only to teach his own materials but also to refute contrary teachings *(aliena)*." [195] Just as surely as all Christians have the right and the duty "to judge doctrine," so a special responsibility is here placed on the preachers of the Word,[196] for they are the shepherds whose responsibility it is not only to "feed the sheep" but also to "resist the wolves." [197] They are commissioned to keep the proclamation and the doctrine pure, as Luther put it in his commentary on Zechariah, "Among the teachers there must be those who keep cleaning and polishing the lamp so that the dirt will not obscure the light." [198] In this sense the incumbents of the evangelical teaching office are the successors of the councils — "though small, they are eternal and beneficial councils." [199] Whenever a council "anathematizes" properly, this is "nothing else than a consistory, the verdict of the imperial or supreme court, or the like." It does not proceed arbitrarily but in conformity with the imperial law of the kingdom of God, that is, the Scriptures.[200] Now, "the servant or judge of this law and kingdom is not only the council, but also every pastor and teacher." "To defend the true Christian faith," this is their office as it was formerly carried out by the ancient councils.[201]

It is known that Luther himself repeatedly drew strength for his battles from the awareness of this obligation. He wrote to Spalatin in July 1520 that he was not at liberty to give up his "office of teaching and his ministry of the Word"; and therefore he should be allowed the freedom to do justice to his office. He continues: "I am already sufficiently burdened with many sins, and I don't want to add this unforgivable one that having been put into the ministry I would fail to perform it and be found guilty of an ungodly silence, of neglected truth, and of so many thousands of souls." [202] He speaks similarly in his writing in which he justifies the book burning at the Elster gate. "Though unworthy, I am a baptized Christian as well as a sworn doctor of the Holy Scriptures and a daily preacher besides. Thus by virtue of my title, status, oath, and office it is my duty to destroy or at least oppose false, seductive, and unchristian teaching." [203] "To move in on doctrine"—this, in view of Rome, Luther regarded as his life's commission.[204] Iwand is correct in his observation that Luther's so-called "self-consciousness" can be properly understood only from the perspective of his call to teach.[205] One who fails to see this will naturally find in Luther nothing but an inhuman arrogance that has so completely blinded him that he has the presumption to equate his own doctrine with God's doctrine and his own "judgment" with God's judgment.[206] The critics of this seeming presumptuousness, from King Henry VIII to modern opponents of Luther,[207] failed to appreciate Luther's understanding of doctrine; else they would have had to realize that he regarded doctrine as not at all subject to human controls, but rather, as nothing less than the preaching of the Gospel commanded by God, and also that he thought of the commission to judge doctrine as directly related to the Word itself.

The Word, the Gospel, was for Luther the criterion according to which he drew the line between pure and false teaching, between true and false church. From the Word he drew for himself and for all Christians the obligation to ward off false teaching by means of the condemnatory verdict. In the Word, finally, Luther also discovered the boundaries set for judging doctrine. As far as the goal and the success of condemnations were concerned, he followed the principle: "A heretic has never been overcome." [208] It is impossible for the church on earth to be entirely without "sects and schisms." It is true, the schismatics who disturb true Christian unity are of the devil; but it is equally certain that these sectaries *must* be, as Luther often stressed in connection with 1 Cor. 11:19.[209]

Above all, however, it was the parable of the tares among the wheat to which Luther referred again and again in this connection. It appeared to him beyond question that here the Lord Himself was forbidding all extirpation of heretics. Already in his first lecture on the Psalms he had stated that the tares were necessary,[210] and later on he had warned the papal condemnators that in pulling up the weeds they would also uproot the wheat.[211] Since the Word must exert its power on the erring, all physical penalties would be a mistake. "By murdering the people we separate them from the Word so that it cannot operate in them." [212] From this the further conclusion is drawn that the preachers are to be advised "to have patience and endure such blasphemy and commit it to God." [213] Christ desires to say: "Do not wish to be without evil men and heretics. You will not be able to change this situation. It will be up to Me to judge this matter in the coming judgment, where I will release you from this forbearance." [214] Hence the command to exercise patience does not demand coming to terms with false teaching and its representatives. Rather, one must learn to view them from the perspective of eternity and not presume to interfere with God's coming judgment on them by imposing physical penalties upon them. In a sermon on Matt. 18:7 Luther observed that in this life the good and the evil are still interwoven and the devil has not yet been fully confined to hell. Not until Judgment Day will it be possible to say: Here is heaven and there is hell.[215]

Under no circumstances is the command to let the tares grow intended to encourage indifference to false doctrine or to relieve the Christian community of the responsibility of passing judgment. Already Augustine, in a notable commentary on Matt. 13:29f., had shown that the parable of the tares did not ask for leniency over against notorious sin, even though love must also be allowed to do its work with a view to betterment. On occasion Luther made explicit reference to this passage.[216] But while patience with heretics is necessary, there must be no "tolerance" in the sense of granting heresy free rein. Luther says, "At the same time, however, we must not tolerate, not approve, not allow the weeds to exist unmolested, but let us reproach, let us excommunicate, let us do whatever we can." [217] "The Lord does not say that we should not counteract the weeds. He says that we should not uproot them. From this it does not follow that we should with open eyes permit the weeds to be sown if we can prevent it." [218] Luther knew that he was not suggesting a fully consistent rule of procedure, but that a tension was created which can be endured only in view of the resolution promised in the final judgment. Meanwhile, we must suffer the tension anew whenever we are faced with concrete decisions. Luther frankly described the tension in this context as a paradox: "Christ did not permit Judas to be without reproof; yet He dismissed him as one unreproved." [219] Does such "permission" apply also to the Romanists? Certainly it does. Yet "we do not suffer them by agreeing with them but rather by repudiating them and by separating ourselves from them." [220] "We must reject the papal preaching, for nothing grows there but tares, and you see only noxious weeds and no wheat." [221]

Perhaps the clearest discussion of this problem is found in a sermon on the parable of the tares that Luther preached in Eisleben shortly before his death, the second-last sermon, in fact. "St. Paul says, 'Avoid a heretic.' That's what the text says. Place him under the ban and have nothing to do with him. How are you going to harmonize this, not uprooting the weeds but letting them grow, and at the same time, avoiding them?" [222] Luther's answer is quite in line with his previous opinions. As he had consistently underscored the "medicinal" purpose of church discipline, so also here he used the metaphor of medical therapy. The church resembles a body with ailing members. "If the body begins to fester and suppurate, we must clean and purify the wound, but so that we do not injure the ailing member." [223] If this will not cure the malady, we must "drag the sick part along and put up with it. We will not on that account amputate and cast off a member, however ailing, infected, atrophied, and corrupted it may be. If we can't do any more about it, we bear it patiently, unless of course it becomes so diseased that it cannot remain on the body and is so completely rotted and dead that it disintegrates and threatens to corrupt also the other members." [224]

Thus also here the "vindicating" aspect of rejection yields to the "protective" aspect. The means of protection takes precedence over the means of punishment. At the same time there is an emphatic rejection of the illusion that the condemnation of heresy could serve to create and gather the true church as a pure church already here on earth. The outwardness of the preached Word does indeed permit and even demand passing judgment on all doctrine. Pure doctrine must always be coupled with the antithesis to false doctrine. This does not mean, however, that pure doctrine must insist on its way against all false doctrine by means of irrefutable evidence. The perceptibility of pure doctrine does not remove the hiddenness that belongs to it as the doctrine concerning faith. Not even the condemnation of false doctrine can cross this boundary line. The same applies to the church: As the church of the external Word it is and remains the visible church and is obligated not to tolerate false teachers in its midst — though the "evil men" may be tolerated.[225] Yet the church dare not hope by a constant practice of doctrinal discipline to become empirically identical with the true church of faith; for this "is not to be seen but believed. Now, faith consists of that which is not seen." [226] Thus the church on earth will always be threatened and attacked by false teaching. This, however, is neither a cause for resignation nor a reason for becoming indifferent to pure doctrine. "Let offenses, sectaries, heresy, and imperfections be and do what they can, so long as the Word of the Gospel is kept pure among us and we love and cherish it, we must not doubt that Christ is on our side and with us." [227]

There are limits for condemnation not only in regard to the end result but also in regard to the procedure. It has already been shown repeatedly that Luther considered it important to draw a line between the doctrinal judgment as such and the possible and prescribed consequences in the domain of church discipline. Throughout his life he saw very clearly the dangers inherent in combining the teaching office with the power to impose penalties, as was done in the papal organization. Furthermore, he regarded the application of force in matters of faith absurd. "We do indeed have the authority of the Word, but we do not have the execution. We are to preach the Word but leave the consequences entirely up to God's good pleasure." [228] Wherever the attempt was made to make unity of faith "a required law," Luther counseled against it, because this seemed to him to imperil the freedom of faith at the same time.[229] Melanchthon's exhortation to the visitors "to compel no one to believe, or to turn no one from his unbelief by means of commandment or force," is in line with Luther's thinking.[230] The distinction between faulty faith and false teaching must be maintained. Luther could say that he permitted everyone to believe what he wished — "yet he is forbidden to teach and to blaspheme with the aim of robbing God and the Christians of their doctrine and Word." [231] For the visitation, too, the rule applied that where "unruly heads" willfully opposed the preaching of the Gospel they are not to be tolerated but expelled.[232] "Let them make their noises in their own little corner, but as far as possible you may not permit them to take the platform, mount the pulpit, or step before the altar." [233]

Even the law of love did not for Luther permit blurring the border line between the innocently erring and the stubbornly heretical. Over against the condemning judges of Louvain and Cologne Luther had himself urged the requirements of love and had offered to subject himself to the same requirement; but he did it only because their attacks were without due objectivity directed against his person, while he in turn was concerned about dogmas, not names. In the background was his conviction that personal attacks could have no place in disputations concerning doctrine.[234] Thus he could interpret Ps. 26:5 ("I hate the company of evildoers") to mean that such hatred was there not because of the person but for the sake of the doctrine.[235] This love, moreover, is only something self-evident (significantly Luther speaks to the Louvain theologians about "the rule of love, indeed of *natural law*"). It is also a self-evident law of love that men do not hereticize each other merely for the sake of words [236] and that in externals men have consideration for the weak.[237] But what if love demands unity, whereas doctrine and faith are opposed to this desire? The thing to do then is to observe the proper order of faith and love. "It is the part of love to put up with everything, but of faith, with nothing." [238] Certainly Luther did not want to repudiate the willingness toward unity that love dictates. However, where love injures the responsibility for pure doctrine, love is exceeding its limits.[239] The prohibition concerning the passing of judgment, which must always prevail in "the spiritual life and conduct among Christians" — particularly for the purpose of preventing schism among Christians — is not to be applied to judgment concerning doctrine,[240] provided that such judging proceeds "from an office and command." [241] Luther, too, valued "the virtue called tolerance," yet it must always be practiced so as to do no injury to doctrine. Not until "we have discharged our office, be it preaching or public rebuke or fraternal admonition," may we "bear, conceal, and extenuate the neighbor's faults." [242] Carlstadt demanded the very opposite of Luther, but this could not change Luther's attitude.[243] For him it was the same with the "mercy from the heart," according to which the apostle wanted the communal life of Christians to be governed.[244] It was the same with "Christian charity." We must "not apply it in matters of doctrine but only in deeds or life, as has often been said that there is no place in doctrine for love with all its works and fruits. . . . In this remarkable way the two, faith and love, are separated and distinguished. Love desires to be and must be kind even to the worst enemy as long as he does not attack doctrine and faith. Faith, however, neither will nor can put up with even father and mother and the dearest friend, if he attacks doctrine and faith." [245] Moreover, it was precisely Luther's love for those who were in danger of being led astray that drove him to condemn perverse and ungodly doctrine, and for that reason he could in good conscience say in his writing against the bull *Exsurge,* "I have omitted nothing that I owed to Christian charity." [246] He never doubted "that the preacher who fails to speak up sins most grievously and shows no concern for his neighbor's salvation, which is the highest treasure." [247]

The fact that Luther could not acknowledge the law of love as setting bounds to the condemnation of false doctrine indicates incidentally also that he saw no problem in the separation of false teaching and false teacher, of things and persons — a problem to be treated in so much detail at the time of the Formula of Concord. As little as he entertained the thought of an imprecatory effect of excommunication and condemnation, so firmly was he convinced that both, properly applied, confirmed an already existing state of affairs, which was by no means concerned only with the doctrine but included the person of the heretic. If Luther could reduce the judgment of condemnation to the formula that the culprit was "separated from Christ and under the devil," [248] if he taught that the properly applied ban should be regarded as the self-evident sequel to the spiritual self-excommunication that had already taken place through sin and spiritual death,[249] there was simply no room left for any strict distinction between the judgment applied to things and that applied to persons.

An item of Table Talk transmitted by Schlaginhaufen confirms that Luther committed to God the solution of the problems raised here without letting himself be shaken in his certainty: [250] "We judge according to the Gospel: He who does not believe this cannot be saved. Therefore we must be certain that such people are in error, etc. But God can act beyond the prescribed rule. We, however, cannot judge otherwise." Thus once again the condemnation is placed emphatically on the foundation of the Gospel as the only norm without doing injury to the eschatological reservation that remains constant: The invisible church of this age, living by the Word alone and obligated solely to the preaching of the Word, is not yet the Church Triumphant. If the church should forget this, if with the help of judgment on doctrine it either attempts to transcend the stage of its hiddenness here and now or desires to exist without doctrinal discipline as a pure fellowship of the Spirit and of love, the church has forsaken the way of the cross of its Lord.

It is hardly necessary to point out that Luther did not start out with this basic evaluation of the condemnation of heresy. Rather, his attitude grew gradually out of his concrete dealings with false teaching, beginning with his conflict with Rome and continuing to his struggle with the Sacramentarians. It is no less clear that in this development special importance attaches to Luther's repudiation of the Enthusiasts, through whom he was led to the primacy of the external Word. In any case he never doubted that all of his opponents—the pope, Carlstadt, Muentzer, Zwingli—had to be regarded and treated as false teachers. In other cases this decision could not always be made so clearly. This fact may, in conclusion, be briefly demonstrated by Luther's vacillation with regard to John Agricola.

Luther often expressed his grief over his quarrel with his former student and friend. In 1539 he remarked that no papist or Enthusiast had grieved him more than Agricola.[251] Already at the end of 1537 Luther intended to publish the antinomian theses that were going the rounds in Agricola's circle and to add his own explicit condemnations;[252] but he did not carry out his resolve. On the other hand, in his book *Against the Antinomians*, 1539, Luther left no doubt that it was impossible for one thinking in antinomian terms to remain loyal to the pure doctrine.[253] It was for him certainly not only a matter of adiaphora, but of the center of saving faith, the work of Christ; for where the Law is not properly applied, there can be no true appreciation of what Christ has done for us.[254] None other than the devil, says Luther, has blown up a new tempest through Agricola, just as in the past he had done through the papacy, through Muentzer and Carlstadt, yes, even through Servetus and Campanus.[255] Significantly enough Luther also pointed out that "this dissimulator and extremely vain man," Agricola, had never clearly defined his true position negatively and positively.[256] Nevertheless, Agricola was plainly enough marked as a heretic, or so it would seem. And yet Luther evidently did not wish to apply the principle of Titus 3:11 to him. Even though the various reconciliations with Agricola never lasted very long, they cannot be brushed aside as inconsistencies. Seemingly Luther could never bring himself to a radical separation in spite of all personal exasperation with the erring pupil who ever again became the victim of his own ambition and occasionally felt himself rebuffed by Luther. His feeling was not without some justification. Luther could not take the final step because he believed that in principle Agricola still acknowledged the "chief article" of justification and of Jesus Christ, even though Luther was certain that a consistent antinomianism could only result in undermining this center of the faith. And though Luther stood personally much closer to Melanchthon, it was undoubtedly this same conviction that kept him committed to Melanchthon to the end. In one point the Gnesio-Lutherans at a later date may well have been correct: If Luther had lived to see how both of them, primarily Agricola but also Melanchthon, yielded to the Interim, he would very likely have given up his restraint and definitively have denied them the fellowship of the pure doctrine.

To sum up, looking back over Luther's position with regard to the condemnation of false teaching, we are justified in saying that because this position is strictly oriented to the living voice of the Gospel it fits well into the broad framework of his total reformatory activity. As Luther liberated the ban from an externalizing of the motives, from a mechanical procedure, and from its association with unspiritual ends, so he also restored the proper significance to the condemnation of heresy. He went back beyond the medieval anathema with its fixed penalties and focused on the first age of Christianity and the time of the New Testament. There, in the form of the condemnatory judgment, the sign of separation was established in relation to Christ and for the sake of Christ as the incarnate Word. Luther could still perceive this clear, strict note in the antitheses of the ancient councils, but he no longer found it in the schematized censures as practiced by the church of his time. As he had experienced in his own case, the church of his day thought it could enclose the judging and separating function of the efficacious Word in a rigidly graduated scale of judgments. Yet thereby the church only rendered the Word's function powerless, because it placed its own hierarchical authority above the authority of the Word. The primacy of the pope was the foundation for this system, and canon law was its most important instrument. Questioning the authority of the condemnors of doctrine led Luther logically to a denial in principle of the spiritual supremacy of the pope and the validity of canon law. Consequently the way was opened for him to reestablish the act of condemnation in the Word of the Gospel itself. If pure doctrine means nothing else than the proper preaching of the Gospel, then the criterion for false doctrine is no longer opposition to the dogma established by the church, but rather departure from *sola gratia* and *sola fide*. This point of view is decisive also for judging those who deny the dogmas of the ancient church. In this sense the rejection of false doctrine simply gives expression to the separation the Gospel itself creates. The rejection itself then stands in the context of the manifestation of the external Word and, as a judgment proceeding from faith to faith, does not abolish the fundamental hiddenness of God's revelation in the Word. Hence it cannot serve the purpose of making the separateness of the true church from the false church perceptible to all. It does, however, represent the necessary defense of the visible church against all attempts to displace the external Word from its fundamental validity in the church and to lay another foundation in place of the one that is laid.

By virtue of the authority he knew to be his and that of all Christians through Baptism, Luther had himself rejected the unspiritual, antichristian authority of the hierarchy. Even so he now made it the obligation of the whole Christian community to "judge all doctrine" in this sense. For the congregation and each of its members is entrusted with the responsibility to proclaim the Gospel in the right way. This basic principle is not affected by the fact that for primarily practical reasons this implication of the priesthood of all believers is specifically committed to the called servants of the Word.

Luther, too, regarded it as possible and necessary that the judgment of doctrine should lead to measures of church discipline. But for him the rejection of heresy for the purpose of identifying it for the Christian community was more important than penal measures taken against the heretics. The condemnation is not so much a means of punishment as it is a means of protection, not so much punishment of the heretic as warning for the congregation. In this way the rejection of heresy is given limits that must preserve it from becoming a war of extermination against heretics and the application of coercive measures in matters of faith. Luther could not acknowledge the law of love as a limitation on the rejection of heresy because that would mean a disruption of the fundamental primacy of doctrine over life.

Apart from a few shifts in accent (as, for example, in his assessment of the ministerial office or in the question regarding the punishment of heretics by the government), Luther remained committed to his basic attitude toward the condemnation of heresy. He acquired this attitude during his experience with the heresy trial Rome had conducted against him. How Luther applied his principles also to the false teachings of Zwingli and his followers must be considered in the larger framework of condemnations in the Lutheran Confessions, which we shall now investigate.

Notes to Chapter 7

[156] "He, therefore, is a faithful shepherd who not only feeds but also guards the sheep. This is done when he points out heresies and errors" (WA 25, 29, 1).

[157] WA 24, 86, 24.

[158] WA 32, 506, 24 (Week-day sermons on Matt. 5 – 7, 1530 – 32. The value of these sermons as source material is disputed; cf. H. W. Beyer, Luther-Jahrbuch, 1932, pp. 39f. However, the cited passage may be regarded as genuinely true to Luther in both content and language).

[159] "If you fight, you will see what wisdom and strength there is in the Word of God and what folly there is in the world. In this way the Word of God is made manifest" (WA 17 I, 357, 1, Sermon on Matt. 7:15ff., July 30, 1525).

[160] WA 50, 474, 1 (Against the Antinomians, 1539).

[161] WA 18, 418, 17; 38, 602, 1.

[162] WA 51, 476, 23.

[163] WA 38, 591, 16. See also 7, 431, 5, where the "despising" is brought into relation to Gal. 1:8f.

[164] WA 17 II, 117, 2, on Col. 3:13.

[165] WA 51, 476, 25.

[166] Cf. 17 II, 120, 36; 32, 477ff. The fact that in his last exchange with the Swiss Luther departed from these principles weighs heavily and will require special treatment.

[167] WA 31 II, 679, 9 and 19 (Lectures on Song of Solomon, 1530/31).

[168] WA 8, 667, 19 (De votis monasticis, 1521).

[169] Cf., above all, G. Hoffmann, "Lehrzucht und Glaubensduldung bei Luther und im Luthertum," Luthertum, 1939, pp. 161ff., 193ff. Ibid. for further literature on the problem of toleration in the age of the Reformation.

[170] WA 50, 9, 21; 51, 433, 20.

[171] Cf. Lectures on Romans, Ficker, II, 216f.

[172] Ibid., 218, 6.

[173] WA Briefe, 1, 148, 17 (Letter to John Lang, Feb. 19, 1518).

[174] WA 40 I 116, 4.

[175] Ibid., 117, 9.

[176] WA 7, 431, 7; 9, 626, 14; 10 II, 84, 1; 12, 187, 35; 51, 521, 26; 534, 21; and in other places.

[177] WA 50, 474, 1.

[178] "To overshadow means to place a shade over them, that is, to teach the true faith. Through this doctrine of faith they are truly protected against the devils" (WA 4, 68, 27).

[179] "It is a matter of great concern to us again and again to condemn and declare condemned the same people (that is, the Sectarians and Sacramentarians), so that our descendants may be frightened away from their heresies,

and doubting and wavering consciences may be helped, or those who are at present in their error may be recalled so that they will not remain in it any longer" (WA *Tischreden*, 1, 527, 31, about 1530/35).

[180] WA 25, 29, 1; 31, 25; *Tischreden*, 2, 444, 11.

[181] Kohlmeyer, p. 505.

[182] WA 51, 75, 12.

[183] WA 11, 410, 16.

[184] WA 4, 267, 18. Cf. 3, 179, 11; 4, 353, 17. Further passages in Holl, p. 305 n. 4.

[185] WA 6, 412, 37 (*To the Christian Nobility*, 1520). Cf. ibid., 412, 22; 413, 2; 12, 180, 4; 12, 187, 29; 14, 260, 10.

[186] WA 6, 228, 3.

[187] WA 7, 95, 4.

[188] WA 29, 481, 6; 30 I, 128, 22.

[189] WA 6, 561, 9 and 13. Cf. 33, 146, 20; 45, 622, 3.

[190] WA 33, 365, 8.

[191] Ibid., 364, 38.

[192] WA 10 III, 174, 2.

[193] WA 25, 16, 23. See also Holl, pp. 318f.

[194] Cf. the Wittenberg faculty certificate, WA *Briefe*, 6, 229, 1. The certificates of ordination mentioned by H. Preuss, pp. 192f., were signed by Luther but not prepared by him.

[195] WA 5, 339, 1.

[196] "'Prove all things.' The judgment must be with the preachers and the faithful" (WA 27, 511, 17. *Sermon on Luke 2:15ff.*, Dec. 26, 1528).

[197] WA 48, 215, 20. Cf. 25, 29, 1.

[198] WA 23, 565, 19 (*Exposition of the Prophet Zechariah*, 1527).

[199] WA 50, 617, 23 (*Of the Councils and Church*, 1539).

[200] Ibid., 615, 28.

[201] Ibid., 616, 8.

[202] WA *Briefe*, 2, 135, 25.

[203] WA 7, 162, 8.

[204] "Moving in on doctrine has never happened. This is my calling. Others have attacked life only, but to deal with doctrine, this means to grab the goose by the neck. . . . Everything depends on the Word, because the pope put aside the Word and produced another word. With the Word I have won the victory, and I have won nothing else except what I teach correctly" (WA *Tischreden*, 1, 294, 23; 295, 3. Autumn, 1533).

[205] Iwand, p. 5, note.

[206] Cf. WA 10 II, 106, 1; 24; 107, 7; 229, 29 and 33.

[207] Cf. H. Denifle, *Luther und Luthertum in der ersten Entwickelung*, I (Mainz, 1904), p. XIV; II (1909), 161f., 226ff.; Joh. Janssen, *Geschichte des deutschen Volkes*, II (Freiburg, 1879), 219f.

[208] WA 25, 28, 26.

[209] E.g., WA 18, 417, 22; 32, 474, 37.

[210] WA 4, 240, 20.

[211] WA 6, 604, 10.

[212] WA 17 II, 125, 2 and 17 (*Lenten Postil*, 1525).

[213] Ibid., 126, 18.

[214] WA 38, 561, 10 (*Annotations to Some Chapters of St. Matthew*, 1538).

215 WA 47, 264, 1 *(Matt. 18—24 Explained in Sermons*, 1537—40. Aurifaber transcript).

216 For the text of the passage from Augustine see above, n. 51. Luther quotes: "Let not the severity of discipline sleep when some one's crime is known and appears repulsive to all" (WA 52, 135, 10. Veit Dietrich's *House Postil).*

217 WA 38, 561, 35.

218 WA 52, 835, 11 and 23 *(Sermon on Matt. 13:24ff.*, Dec. 9, 1528).

219 WA 38, 561, 39.

220 Ibid., 562, 10.

221 WA 52, 834, 23.

222 WA 51, 176, 15.

223 Ibid., 177, 1.

224 Ibid., 177, 12.

225 Frequently Luther did not distinguish sharply between heretics and evil men (e. g., WA 38, 561, 10, quoted above, p. 67). However, his expressions concerning the difference between doctrine and life already indicated that in principle he could not think as generously about false teachers remaining in the congregation as he could about tolerating those who had sinned in the area of life. What he had written in 1522 about the radicals and fanatics in Wittenberg he could not apply to the Enthusiasts without further ado.—Yet even here it should be noted that Luther wished to see a distinction made between false teachers and those whose faith was faulty (see below).

226 WA *Deutsche Bibel*, 7, 420, 3 *(Preface to Revelation*, 1530).

227 Ibid., 420, 11.

228 WA 10 III, 15, 10 *(Invocavit Sermons*, 1522); cf. WA 52, 833, 20.

229 WA 18, 418, 1 *(Open Letter to the Christians in Livonia*, 1525).

230 WA 26, 214, 15; cf. ibid., 200, 10; WA *Briefe*, 4, 330, 18.

231 WA 31 I, 208, 31 *(Exposition of Psalm 82*, 1530); cf. Hoffmann, pp. 173f., 180.

232 WA 26, 200, 22.

233 WA 51, 184, 18 *(Sermon on Matt. 13:24ff.*, Feb. 7, 1546).

234 "It would have been the part of love if the dodgers distributed among the people had tried to persuade them in this manner: 'Don't be offended by Luther's writings, brethren. He has argued about many things and perhaps has said some things more sharply than all might understand. Even the divine Scripture has its dangerous passages, how much more the writing of a man.' I say, this rule of love, indeed of natural law, they would undoubtedly have expected me to observe toward them in a similar situation, and I would have done it too, if in the style of those fellows I would have undertaken publicly to attack not so much someone's doctrine as his name. I myself haven't ever called anyone by name whenever I attacked teachings. Wherefore they would have harmed neither me nor the truth, but rather profited all in the best possible way, and would have received for themselves and their followers honor and the love of both God and men" (WA 6, 185, 27).

235 WA 17 I, 242, 4.

236 WA 18, 103, 4; 12, 468, 14.

237 WA 18, 419, 7.

238 WA 40 I, 21, 7 *(Notes on Gal. 5:9*, 1531); cf. WA 17 I, 242, 6; 40 II, 46, 8.

239 WA 40 II, 47, 8; cf. ibid., 531, 8; 50, 10; 51, 75, 6.

240 WA 32, 473, 34; 475, 11.

241 Ibid., 475, 19.

242 WA 32, 476, 3; 477, 22.

243 WA 15, 336, 28.

244 WA 17 II, 113, 5 ("Sermon on Col. 3:12ff.," *Lenten Postil*, 1525).

245 WA 17 II, 114, 6.

246 WA 6, 612, 17; cf. ibid., 320, 27.

247 WA 10 II, 108, 21.

248 Cf. supra, p. 62.

249 Cf. supra, pp. 31–32.

250 WA *Tischreden*, 2, 102, 3 (April 1532).

251 WA *Tischreden*, 4, 433, 26.

252 *Corpus Reformatorum* (hereafter cited as CR) 3, 454.

253 WA 50, 472, 14; 51, 438, 22.

254 WA 50, 473, 7.

255 Ibid., 475, 16.

256 WA *Tischreden*, 4, 390, 5.

Part 3

The Period of the Augsburg Confession
(1530 – 1565)

Chapter 8

The Condemnations in the Augsburg Confession

Remembering Luther's basic attitude toward condemnations and considering that the Augsburg Confession consciously aims at preserving the continuity with the one holy catholic church and its ancient confessions, we are not surprised that the Augsburg Confession has no inhibitions about pronouncing numerous anathemas. Article I condemns all the heresies that conflict with the correct doctrine of God and of the Trinity – in addition to the heresies of the Manichaeans, Arians, and other ancient heretics, also those of the "Mohammedans." Article II condemns the Pelagians, Article VIII, the Donatists, Article XII, the Novatians.[1] In Articles V, IX, XII, XVI, and XVII the Anabaptists are condemned.[2] Article X expresses disapproval of all opponents of the Lutheran teaching regarding the Lord's Supper.[3] Finally, in Articles II and XII individual Roman teachings are condemned without, however, identifying them by name.[4] The *textus receptus*, that is, the authentic *editio princeps* of 1531, has in Article XIII a condemnation of those who teach "that the sacraments justify *ex opere operato* without faith," quite in line with Luther's position. Yet this item must be excluded from our study for the present because it is found in no known manuscript and hence must have been missing in the text presented to the emperor. Nor, apparently, did the papal confutators see it. The same is true of the rejection of the Semi-Pelagian doctrine of free will in Article XVIII of the *editio princeps*.[5]

It is notable that the known sources Melanchthon was able to use in his work are consistently more sparing with their anathemas than the Augsburg Confession itself. There is, first of all, the "Instruction for the Visitors," written by Melanchthon and reviewed by Luther. This writing was published in 1528 with a preface by Luther. Its fundamental significance for the genesis of the Augsburg Confession was first demonstrated by G. Hoffmann.[6] The points of contact between the two documents are both numerous and of varying degrees of importance. For the condemnatory clauses, however, there are no correspondences. The Schwabach Articles, which were completed in September 1529 and are also the joint product of Luther and Melanchthon,[7] mention the heresies of the Patripassians and the "Photinians," as well as the "blasphemers of Baptism," but do not pronounce any explicit condemnations. Only Article XV states that the teachings concerning celibacy, the distinction of foods, and monastic vows are "nothing but condemned and devilish doctrines."[8] The article concerning the Lord's Supper repudiates the content of the teaching of Zwingli but does not condemn it, even though the Schwabach Articles were particularly concerned about drawing a clear line of demarcation against the Swiss and the South Germans as well.[9] The Marburg Articles, written by Luther himself at the close of the Marburg Colloquy in the beginning of October 1529, had the purpose of formulating the areas of agreement with the Swiss in spite of the differences. Understandably they were especially chary of condemnatory clauses. Article 7 condemns "all monastic life and vows," as far as they are intended to be "useful for righteousness," and Article 13 condemns the prohibition of clerical marriage as "devil's doctrine."[10] But it is noteworthy that these condemnations are missing in Luther's original draft and were only subsequently inserted by him while he was still at Marburg.[11] Finally, the article concerning the Lord's Supper states the divergent teachings without any word of condemnation.[12]

The memorandum intended as a basis of the Saxon elector's reply to the emperor — it is a moot question if the name "Torgau Articles" is appropriate — is another source of the Augsburg Confession; it contains no condemnations of false doctrine at all. It is true that the nature of this report as an opinion regarding the purity of church practices in electoral Saxony hardly provided the opportunity for explicit anathemas. Only in the article concerning the Mass the statement is made that in Saxony "the Zwinglian doctrine is most strenuously resisted," as is evident from the books published on the subject, i. e., Luther's polemical writings against Zwingli.[13]

Thus all the listed sources of the Augsburg Confession offer scarcely any points of contact for the origin of the condemnatory clauses in the confession. The situation is changed when Luther's personal confession, appended to his *Confession Concerning Christ's Supper* of 1528 (of which it forms the third part), is drawn into the discussion, as suggested by the newer Augustana researches.[14] Hoffmann's investigations in the "Instruction for the Visitors" have shown that Luther's personal confession can no longer be regarded as "the last direct source for the construction of confessions that resulted in the Augsburg Confession."[15] Yet the specific relevance of Luther's personal confession in the context of the source materials for the Augsburg Confession cannot be questioned. It is true, in the majority of cases there are no clearly demonstrable lines leading from Luther's condemnations to the individual anathemas in the Augsburg Confession. Moreover, the Augsburg Confession contains rejections that Luther does not have. The net result seems to be the following: It is in the nature of the case that both Luther and the Augsburg Confession, Article I, condemn the Arians. Otherwise the two lists are supplementary. (Luther: "Arians, Macedonians, Sabellians, Nestorians." AC I: "Manichaeans, Valentinians, Arians, Eunomians, Mohammedans, Samosatenians").[16] Luther's rejection of all teachings "that praise our free will" is not included in the original text of the Augsburg Confession, Article XVIII.[17] Above all, the Augsburg Confession has nothing to correspond to Luther's sharp condemnation of all "orders, rules, monasteries, foundations, and whatever else has been invented and established by men beyond and without Scripture."[18] On the other hand, Luther has no explicit condemnation of contrary teachings regarding the Lord's Supper. Thus the cases of undoubted correspondence between Luther and the Augsburg Confession in the area of condemnations are reduced to two — the rejection of the Pelagians as well as that of the Anabaptists and Donatists. In the first case it may be assumed that Melanchthon derived his formulation, down to the choice of words, from Luther's personal confession (Luther: "Thus I also condemn both, new and old Pelagians, who refuse to call original sin sin but say that it is a weakness or lack." AC II: "Also condemned are the Pelagians and others who do not regard original sin as sin").[19] In the second case Luther lists the "Anabaptists and Donatists and whoever they may be who rebaptize," while the Augsburg Confession condemns the Donatists in Article VIII and the Anabaptists in Article IX.[20] But we must not put too much emphasis on the connection because, as G. Hoffmann has shown,[21] Luther's accent differs from that of AC IX. While the condemnation in the Augsburg Confession is aimed at the rejection of infant baptism, Luther has the denial of the sacramental character in view. These are two different matters, though of course they are most intimately related.

In reviewing the situation, we must make two weighty qualifications in spite of the striking correspondences between Luther's personal confession and the Augsburg Confession. For one thing, precisely those rejections of Roman doctrines and church customs that Luther had added to his condemnations of ancient heresies are omitted in the Augsburg Confession (apart from Articles XIII and XVIII in the *editio princeps*). Secondly, Luther does not have the explicit rejection mentioned in the Augsburg Confession's article on the Lord's Supper. As for the first point, it will suffice to recall the thrust of the Augsburg Confession. Melanchthon could not and would not incorporate these condemnations because he was to prepare not so much a confession of faith as rather an apologetic document designed to emphasize the consensus of the estates that had "protested" at Spires in 1529 with the universal Christian church in the presence of the emperor and the estates of the empire.

The condemnations of heresies that Melanchthon retained promoted this purpose very successfully, as can be seen in the approving opinions expressed in the "Pontifical Confutation," the counterdocument of the Roman theologians handed to the emperor.[22] Eck and his co-workers expressly applaud not only the condemnation of the heretics mentioned in Article I and the Donatists, Anabaptists, and Novatians, but also that of the Pelagians. At the same time it was apparently also Eck who by his kind of polemics gave the impetus for the inclusion of more and more anathemas as Melanchthon progressed with the confession. Originally Eck had suggested a disputation [23] — still regarded as a possibility in Augsburg at the beginning of June — and for that purpose had compiled 404 excerpts from the writings of Luther and his adherents, items that seemed to him most heretical, in order to unmask the Lutherans as heretics and thus at the same time as enemies of the empire and disturbers of the peace.[24] Eck had diligently placed on the same level with Luther's and Melanchthon's teachings not only the utterances of Zwingli, Oecolampadius, and Carlstadt, but even those of the notorious Enthusiasts Hubmaier and Denk. Even more: In his copy of the articles intended for the emperor Eck had here and there inserted the names of ancient heretics, whose teachings had allegedly been taken up again by the Lutherans. Finally, to make completely sure, in a covering letter to the emperor, March 14, 1530, Eck had explicitly accused the Lutherans of "renewing the ancient heresies, condemned a thousand and more years ago, and of following heretics who had been burned long ago and whose memory was accursed." [25]

True, not every one in the Roman camp approved of such tactics. Yet Melanchthon was compelled to recognize the deadly peril that threatened the cause of the "protesting" estates if the emperor would allow himself to be pushed in the direction indicated by Eck. In that case every prospect of conciliation would be ruined. One did not negotiate with heretics. The emperor could only deal with them as the executor of the judicial verdict. This made it necessary for Melanchthon to parry the thrust in the way he did and to refute the equation of Lutheran teaching with ancient heresies by explicitly condemning these same heresies also in the confession of the "protesting" estates, even though this had not been done in the documents on which the confession was based.[26]

This background history of condemnations will at least have made it clear that neither Luther nor Melanchthon had any serious problem with the condemnation of heresies the church had always condemned. Where they did omit anathemas, they did it not because they had any basic doubts about their propriety. Nor was it necessary to furnish any explanations for the condemnations. The *Damnamus* is nowhere defined or clarified. Everyone knew what was intended, and Melanchthon was saying nothing new when in Article I of the Apology he circumscribed the rejection of heretics in the following manner: "We steadfastly maintain that those who believe otherwise do not belong to the church of Christ but are idolaters and blasphemers." [27] Though severe, this was entirely in the spirit of Luther, and it may serve as the legitimate interpretation of all other condemnations to the extent of their involvement with ancient heresies or with the Anabaptists. Thus understood, the *Damnamus* implies something more than Vilmar was willing to concede. He defined the *Damnamus* as the "usual, unequivocal formula: We have nothing to do with those people." [28] It is also apparent that there was no thought of distinguishing explicitly between the condemnation of false teachings and of false teachers, simply because this question was not up for discussion. The action taken followed from the self-evident conviction that the thesis must have its antithesis, and it was possible to do this with an even clearer conscience, because at least on this point they knew themselves to be in harmony with the Roman Church, and the case of the heresies under discussion, at least with reference to ancient heretics, had been closed long ago.

The situation was less clear when the question was raised whether they could and must give expression in the same manner to the doctrinal divergence from Zwingli and his followers. It certainly does credit to the fathers of the confession that, as will be shown, they did not operate in this matter with the same lack of restraint as in the case of the other condemnations. Only a careful study of the motivation, however, will keep us from drawing one-sided conclusions.

It is noteworthy, to begin with, that according to the testimony of the Augsburg Confession the doctrine of the Lord's Supper was not the only point in which the Lutherans felt they must separate from the Swiss. Article II condemns not only the Pelagians but also "others who deny that original sin is sin, for they hold that natural man is made righteous by his own powers, thus disparaging the sufferings and merit of Christ." [29] It makes no difference that this condemnation is missing in the document now usually identified as *Na* — Jerome Baumgartner's German translation of the earliest surviving draft of the Latin Augsburg Confession, which the representatives of the imperial free city of Nuremberg sent to their city council on June 3, 1530, as a kind of progress report and which represents an intermediate stage in the series of preliminary drafts.[30]

Just when and how the condemnation of the Zwinglians got into the final form can no longer be determined. Apparently here, as in Luther's personal confession of 1528, Zwingli was included with the Scholastics because he regarded original sin a sickness rather than a sin. Whether a reference to Zwingli may be assumed in the rejection of the Spiritualists in Article V cannot be definitely asserted.[31] In any case it would hardly be accurate even for the period around 1530 to say that nothing but differences in the doctrine of the Lord's Supper provided the deep cleavage between the Lutherans and the Swiss. As early as the beginning of the Marburg Colloquy Luther had pointed out that the Lutherans had their serious misgivings not only about Zwingli's understanding of the sacraments but also about his doctrine of original sin, of the Word of God, and of the means of grace.[32] But it is particularly the Augsburg Confession that demonstrates clearly that the difference in the doctrine of the Eucharist was especially irritating and, even more important, that the problems raised by the condemnation became really acute for the first time in this context.[33]

The formula of disapproval in Article X evidently takes a significant step beyond the preliminary documents known to us. True, already the Torgau Opinion had underscored the opposition to Zwingli's doctrine of the Lord's Supper. Also the Schwabach and Marburg Articles had in their way emphasized the point of controversy. The former had stated that in the Supper "there is not only bread and wine, as now the opposition alleges." At Marburg the question remained unsettled "whether the true body and blood of Christ were corporeally present in the bread and the wine." [34] Yet there had been no condemnation of the opposing doctrine. We find it for the first time in *Na*, the oldest surviving draft of the Augsburg Confession. There the article reads: "In the ninth place, (they teach) that the body and the blood of Christ are truly present and distributed in the Supper, and that those who teach otherwise are rejected." [35] If we are not satisfied to accept the figment of the later anti-Lutheran polemic that this reference is to be restricted to the Anabaptists and to Schwenckfeld,[36] we are confronted with the urgent question: How did the condemnatory formula get into the draft of the confession?

An answer crops up at a relatively early time, first of all in the writings of the Strasbourg theologian Johann Marbach. He states that Luther himself had inserted the formula.[37] There is, however, no proof for this claim. Nevertheless, it must be said that in an indirect way Luther's voice sounds through in the condemnatory statement in Article X and that it is authentically Lutheran at least in sense. As early as the autumn of 1525, at a time when the controversy with Zwingli had not yet come out into the open, Luther expressed himself specifically with reference to the Lord's Supper in a very informative, even exemplary manner on the question of condemnations. At that time the Strasbourg preachers, led by Bucer and Capito, made a determined advance in order to forestall a threatened break between Wittenberg and Zurich. Gregory Casel, professor of Hebrew in Strasbourg, was sent to Luther with a letter full of deep anxiety. Only if both, the Wittenbergers and the Zurichers, would get together in full harmony for "the work of transmitting the purity of Christ" and would put an end to fighting about words and shouting at each other, would they be able to face the opponents of the new teaching with a united front. This was both the theological and the tactical concern of the Strasbourgers.[38]

Luther saw things in a completely different way, as may be seen from the answer he sent back with Gregory Casel. Now, confronted with the antithesis to Zwingli's doctrine of the Eucharist, the principles that had always been decisive for Luther in the matter of condemnations were applied no less clearly than in his disputes with Rome. In interpreting the words of institution Luther was not interested in fighting about words, in something neutral or indifferent, but he was concerned about salvation. "We have never said that the flesh and blood of Christ are a neutral thing or do not bring salvation." On the contrary, "It is here above all a matter of danger to salvation." [39] From this perspective Luther could even say that the difference was the same as between Christ and Belial. Hence one of the parties must surely be a party of Satan's henchmen (a remark that deeply offended Bucer),[40] and there was no room for deliberation or a forum for debate. There was only one thing to do now, namely, to confess ("Each side must tell the other what it believes"). "We gladly embrace peace, but not at the expense of the peace with God that is given us through Christ." [41] Whoever makes concessions here or attempts to smooth over the differences only proves that he is not sure of salvation and that he does not understand the responsibility connected with the assurance of salvation, no matter how much he may talk about his "experience of faith." Nothing but the certainty that what is said is spoken as the Word of God (1 Peter 4:11)—indeed an extremely presumptuous certainty in the opinion of the flesh—justifies and demands the antithesis. Now, this antithesis is something quite different from a mere clamor, a reproof growing out of an arrogant dogmatism and contentiousness. "It is proper to refrain from clamor, but how can we answer and contradict if we may not condemn, or if the word of condemnation is construed as mere clamor?" So Luther asked.[42]

That he desired peace and knew how necessary and important a united front among all Evangelicals would be was no less evident now than it would be later at Marburg and still later in connection with the Wittenberg Concord in 1536. For a long time Luther felt he ought to keep silent, and it was only the offensive talk of his opponents about "cannibals" and "the bread God" that called him into the arena. Yet he came not to pit clamor against clamor but rather to exhibit the fundamental cleavage, which dare not be ignored once the church has been troubled and the authority of the teaching office is endangered.[43] Drawing such boundaries was intended also to serve the purpose of leading the others out of error into the certainty of the truth. "We are sure that they are in error. Let them see for themselves how sure they are that they are not in error. The Lord grant that they truly may not be in error, that is, that they may come to their senses." [44] So ends the letter that like scarcely any other utterance of Luther uncovers the roots and the essence of the condemnatory judgments expressed by him. This does not say that the addressees received Luther's words in the sense intended by him. Bucer had only a feeling of revulsion against the harshness with which Luther drew boundaries and which he thought conflicted with the spirit of Christ and the apostles.[45]

As we turn from this situation to Luther's personal confession of 1528 and to the Augsburg Confession, we note that it is of little moment that Luther's writing has no verbatim model for the condemnatory formula used in Augsburg Confession X. The whole tenor of that article points in the direction indicated in Luther's letter of 1525 and followed by Melanchthon in the Augsburg Confession. In view of what Luther had written in his book on the Lord's Supper in 1528, which was definitive up to that time and which closed with his personal confession, as well as in view of his earlier publications against Zwingli, there was hardly a need for a specific model of condemnations. Luther had shown unmistakably what the aim of his personal confession was. He desired to confess all the articles of his faith against the Zwinglian and other new heresies. Just before that he had for good measure so characterized his attitude toward the Swiss that it was tantamount to an explicit condemnation. "Therefore I will now break with them according to St. Paul's teaching in Titus 3, 'As for a man who is factious, after admonishing him once or twice, having nothing more to do with him.'" [46] Besides, at the close of his personal confession he had expressly stated that it should be interpreted and even supplemented in the light of his previous writings. "What I have neglected to say here my other booklets will testify in sufficient manner, particularly those that were published within the last four or five years." [47] In line with this, Melanchthon evidently also refers to the Eucharistic controversy in his first draft of a preface to the confession, as it is preserved for us in *Na*. Speaking of Luther's teaching, Melanchthon says that "more than one heresy that has arisen against the holy sacraments in new and unchristian writings has been refuted by it." [48] All of this makes clear that not only is there no difference between the condemnation in Article X and Luther's intention, but the condemnation must be considered also against the background of the whole Eucharistic controversy. More than that, the anathema in the Augsburg Confession follows as the logical conclusion from Luther's controversy with Zwingli and does so entirely in the spirit of Luther.

Luther's readiness for conciliation at Marburg can, on the basis of what we now know,[49] no longer be called into question as to its genuineness. Yet at first glance it seems difficult to fit into the framework of his condemnatory judgments. In offering his formula for agreement Luther surely had neither the consciousness nor the purpose of yielding anything of his basic understanding of the Lord's Supper, as determined for him by the literal sense of the words of institution.[50] "He may no longer be pictured as the *completely* irreconcilable one," and yet his "formula was conceived in the Lutheran sense in all points and made no concessions . . . and only the most clever sophistry could give it a Zwinglian interpretation." [51] In spite of this, as will be shown, we can by no means dispense with Marburg in our understanding of the condemnations in the Augsburg Confession.

Meanwhile it is proper to draw the further conclusion that the condemnation in Article X also reproduces the expression of Melanchthon's personal conviction. At this time he was clearly not yet the "messenger boy for an opinion that was foreign to him," as he felt himself to be at a later date. This conclusion is, in fact, confirmed by other statements of Melanchthon from this period, statements in which he makes plain the cleavage between himself and the Swiss because of the Zwinglian conception of the Communion. In an opinion regarding a religious colloquy with the Swiss and South Germans composed a half year before the Marburg meeting, Melanchthon stated: I "abide by the conviction that I will not side with the Strasbourgers as long as I live, and I know that Zwingel and his cohorts," this "Arius and his sect," as he puts it elsewhere,[52] "write erroneously about the Sacrament." [53] "I would rather die than have our people contaminated by association with the Zwinglian cause. It is a grave matter, but few give it thought," he wrote in June 1529.[54] In the midst of his work on the Augsburg Confession he expressed similar sentiments about the Swiss: "They have teachings that cannot be tolerated." [55]

It was, of course, no easy matter for Melanchthon to draw the dividing line. With all his heart he approved of the protestation that the estates made against the Resolution of the Majority at the Diet of Speyer in 1529, in which the Swiss doctrine of the Lord's Supper was forbidden, and he shared the opinion of the protesting estates that such a decision was not possible without a council, or at least without giving the accused a hearing. Significantly enough, however, the same letter of May 17, 1529, in which he told his friend Camerarius about this, also contains firm words in opposition to any joint endeavor with the Swiss. Melanchthon sincerely regretted that he did not bring about a separation or at least advise such a step. He feared that the "profaneness" — he was fond of calling the Zwinglian teaching "profane" [56] on the basis of 1 Tim. 1:9; 4:7 — might become a fateful epidemic. Yet he had experienced qualms of conscience about pronouncing condemnation on people who had not received a hearing in all due form.[57] Later, above all after the Marburg Colloquy, which in spite of its long-range consequences

remained a mere episode for the Lutherans up until the Wittenberg Concord,[58] Melanchthon's opinion had crystallized to the
extent that he felt conscience-bound to reject especially the
Zwinglian doctrine of the Holy Communion.

Supporting this conclusion is the fact that at that time
Melanchthon believed that the Lutheran view of the Lord's
Supper could be found also in the writings of the church fathers.
In the midst of his preparation for the diet he published a collection of patristic statements that were to provide the documentation.[59] These were not without some influence on the formulation
of Article X.[60]

Nevertheless, it has always occasioned surprise that the
condemnation of the Swiss in Augsburg Confession X was plain
enough in the German text ("repudiated") but apparently took
a considerably milder form in the Latin text (improbant, "disapprove").[61] Even the strict Lutherans who prepared the Formula of Concord expressed concern about this situation.[62] In
more recent times the question has actually been entertained
whether Melanchthon perhaps had nothing more in mind than
"an almost polite expression of disapproval." [63]

However, this can hardly be proved from the substitution
of the milder improbare ("disapprove") for the otherwise customary damnare ("condemn"). There is no evidence in the Augsburg Confession that these terms were clearly differentiated.
Maurer [64] wants to interpret the "disapprove" of Article X in
the light of the same word as used in Article IX and construes
it as "teaching that something is not right." However, in Article IX both the context and the purpose are of an entirely different nature. In Article IX the "disapprove" refers to a doctrinal opinion; in Article X the concern is not with teachings
but with the teachers themselves, and this not incidentally as in
Article IX but by way of a direct judgment. Therefore Article IX
can hardly be of help in arriving at the significance of the "disapprove," especially since a comparison with another passage
leads to the opposite conclusion. Article VIII uses "condemn"
(damnant) against the Donatists, but in the same context in the
Apology Melanchthon writes, "We have spoken out clearly
enough in our confession, where we condemn (improbare, 'disapprove') the Donatists. . . ." [65] He surely had no occasion in the
Apology consciously to temper the harsh rejection of the Dona-

tists in the Augsburg Confession. One could then conclude that Melanchthon regarded the terms "disapprove" and "condemn" (as well as "reject" in Article XII) as synonymous and that therefore the "disapprove" of Article X was not intended to weaken the force of the German *verwerfen*, that is, "repudiate."

It is evident that the comparison of terms does not suffice to fix beyond a doubt the meaning of the rejection in Augsburg Confession X. Nor is that surprising. Undoubtedly the situation with regard to the terminology of the rejections parallels that of the entire doctrine of the Lord's Supper.[66] That is to say, we have no right to expect a fully reasoned apparatus of concepts at that time, such as was evolved later after long years of disputation. Just so, in 1530 certain aspects of the question about rejections were felt to be problems as little as in Luther's earlier utterances. This applies above all to the relation between the rejection of false teachings and the condemnation of false teachers. It is true, Melanchthon expressed the axiomatic opinion that the anathema applies to the doctrines, not to the persons.[67] Among the official duties of the bishops in Augsburg Confession XXVIII he listed the duty to "judge *doctrine* and condemn *doctrine* that is contrary to the Gospel." [68] Otherwise, as indicated, he was able to apply the condemnations in the confession quite generally and unhesitatingly to the persons of the false teachers. Thus he states in the Apology that "we should forsake wicked teachers." [69] Yet it is significant that this directive is not brought into relationship with the *Damnamus*. The authority of implementing the rejection is a matter for itself in the opinion of both the confession and of Luther. It belongs to the area of church discipline.[70] In any event, the problem of referring the condemnations to persons and to things was not yet really acute. This is supported by the fact that later on Jacob Andreae found satisfaction in having overcome the one-sided "condemnation of persons" as in the Augsburg Confession.[71]

In a similarly inconclusive way the Apology distinguishes between "wicked error" and "unprofitable opinion." The former is said to undermine the foundation (that is, Christ) and is therefore intolerable, whereas the latter does not (based on 1 Cor. 3:12).[72] However, this purely Biblical concept of the foundation is not employed as a means to a clear-cut distinction between heretical and nonheretical error, as was done later with the concept of the foundation of faith *(fundamentum fidei)*. Consequently in this respect as in others there remains the impression of a certain simplicity with respect to the problem of condemnations, and it should seemingly not be surprising that the condemnation that bore the gravest implications, namely the one in Article X, should share in this simplicity.

This, however, by no means signifies that we must confine ourselves to the situation derived from the text itself. Recently Wilhelm Maurer has demonstrated in a particularly comprehensive way that there are indications that can be derived from the history of the text and from what we know about the deliberations among the "protesting" estates before the diet. These findings represent a substantial advance.[73] Regarding the condemnations two lines of development may be discerned. The one shows up with particular clarity in the genesis of Article XXIV, concerning the Mass. The various stages in the development of this article can be traced back to an opinion of the Wittenberg theologians prepared by Luther himself. In this opinion Luther says that the emperor ought to help "to make provisions for condemning the Sacramentarians as erring heretics." [74] In what used to be called the Torgau Articles, that is, Melanchthon's recasting of the above-mentioned opinion, which was designed to serve as the decisive apologetic document of the Saxons before the emperor and the empire, it is stated that in electoral Saxony "the Zwinglian teaching is most strenuously opposed." [75] In the draft *Na*, the corresponding passage is no less harsh: "Here we also condemn the unchristian teaching that denies that the body and blood of Christ are truly present." [76] In the next stage, documented in a copy prepared by Spalatin, there is no longer talk of condemnation, but in considerably milder form the statement reads, "There is also instruction directed against the false and erroneous doctrine concerning the sacrament." Here the definite article still makes plain enough what is meant.[77] However, in the final German form of the confession even this has been eliminated, so that the sentence now reads, "The people are also given instruction about other false teachings concerning the sacrament." [78] The Latin text omits this reference entirely, as subsequently do both Latin and German texts of the *editio princeps*.[79]

The record of a similar development may be found in the

preliminary drafts of the preface of the Augsburg Confession. In the form preserved in *Na*, Melanchthon mentions among other favorable results of the Lutheran teaching that "as is apparent, more than one heresy has been overcome by it, heresies which in new and unchristian writings have risen up against the holy sacraments." [80] This undoubtedly refers to the Swiss because the false view of the sacraments held by the Anabaptists is specifically mentioned immediately afterward. In all the other forms of the preface such a direct barb aimed at the Zwinglian teaching is omitted. We have, then, a situation similar to that of Article XXIV. There is an unmistakable trend toward toning down or even eliminating the condemnation directed against the Swiss. How shall we explain this trend, which appears to conflict with Melanchthon's decidedly Lutheran position on the Lord's Supper?

Maurer calls attention to the fact that the lessening of the antithesis against the Zwinglians corresponds to an increasingly clearer expression of the antithesis against the *Roman* doctrine of the Eucharist. "The fuller delineation of the reformatory concern in the Augsburg Confession . . . has helped to overcome the intra-Protestant divergence on the sacrament." [81] It seems natural to assume that the attempts at union in Marburg were still exerting an influence. Already Vilmar had pointed to the "Marburg Concord" to explain the strikingly gentle "disapprove" of Article X.[82] Maurer has now provided strong support for this assumption by pointing to clear textual correspondences between the Latin wording of Augsburg Confession X and the original Marburg union formula.[83] At the very least this would make it very probable that Melanchthon chose the "disapprove" with conscious reference to the Marburg conversations. Hence, the choice of that word belongs into the mediating line that became evident in the development of Article XXIV. What could not be concluded from the linguistic findings becomes clear from the genetic history of the text. The Latin version of Augsburg Confession X does in fact demonstrate a degree of mitigation in its formula of rejection.[84] If we add what Maurer has also shown, that Melanchthon's studies in the church fathers helped to shape his formulations, the origin of this mediating line may be recognized. "Melanchthon, striving for objectivity and eager to dispose of the Eucharistic controversy by having recourse to history, is indeed Lutheran in his Communion formula, but he is a Biblical humanist at the same time." [85] The formal difficulty of letting the Latin form of Article X stand as the bearer of this compromising tendency alongside the different German form finds its solution in the fact that the Latin text was originally designed as a basis for discussion and was not intended, like the German text, to have legally binding force.[86]

It must be remembered, however, that this line of investigation should not obscure consideration of the second line, which is represented by the plain rejection of the Zwinglians in the German text of Augsburg Confession X and which in the long run proved itself to be normative for the future development. This must be kept clearly in view. It was, after all, the strictly Lutheran view of the Lord's Supper that Melanchthon believed to have discovered also in the writings of the fathers. It will not do to interpret the varying accents of rejection in the German and Latin texts of Augsburg Confession X as indicating a concession by Melanchthon in the doctrine itself. The South Germans had good reason for taking also the "disapprove" of Article X in the sense of a full-fledged condemnation.[87] The stubborn altercation between Philip of Hesse and the Saxon representatives before the emperor's arrival in Augsburg [88] shows very clearly that and why the strong rejection of the Swiss in the German wording of Augsburg Confession X had to win out.

The history of the controversy is reflected in an exchange of letters between Melanchthon and Brenz on one hand and Philip of Hesse on the other during the days around June 11, 1530.[89] The 25-year-old prince, determined not to yield to the emperor in anything and to have all negotiations tabled until a future general council, desired to preserve solidarity among the "protesting" estates at all costs. Desperately he tried to prevent the separation of the Wittenbergers from the Swiss and the South Germans. His theses were simple: Basically the Swiss and the Wittenbergers are "thoroughly united and believe in and confess one Christ and seek to be saved through Him." It is true, the Swiss view of the sacrament is different. But this cannot be regarded as a heresy for the sake of which there would have to be a separation. If the Swiss must nevertheless be regarded as false teachers, at least do not lump the errorists and the misguided together and so condemn the whole opposition party. "In case a country should be condemned and penalized, the cabbage would have to suffer along with the wild herbs." [90] And finally, the Lutherans must not deny the spirit of Christ, who desires not to condemn but to save. Therefore Christians, "if something in Scripture is not understood in the same way . . . should have patience and not give up." [91] For that reason Philip practically adjured the Wittenbergers: "Make a friendly, fraternal peace with those who are called Zwinglian, and bear in mind how very kindly the apostle and many of the ancients dealt with each other and with outsiders." [92]

It must have been difficult for the irenic Melanchthon to turn a deaf ear to so urgent a plea for a fraternal attitude. He answered the Landgrave [93] that "we are most desirous of establishing peace." He continued, however, that his conscience did not permit him to set aside the difference in the doctrine of the Lord's Supper for the sake of "fraternity." It was and remained his conviction that "the faith must be certain if it is to stand before the judgment of God," and that this certainty is the most important matter also in the doctrine of the Lord's Supper. "For since the church makes daily use of the sacrament, it would lead to tremendous offense if one should be in error at this point." [94] According to Melanchthon's conviction the Swiss were doing precisely that. "If the arguments advanced by Zwingli could quiet the conscience so that it could be confident before God, we would accept those allegories too. But we know that these cannot give rest to the conscience." [95] Furthermore, it cannot have escaped Melanchthon that Philip's expressed views on the Lord's Supper bore an unmistakably Zwinglian tinge. Hence he could not accept Philip's thesis of a basic doctrinal unity, and the rest followed as a matter of course, for "we may not approve of false teaching." Surely a condemnation dare not strike the leaders and the misled to the same degree. "It is possible that we should tolerate as brothers Christians who err but do not defend the error. . . . Yet those cannot be regarded as brothers who promote and defend teachings that have no Scriptural foundation." [96] It was self-evident also for Melanchthon that one must distinguish between the "teachers" and the "people." He emphasized furthermore that the concern here was not with persons but with doctrine. However, for him as for Luther these limitations on the condemnations were not in the foreground. No matter how embarrassing and inopportune the consequences might be, these limitations could not rescind the primacy of the concern for truth, the inescapable necessity of the antithesis for the sake of the thesis.

At this point, in the matter of consequences, there arose a second serious difference of opinion between Melanchthon and the landgrave, a difference resting on profound divergences in the assessment of the total political situation. Philip refused to concede that the diet could have any competence in spiritual matters, and he therefore urged the convocation of a council. The Wittenbergers, however, together with their elector maintained that the diet could very well be regarded and serve as a council. While Philip aimed at the establishment of a united Evangelical front from Wittenberg to Zurich as the only effective countermeasure against the politics of the emperor, dictated by the Hapsburg dynastic interests, Melanchthon was concerned above all about peace with the emperor. The very thought of a religious war was for Melanchthon a bogey man, and under no circumstances did he want to see the peace endangered by a merger with the Swiss, whom the emperor detested. There is no doubt that this longing for peace led Melanchthon, especially toward the close of the Augsburg events, to participate in questionable diplomatic maneuvers and attempts at compromise. But from all that we know it is equally certain that his clear-cut aloofness from the Swiss did not rest primarily on those political considerations. On the contrary, it was based primarily on the factual theological difference, in which he felt conscience-bound to stand firmly beside Luther.

With Philip of Hesse the situation was different in principle. For him the priority of the political goals was beyond argument. This is perfectly clear from the instructions which he planned to give his emissaries to Augsburg when he himself thought of staying away and which he still regarded as being in force when, contrary to his original intention, he did go to Augsburg in person.[97] Not to support any kind of separation or isolation among the Evangelicals—that was declared to be the summit goal of Hessian policy. To that end the delegates should in every case strive for the suppression of differences. "By no means and in no way" should they allow themselves to be separated from the Strasbourgers and others of like mind because of the Zwinglian or other controverted teaching. Finally, they were also instructed to refuse their consent as a matter of principle when it concerned "banning, condemning, judging, or disposing of" someone who does not "follow the party that is called Lutheran in believing that Christ is bodily present in the bread." [98]

It is these principles that really show up Philip's behavior at the diet in its true light. They provide the key to his correspondence with Melanchthon and Brenz, as well as his conversation of several hours with Urbanus Rhegius. As the latter reported to Luther, he was deeply impressed by the landgrave's will to peace.[99] Philip's emphatic support of the Strasbourgers belongs here too, as does all of his endeavor in general to suppress as much as possible all opposition to the Swiss and the South Germans. Thus he ordered his court preacher, Schnepf, to refrain from attacking the Zwinglian doctrine of the Lord's Supper in his sermons, and he himself regularly attended the services of the Zwinglian Keller and ostentatiously avoided those conducted by the Saxon preacher Agricola.[100] Yet Philip was unable to prevent the retention of the condemnation at its decisive place in Article X of the confession. The force of circumstances, especially the necessity of presenting a united front to the emperor's ban on preaching, finally led even Philip to subscribe to the entire confession, including the article on the Lord's Supper. And that was the article that was worded "so as to express Luther's position," as Melanchthon was careful to emphasize once more in his report on the subscription.[101] Jonas informed Luther that the landgrave did indeed subscribe, not, however, without saying that he "was not satisfied on the matter of the sacrament." [102] It is readily understandable that Philip gave in only with the greatest reluctance, for with his signature he had for the moment dealt the death blow to all his political plans.

But though he was unsuccessful in his opposition to the condemnations, he fared better in another area. The idea of a general council was everywhere gaining ground. The estates, the emperor, and finally even the pope took up the idea. It was, of course, not a new idea, either for the imperial politics or for the "protesting" estates. But in Augsburg it was above all others the landgrave who tirelessly promoted this plan. It seems that he, too, entertained the special turn of thought that was to play a significant role in the problem of condemnations, namely, that a condemnation of false teaching, such as the Zwinglian doctrine of Communion, could be pronounced only by a council after a hearing. But Melanchthon, too, had been troubled by this consideration after the Diet of Speyer in 1529.[103]

If we now try to draw conclusions from the whole Augsburg argument about the condemnation of the Swiss, we shall find the net results to be quite meager. The people involved had experienced something of the immanent problems and had been compelled to do some mature thinking about them. But both the force of circumstances pressing upon all the "protesting" estates as well as the one-sided political orientation of the land-grave severely limited the discussion from the outset. Philip's opposition to the rejection of Zwingli and his followers was basically only one fragment of his grandiose political schemes, which dominated him completely and in which he was far ahead of his time. This was also to have great significance for the sub-sequent Evangelical political history. Philip's own position on the controverted doctrines remained uncertain. He wavered constantly in his understanding of the Lord's Supper, although on the whole he felt himself more attracted to Zwingli's teach-ing.[104] He wrote to Melanchthon that he could not be convinced of the Lutheran conception "on the basis of a clear text, without explanation," [105] and it is significant that later he made himself the advocate and protector of Bucer's policy of mediation. Hence his stature remains ambiguous for historical assessment. "As a politician who assumed the right to measure religious questions by worldly standards, he did not grasp the absoluteness of the Gospel, the cutting edge of personal decision in matters of faith." [106]

With reference only to the question of condemnations, it may be said for Melanchthon, on the other hand, that in Augs-burg he knew himself to be conscience-bound to the decision that forced itself upon him in submission to the Word of God. He was far from excluding political considerations altogether. But it remained clear for him that the responsibility for the cor-rect preaching of the Gospel must have priority in this matter. It must be admitted that Melanchthon's readiness to make compromises and concessions, as demonstrated over against Rome, casts a shadow over his condemnation of the Zwinglians. It is and remains embarrassing that in the Augsburg Confession "there is no decisive *damnant* against the Roman errors, an inclusion that would have given full weight to the other condemnations." [107] In spite of general approval Luther's criticism of the confession at this point is clear and certainly not without foundation. "Satan is still alive," he wrote on July 21, 1530, from the Coburg, "and he well knows that your apology is treading softly and is not being frank in the articles on purgatory, on the cult of saints, and especially on the Antichrist, the pope." [108] How much more believable the "disapprove" of Article X would have been and would still be if Melanchthon could already in Augsburg have achieved the clear-cut rejections of Roman teachings he incorporated later in the text of Articles XIII and XVIII. And this takes nothing away from the fact that the basic concerns of the Reformation are in substance given their due everywhere in the Augsburg Confession.[109] The Apology did a thorough and plain job of coming to grips with Rome. Yet this could not remove the unresolved issue present in the confession itself. A point had become manifest at which Melanchthon on his part sacrificed theological consistency to a mirage of church politics. This he did in that embarrassing fiction at the close of the first part of the Augsburg Confession, a statement later toned down, that the whole dispute between Rome and the "protesting" estates had to do with "a few abuses." [110] This discordant element has for all time created serious problems not only for the subsequent debate about condemnations but also for the whole relationship between the Lutherans and the Reformed.

Since the day of Augsburg it was no longer possible to force the *Damnamus* back into the domain of unauthorized theological polemics, as Melanchthon would have been only too happy to do later on. Henceforth the full weight of the teaching churches of the new faith, of the parishes that had been led by Luther away from the domination of the Roman teaching office to the liberty of independent decision in matters of faith and life in obedience to the Word and could for that very reason recognize themselves to be *the* church—this full weight now stood behind both the condemnations in the opening articles of the

Augsburg Confession that attach themselves to the doctrinal decisions of the ancient church and also the condemnation in Augsburg Confession X. [111] In 1530 Melanchthon was undoubtedly sincere in his condemnation of the Swiss teaching on the Lord's Supper, even though he continued to feel himself bound to take the concerns of the Marburg Colloquy seriously. Yet he would probably not have agreed to the condemnation if he had not felt confident that this point, too, would serve to divert suspicion from the cause of the "protesting" estates before the emperor and the empire. But now the "apology" had inadvertently been turned into a confession, the defensive document had become a basic witness to the faith. Time would have to tell whether the confessional formulation could survive the tempests the coming discussions would raise. Melanchthon could not prevent the application of this test also to Article X. This test came in a resurgence of the Eucharistic controversy that seriously shook Melanchthon's convictions, while it gave Luther the opportunity decisively to reaffirm his earlier position and thus also to confirm for the future the judgment of the condemnation in Article X in its inviolable validity.

Notes to Chapter 8

[1] *Book of Concord* (Tappert) pp. 28, 29, 33, 35.

[2] Ibid., pp. 31, 33, 35, 37, 38.

[3] Ibid., p. 34.

[4] Ibid., pp. 29, 35.

[5] Ibid., pp. 36, 40.

[6] "Zur Entstehungsgeschichte der Augustana. Der 'Unterricht der Visitatoren' als Vorlage des Bekenntnisses," ZsystTh, 15 (1938), 419ff. For the text of the instructions see WA 26, 175ff.

[7] Cf. H. v. Schubert, *Bekenntnisbildung und Religionspolitik, 1529 – 30 (1524 – 34)* (Gotha, 1910), pp. 21ff.

[8] WA 30 III, 87, 4; 89, 5; 90, 23.

[9] WA 30 III, 89, 17. – W. Koehler *(Das Religionsgespraech zu Marburg, 1529* [Tuebingen, 1929]) writes of the Schwabach Articles, p. 30: "Zwingli's doctrine of the Lord's Supper was here firmly rejected." One cannot, however, speak of a rejection in the strict sense of the term.

[10] WA 30 III, 171, 10 and 23.

[11] Cf. O. Seitz in WA 30 III, 97f.

[12] WA 30 III, 169, 5.

[13] The text is found in Th. Kolde, *Die Augsburgische Konfession lateinisch und deutsch* (Gotha, 1911), 134ff. On the problem of the "Torgau Articles" see W. Maurer, "Zum geschichtlichen Verstaendnis der Abendmahlsartikel in der Confessio Augustana *(Festschrift fuer Gerhard Ritter zu seinem 60. Geburtstag*

[Tuebingen, 1950], 161ff.); also: J. v. Walter, "Was sind die Torgauer Artikel?" in: *Christentum und Froemmigkeit* (Guetersloh, 1941), 203ff.; H. Bornkamm, "Die Literatur des Augustana-Gedaechtnisjahres," ZKG, 50 (1931), 209f.; G. Hoffmann, "Zur Entstehungsgeschichte der Augustana," ZsystTh, 15 (1938), 419ff.

[14] H. Bornkamm *(Die Bekenntnisschriften der evangelisch-lutherischen Kirche,* 4th ed. [Goettingen, 1959], p. XV, n. 8) here calls attention to P. Wernle, *Der evangelische Glaube nach den Hauptschriften der Reformatoren,* I, *Luther* (1918), pp. 268ff., and also refers to a communication from E. Hirsch. Of the recent literature see also W. E. Nagel, *Luthers Anteil an der Confessio Augustana* (Guetersloh, 1930), pp. 14ff.; furthermore, H. H. Wendt, *Die Augsburgische Konfession* (Halle, 1927), p. 11.

[15] So Bornkamm, *Bekenntnisschriften,* p. XV. Cf. Hoffmann, p. 489.

[16] WA 26, 500, 30; 501, 32.

[17] Ibid., 503, 35.

[18] Ibid.

[19] WA 26, 503, 25.

[20] Ibid., 506, 19 (Bornkamm: "The reference to the Donatists is taken from Luther's Confession of 1528," *Bekenntnisschriften,* p. 62, n. 2).

[21] P. 466.

[22] Printed in Kolde, pp. 146ff.

[23] See Maurer, p. 195, for the documentation.

[24] Cf. W. Gussmann, *Quellen und Forschungen zur Geschichte des Augsburgischen Glaubensbekenntnisses* II: *D. Johann Ecks Vierhundertvier Artikel zum Reichstag von Augsburg, 1530* (Kassel, 1930).

[25] Gussmann, p. 102.

[26] Cf. W. Gussmann, "Melanchthon und Eck," *Neue Kirchliche Zeitshrift,* 1930, pp. 307f., 310.

[27] *Book of Concord,* p. 100.

[28] *Die Augsburgische Confession* (Guetersloh, 1870), p. 48.

[29] *Book of Concord,* p. 29.

[30] In his edition of *Na (Die aelteste Redaktion der Augsburger Konfession,* Guetersloh, 1906) Kolde calls this "striking," p. 49, but does not pursue this matter further.

[31] The opinion of Nagel, p. 88.

[32] W. Koehler, *Das Marburger Religionsgespraech 1529. Versuch einer Rekonstruktion* (Leipzig, 1929), pp. 7f.; H. v. Schubert, pp. 56ff. See also the much earlier V. E. Loescher, *Aussfuehrliche Historia Motuum zwischen den Evangelisch Lutherischen und Reformierten,* I (Frankfort and Leipzig, 1707), 159.

[33] As a matter of fact, in the complicated church-political history leading up to the Diet of Augsburg the question of condemnations recedes completely into the background (cf. the whole presentation by H. v. Schubert, as well as his *Buendnis und Bekenntnis 1529/30* [Leipzig, 1908]).

[34] WA 30 III, 89, 17; 170, 6.

[35] Kolde, *Aelteste Redaktion,* p. 13.

[36] Loescher, I, 181; cf. Rudolf Hospinian, *Concordia Discors* (Geneva, 1678), p. 285.

[37] *Christlicher und wahrhafftiger Unterricht von den Worten der Einsetzung des h. Abendmahls* (Strasbourg, 1565), p. 149. Cf. Th. Kolde, "Historische Einleitung in die Symbolischen Buecher der ev.-luth. Kirche" (12th ed. of Mueller, p. VIII). W. Gussmann, *Quellen und Forschungen* I/1 (Leipzig and Berlin), 1911, p. 398.

[38] WA *Briefe,* 3, 586, 25.

[39] Ibid., 604, 37; 606, 84.

[40] Ibid., 600, n. 2.

[41] Ibid., 605, 42 and 48.

[42] Ibid., 606, 93; 604, 15.

[43] Ibid., 604, 12.

[44] Ibid., 606, 97.

[45] Cf. the quotations in the notes on Luther's letter, pp. 606f.

[46] WA 26, 262, 3 and 22.

[47] Ibid., 509, 20.

[48] Kolde, *Aelteste Redaktion*, p. 8.

[49] H. v. Schubert, *Bekenntnisbildung u. Religionspolitik*, pp. 96ff.; W. Koehler, *Religionsgespraech zu Marburg*, pp. 36ff.; Maurer, pp. 205ff.

[50] Cf. Koehler, p. 37, note: "In my opinion v. Schubert makes too much of the conciliatory attitude of the Lutherans, whose only concession, after all, was the removal of a misunderstanding. In other respects they held firm to their whole position."

[51] Koehler, pp. 36, 38. — A sample of how some Lutherans could assess the situation immediately after Marburg is afforded by the draft of an ordination pledge, which is contained in the "Reformatory Articles of an Ordinance" set up by Heinrich Winckel for Goettingen toward the close of 1529. There we read: "I also curse and condemn Zwingli and all his associates" (reported by P. Tschackert, ZKG 20 [1899], 371). And yet Winckel was a man "who otherwise throughout his life, both public and private, manifested a most peaceable disposition" (Tschackert, *Die Entstehung der lutherischen und der reformierten Kirchenlehre* [Goettingen, 1910], p. 373).

[52] CR 1, 1083 (Letter to Camerarius, July 26, 1529).

[53] Ibid., 1067 (May 14, 1529).

[54] Ibid., 1077 (June 20, 1529).

[55] CR 2, 104 (June 13, 1530).

[56] CR 1, 1043 and 1070. Cf. H. Sasse, "Die Lehrentscheidung der Konkordienformel," in: *Vom Sakrament des Altars* (Leipzig, 1941), p. 143, n. 1.

[57] "Since I would do nothing against conscience, I was very hesitant about condemning those whom we had not yet given a proper hearing" (CR 1, 1068).

[58] Cf. H. v. Schubert, *Bekenntnisbildung und Religionspolitik*, pp. 96ff.; Koehler, *Religionsgespraech zu Marburg*, pp. 40—42.

[59] CR 23, 733ff.

[60] Cf. Maurer, pp. 201ff. Maurer makes a plausible case for the view (p. 205, n. 148) that Melanchthon was to some extent influenced by a compromise formula drafted by Erasmus for the purpose of uniting the warring factions in their understanding of the Lord's Supper. Be that as it may, this does not minimize the antithesis against the Swiss, for in the same context Erasmus himself expressly rejects their doctrine (pp. 205f.).

[61] Maurer thinks that also the German wording of *Na* already manifests a special "considerateness," since the rejection is made without naming names (p. 185); however, the same kind of rejection in *Na* 11, also noted by Maurer (p. 185, n. 78), renders this conclusion somewhat uncertain.

[62] See below, p. 170. Accordingly, we need to revise Maurer's judgment that orthodox Lutheranism, motivated by legal concerns, always appealed only to the legal validity of the German text (p. 162).

[63] O. Ritschl, *Dogmengeschichte des Protestantismus*, I (Leipzig, 1908), 284.

[64] Maurer, p. 162.

65 *Book of Concord,* p. 173.

66 H. Sasse, p. 155.

67 See below, pp. 99 – 100.

68 *Book of Concord,* p. 84.

69 Ibid., p. 177.

70 Cf. E. Schlink, *Theology of the Lutheran Confessions,* trans. Paul F. Koehneke and Herbert J. A. Bouman (Philadelphia: Fortress Press, 1961), pp. 212f.

71 See below, p. 170.

72 *Book of Concord,* pp. 171f.

73 See p. 33, n. 13.

74 WA *Briefe,* 5, 433, 110f.

75 *Bekenntnisschriften,* p. 96, 45 (cf. Kolde, *Augsburgische Konfession,* p. 140).

76 Kolde, *Aelteste Redaktion,* p. 20.

77 *Bekenntnisschriften,* p. 91, apparatus to line 31.

78 *Book of Concord,* p. 56.

79 Ibid. – The variant readings are in part reproduced in Kolde, *Aelteste Redaktion,* p. 46, n. 2; fully in Hoffmann, *Zur Entstehungsgeschichte der Augustana,* p. 447, n. 1, and Maurer, p. 183.

80 Kolde, *Aelteste Redaktion,* p. 8; *Bekenntnisschriften,* p. 42, 1.

81 Maurer, pp. 183f.

82 Vilmar, p. 107.

83 Maurer, p. 205ff.

84 It would be worth a special investigation to determine if from this situation certain fluctuations also in the transmission of the *German* wording of Augsburg Confession X might be explained. They could, however, be simply scribes' and copyists' errors. Thus, in the first Ansbach copy the word *gegenleer* ("contrary doctrine") was obviously added to Art. X later (K. E. Foerstemann, *Urkundenbuch zur Geschichte des Reichstages zu Augsburg im Jahre 1530,* I [Halle, 1833], 349. Cf. Gussmann, I/1, 398). In the second Ansbach manuscript there had been about half a line of text (later erased) between the rejection at the end of Art. X and the beginning of the following article. A Munich manuscript has *gegenlerer* ("contrary teachers") instead of *Gegenlehr* (Foerstemann, p. 387).

85 Maurer, p. 204.

86 Ibid., pp. 195f.

87 "Such is the Lutherans' 'disposition toward disapproval' over against us, and such is the rage of the papists, that in men, to be sure, we see nothing that might fairly promise peace" (Bucer and Capito to A. Blaurer, July 22, 1530, cited by Maurer, p. 194, n. 107a).

88 Detailed presentation by Gussmann, pp. 47ff.; Maurer, pp. 185ff.

89 CR 2, 92ff.

90 CR 2, 97.

91 Ibid., 98.

92 Ibid., 99.

93 Ibid., 102.

94 Ibid., 94.

95 CR 2, 95.

96 Ibid., 93.

97 Reprinted in Gussmann, I/1, 326ff. It is significant that exactly 100 years

later the attempt could be made to use this instruction as proof for the land-grave's Zwinglian inclinations.

[98] Gussmann, p. 327.

[99] WA *Briefe*, 5, 334f.

[100] See the documentation in Gussmann, pp. 60, 397f.

[101] WA *Briefe*, 5, 396.

[102] "The landgrave subscribed along with us, but he said at the same time that our people had not satisfied him with regard to the sacrament" (WA *Briefe*, 5, 427, 29). Maurer correctly emphasizes that no legally valid reservation with regard to the subscription itself can be deduced from this fact (pp. 193f.). It will therefore not be possible to agree with Gussmann's conjecture that the land-grave did not regard the confession as legally binding and only for that reason was willing to subscribe (p. 58).

[103] CR 2, 98.

[104] Cf. Melanchthon's letter to Luther, May 22, 1530 (WA *Briefe*, 5, 335f., especially lines 33 and 38).

[105] CR 2, 100.

[106] Gussmann, p. 62.

[107] G. Hoffmann, "Luther und Melanchthon," ZsystTh, 15 (1938), pp. 102f.

[108] Letter to Jonas, July 21, 1530 (WA *Briefe*, 5, 496, 7). Cf. H. v. Schubert, *Luther-Jahrbuch*, 1930, p. 151f. [Translator's note: It may be argued that Luther had forfeited his right to express such an opinion in July by his failure to comment on the draft of the Augsburg Confession sent to him for examination in May, prior to its final revision and subsequent presentation.]

[109] Maurer, pp. 164f.

[110] *Book of Concord*, p. 47. [Translator's note: It may not be amiss to point out that not all students of the Lutheran Confessions are willing to accept the judgments expressed by the author above. These scholars do not agree that Melanchthon "sacrificed theological consistency," or that the statement at the close of Part I of the Augsburg Confession is a "fiction," especially since the principal items in controversy had not yet been dogmatically defined by the Roman Church.]

[111] Cf. Thieme, pp. 4f.

Chapter 9

Luther, Melanchthon, and the Swiss

The period following the Diet of Augsburg seemed at first to press toward a development in conformity with the view of Philip of Hesse. It is marked by a general attempt at conciliation among the various Evangelical parties. As early as 1531 the cities of South Germany subscribed to the Augsburg Confession, though at Augsburg they had submitted their own confession, the *Tetrapolitana,* and had thus held aloof from the Wittenbergers. They also joined the Smalcald League, which had brought Saxony and Hesse together. The Swiss continued to isolate themselves. Yet there were always some voices raised in support of a political alliance, without suggesting that on its account the doctrinal differences should be glossed over. Could the condemnation that was valid in doctrinal matters really stand as a permanent barrier to meeting the political exigencies? So, for example, Urbanus Rhegius argued in a joint opinion with Schnepf,[112] asking if it were not possible "for the sake of necessary assistance to preserve peace and protection, to make treaties and reach an understanding even though the parties differed in matters of faith, so long as their agreement did no injury to the Christian faith and doctrine and so long as not doctrinal but only temporal matters were involved, such as peace in the land, protection and mutual assistance against force and injustice?" Again: Was the difference in the doctrine of the Lord's Supper really as far-reaching as the action at Augsburg seemed to indicate? It was above all others Martin Bucer who by means of interviews, essays, and letters strove untiringly to mediate and who worked zealously to provide a sound basis for the political plans of the landgrave of Hesse through the establishment of a doctrinal consensus between Wittenberg and

Zurich. The Wittenberg Concord of 1536, which reconsidered
the Marburg issue, succeeded in confirming and strengthening
the South German cities in their adherence to the Wittenberg
position, but it did not bring about a union with the Swiss, so
earnestly desired by Bucer.[113] Luther had left no doubts that
he could make no concessions in the doctrine of the Communion,
however much he longed for concord with the Swiss. The Zurich
people on their part accused Bucer of changing the nature of
the doctrine by coming to terms with the Wittenbergers.[114]
Luther continued to correspond with the Swiss until 1538, but
the issue could not be resolved. In the end, the Swiss refused
to subscribe to the Wittenberg Concord and, as a result, their
isolation became even more palpable, because the condemnation the Augsburg Confession expressed about their Communion
doctrine remained unchanged.

Meanwhile, the author of the Augsburg Confession had
himself experienced an about-face. Negotiations with Bucer, the
prospect of a union with the Swiss, possibly his acquaintance
with Calvin, but above all his studies in the church fathers – all
these influenced Melanchthon privately to begin to have doubts
about the sense and correctness of the Lutheran doctrine of
the Eucharist. There are indications of this as early as 1531.[115]
In February 1535 Melanchthon wrote to Bucer: "I have gathered all the testimonies I could find for both sides, so that we
could talk about them. The difference is remarkable." [116] At the
turn of the year, 1534 – 35, Melanchthon represented Luther at
the Communion colloquy at Cassel and at his request defended
the Lutheran position against Bucer. Then Melanchthon wrote
to his friend Camerarius: "Don't ask me for my own opinion
now, for I was a messenger delivering the opinion of another." [117] He subscribed to both the Wittenberg and the Smalcald Articles the following year, articles which unequivocally
affirmed the sacramental union as well as the reception of the
Lord's body and blood by the ungodly (without condemning the
Swiss, however, since the Smalcald Articles were addressed
principally to Rome). In his will, written at the end of 1539,
Melanchthon declared that he held to the Eucharistic doctrine
of the Wittenberg Concord.[118] In the next year, however, he
issued a new quarto edition of the Augsburg Confession in Latin,
in which he came out into the open for the first time with his

changed views. This document represents a highly significant turning point especially in the matter of condemnations. In Article X the condemnation was dropped entirely. The immediate motives behind this change can hardly be uncovered in detail at this date. It is certain that Melanchthon did not intend to support the Swiss teaching (as subsequent Reformed polemics endeavored to assert). It is just as certain that precisely in this apparently inconsequential change in Article X we have strong support for that uncertainty in the doctrine of the Lord's Supper from which Melanchthon never again freed himself as long as he lived. In giving expression to his doubts in the normative Lutheran Confession rather than in a private remark Melanchthon gave the entire process a scope he himself had not envisioned.

It is surprising that for a time Lutherans did not see through the range of this alteration. V. E. Loescher probably assessed the situation correctly when he said that "because of his great prestige" Melanchthon's actions were at first not resented.[119] Luther himself had seen no reason for a formal break with Melanchthon. The first objection was raised not by the Lutherans but by the Roman Catholics. This protest called attention to the fact that Melanchthon had not simply made some insignificant revisions in formulation but had introduced far-reaching changes in substance. Once again it was Eck who played a role in the development of the problem of condemnations. Of Eck Melanchthon might have said, as did Luther, that he "kept him on his toes." [120] During the first brief Colloquy of Worms, in January 1541, Eck repeatedly called attention to the differences between the 1530 edition and the *Variata* now offered by Melanchthon. The latter defended himself by contending that the sense had not been changed anywhere, but that expressions had been modified and clarified here and there (*vel magis mitigata vel explicatoria*). Eck on his part insisted that he could easily point to considerable differences in content and would do so in due course, expressly naming Article X as an example.[121] It may be that Eck was thinking for the moment of the opposition to the dogma of transubstantiation, an opposition that appears stronger in the *Variata* than in the original. Yet the question of the omitted condemnation would undoubtedly also have been raised — if the premature adjournment of the colloquy had not prevented a thorough discussion of this point.

The Regensburg Colloquy of the same year did not again raise the issue and brought no new development in this matter. Quite a number of older and more recent historians of the Augsburg Confession report an episode which, if trustworthy, would offer a characteristic illustration of Melanchthon's lack of certainty with regard to condemnations. It is reported that in the course of the conversation Melanchthon yielded to the urging of the estates and with his own hand wrote the "disapprove" (*improbant*) of Article X, omitted in the *Variata*, back into the copy of the confession before him.[122] But since there is no hint of this alleged incident in the printed proceedings of the Regensburg Colloquy and since there was still no mention of it in the Altenburg Colloquy of 1568, where the Gnesio-Lutherans and the Philippists discussed in detail the alterations in the Augsburg Confession,[123] we must be skeptical about the story. It is, of course, equally improbable that it was a lie invented for a purpose by apologists of the Formula of Concord.[124] Whatever may be the truth about this alleged "restitution" in Article X, even without it Melanchthon's hesitation and wavering are manifest, not only as methodological doubts motivated by Christian love, as an attempt to avoid the danger of passing unbrotherly judgments, but as symptomatic of shaky convictions concerning the doctrine itself. Augsburg in retrospect clearly demonstrates the difference: At first it was Melanchthon who supported the antithesis because his conscience was committed to the thesis, while Philip of Hesse would have liked to see this combination of thesis and antithesis yield to the goals of his church politics, though he raised no public objections. Now Melanchthon was about to jettison the stand he had defended against Philip. His retreat from this position had begun already in Augsburg. There he had evaluated the total situation of the Evangelical movement in the light of the church-political realities and had found it impossible to agree to a clean-cut condemnation of Roman errors. But while his conduct at that time might still appear as a restraint forced on him by the circumstances, a restraint that did not seriously impair the integrity of the doctrine, his later attitude, following his incontestable approach to the doctrinal position of the Swiss, has the earmarks of a compromise in the issue itself. The inner connection between thesis and antithesis is still in evidence, but now with an inverse signature: Modifying the thesis conditions and compels also a modification of the antithesis, though the change in the thesis itself is not yet expressed. Melanchthon's understanding of the Lord's Supper was never consistently in the pattern of the Swiss doctrine; by the same token he was never quite consistent in abolishing the antithesis. He never explicitly and definitively renounced the "disapprove" of the Unaltered Augsburg Confession. Characteristically the both-and remains, the evasion of definitive decisions, a trait that remained with Melanchthon as long as he lived. In fact, he referred to himself as a "Peripatetic who loves the golden mean." [125]

With all this Melanchthon was moving ever farther away from Luther, as became evident soon after the appearance of the *Variata*. Luther still saw no reason in Melanchthon's attitude for a break in their relations. He did not feel himself deceived by Melanchthon as he did by the Zwinglians, and he surely did not question his friend's personal honesty. Yet his silence could certainly not be construed as approval. His opinion of the Swiss had, if anything, become even more critical.[126] His "Short Confession Concerning the Holy Supper," which appeared in 1544, is characterized by an emphatic and unequivocal development of the antithesis. Looking back on what happened since Marburg, Luther saw only a single, unbroken chain of disappointments for his good will, yes, of conscious deceptions on the part of the Swiss. In his opinion Marburg could have furnished the springboard for a reciprocal "understanding." True, "in the article concerning the Sacrament they got nowhere," yet there was some hope that "in time this one article might be settled too." [127] But the posthumous publication of Zwingli's "Exposition of the Christian Faith" more than anything else dashed Luther's hopes. He regarded the document as a basically "pagan" one and realized now that all honest brotherly love, all Lutheran readiness to forget the evil legacy of the Eucharistic controversy had been a waste of time. The old charges of "cannibalism" and "bread worship," which they had tried to forget, reopened the wounds. If, then, the condemnation was to be in full force again, the blame must rest entirely on the Swiss, whom he had convicted "time and again as manifest blasphemers and liars" — no different, in fact, than Schwenckfeld, whom Luther attacked in the same context. He stated explicitly: "I put them all together in the same pie." [128] There had surely been no lack of explicit warnings. Their own disunity in the doctrine of the Supper should have given the Swiss pause (in this connection Luther also pointed out the particularly dubious opinion that "there is here no article of faith, hence we ought not to quarrel about it").[129] Above all, Luther's polemical writings should serve to warn them, as also the judgment of God expressed with such shocking clarity in the death of Zwingli and Oecolampadius. After all this proved to be in vain, there was only one thing left to say. Luther wrote: I have "lost all hope of their amendment and have so completely ignored them that I have had no desire to write anything against that booklet (Zwingli's 'Exposition') or to pray for them further." In fact, no Christian should pray for them anymore, because "they have been abandoned and 'are sinning unto death.'" [130] According to Titus 3:10f., one must "let them go and avoid them as people who have judged themselves, who knowingly and wantonly desire their own condemnation. One can have no fellowship with any one of them." [131] "They want nothing to do with me, so I want nothing to do with them" — this one sentence now summarizes Luther's experiences with the "sacramentarians." [132] It simply establishes the rule: "Love will be and must be deceived. . . . But faith dare not go wrong." [133]

This sentence transcends the startling embitterment and animosity that at first seem to dominate Luther's insistence on the condemnation of the Swiss. Yet however closely personal pique and lines of demarcation based on facts may be intertwined here, what remained normative was zeal for the Word and its truth, particularly their indivisible unity. "It is certain that he who does not believe one article correctly, or refuses to do so (after he has been admonished and instructed), will surely not accept any article seriously and in true faith." One who dares to call God a liar in *one* word, and does so "wantonly" and in spite of repeated admonition, will do it in other words too. This is the context of the sentences quoted above that establish the basic unity of the saving faith and clarify it with the illustration of the ring and the bell, although there is no explicit reference to the foundation of faith and certainly not to fundamental doctrines. That these statements were exposed to the twofold misunderstanding that the faith-creating Word of salvation should be turned into a firm quantity of things that must be believed and that all segments of this doctrinal quantity should be given the same value — this danger did not worry Luther. As will be seen, even the Swiss took no offense at this thought. Once more Luther wanted to make perfectly plain that in the doctrine of the Lord's Supper as taught by the Swiss he was not fighting discussable, though divergent, partisan theological opinions, but rather a manifest injury to the "chief article" concerning Jesus Christ. Only from this perspective, from this burning anxiety for the integrity of the central doctrinal truth, must we ultimately interpret the almost terrifying rigor with which Luther at the beginning of his essay supports the condemnation of his opponents and sets the tone for the entire work: "As one who is now on the way to his grave I desire to bring this testimony and this reputation with me before the judgment seat of my dear Lord and Savior Jesus Christ that, in accordance with His command, Titus 3, 'As for a man who is factious, after admonishing him once or twice, have nothing more to do with him, knowing that such a person is perverted and sinful; he is self-condemned,' I have in all earnestness condemned and avoided the Enthusiasts and enemies of the sacrament, Carlstadt, Zwingli, Oecolampadius, Stenckfeld, and their disciples at Zurich and wherever they may be." [134]

Here, too, Luther did not lose sight of the distinction between the misled and the misleaders. The condemnation does not apply "where the weak are, who are ready to receive instruction and who will not offer stiff-necked contradiction." It is only stubbornness that makes one a heretic. "I am speaking of the leaders. May the dear Lord Christ preserve the poor people from such spiritual murderers." [135] In spite of this qualification, however, the intensification of the antithesis over all is inescapable. The aspect of personal disappointment and embitterment is more prominent than before. Titus 3:10f. had always determined Luther's attitude toward false teachers, yet never had the lines been drawn so strictly, or the rift declared to be so irreparable, or the finality of the rupture asserted so categorically and cuttingly. Formerly, in spite of the unabated validity of the condemnation, the bridge to conversations with the opponents had never been completely destroyed, if only because the hope for amendment and the prospect for the return of the erring had never been given up entirely. Now we search in vain for a good word of hope; now we miss that caution that always kept the mind open for the limits of the condemnatory judgment. "God grant that they may find their way out of their error" — this was the word two decades earlier; now, however, the intercession for the heretics is expressly withdrawn and advised against.

It might be expected that this last writing of Luther's on the Holy Communion would be awaited with trepidation by both friend and foe, although Melanchthon's fears, entertained in all seriousness, that there would be attacks that would compel him to leave the country, proved to be greatly exaggerated.[136] Even a peacemaker less inclined to compromise than Bucer might have thought of warning Luther, as he worked on this document, to consider the danger of a new controversy on the sacrament (Bucer's admonition did indeed arrive too late because Melanchthon could not muster the courage to deliver it to Luther on time).[137] In any case, the Swiss could publish their response under auspices that were not unfavorable.[138] Part one is historical and throws the charges of insincerity and peacebreaking back at Luther. The second part is dogmatic and attempts to furnish proof that the Swiss view of the Lord's Supper is by no means heretical but rather the only Scriptural one. With that the presupposition is given for a special third part, in which a rejection of the condemnations is undertaken.

The heart of this rejection is to be found above all in the claim that Luther's authority is an act of presumption and is denied. He who dares to boast of himself as the German prophet and apostle deals with his opponents "not in a Christian but in a popish manner," [139] for he proposes his own cause and opinion as "a universal teaching of the church," he "puts on a great display of pomp and promptly consigns to the devil all who do not fully submit themselves to him.[140] . . . Whoever does not speak his language or desires to speak otherwise is a heretic, banned and anathematized." [141] Like Luther, the Swiss regarded as heretical any rebellion against "clear Scripture and explicit Word of God," against the "true articles of our ancient Christian faith" and "the orthodox doctrine of the holy church," together with the stubbornness that refuses to receive instruction. How-

ever, so they insist, "neither we nor our fathers are such people." [142] They do not falsify God's Word, as Luther charges, but
permit it to "stand firm and immovable, as it is in itself," [143]
as they claim to have proved in Part II. The fact remains, therefore, that Luther had "no valid cause at all" and certainly no
"divine mandate" to condemn the Swiss as heretics, because he
had "never convicted" them "or discovered them in lies." [144]

Nor did the Swiss neglect to brand as particularly unchristian the manner in which Luther uttered his condemnatory
judgment. His writings could not serve to warn them, as he
claims, because they are not what such warnings ought to be,
"genuinely Christian, conforming to the Scriptures and the
faith, drawn from the divine truth, and expressed in a modest,
friendly way with brotherly love, for the salvation, not the destruction, of the erring.[145] His condemnation is nothing but
name-calling and scolding, 'sacrilege and excess.'" May God
forgive him for refusing even to pray for them! [146]

Emphatically and not without some irritating self-satisfac-
tion the Swiss pointed out that they conducted themselves in a
far different manner. They, too, want to condemn the heretics
and have "no partnership or fellowship" with them. But they
made even more of the fact that they "part company with no one
anywhere. For," so they continue, "we are well satisfied with
all of them, yes, we acknowledge all those as our dear brethren
who are one with us in the substance, essence, and main points
of our confession. . . . If it is a matter of words or some few formulations that do not overthrow the substance and basis of the
doctrine, we will come to blows with no one." [147] Although they
proceeded against Luther in self-defense and must uphold their
good name, they feel "no envy, hatred, or anger against Luther's
person but wish him well and pray that the Lord would grant
him humility and the Spirit, so that he can know himself." [148]

Yet they did address some rather massive warnings to
Luther. If Luther is so intent on speaking about the devil as
being active in false teaching, they rejoin: "God grant Luther
grace that it may not happen to him according to the Lord's
Word, 'Out of the fullness of the heart the mouth speaks,'" — and
here, too, they state how much better off they are: "By the grace
of God we have nothing to do with the devils at all." [149] As for
Luther, "Let him take care, lest with all his unchristian and

wrathful remarks he condemn himself. And since he has no desire to be at one with those who correctly confess and preach Christ, let him take care lest he separate himself and thereby become a schismatic." [150]

For Luther this response could signify no essential change in the situation. The Swiss refusal to acknowledge that the difference in doctrine concerning the Lord's Supper and Christology touched the substance of faith and doctrine and their insistence that their teaching was Scriptural only confirmed what Luther knew all along, and he saw no reason for changing his attitude or especially his condemnation. The pedantic tone of the Zurichers was ill designed to convince him of having gone too far in his "name-calling and scolding." For that reason he did not reply. He wrote to Amsdorf that he would deal with the "Zurich fanatics" only "briefly and obliquely." [151] This he did in a series of theses directed against the Louvain faculty in which he condemned as "heretics and aliens from the church of God" also the Zwinglians and all Sacramentarians who denied the oral reception of Christ's body and blood. [152] The same note is sounded in his ejaculation in a letter to his old Bremen friend, Jacob Probst, Jan. 17, 1546: "Blessed is the man who does not walk in the counsel of the Sacramentarians, nor stands in the way of the Zwinglians, nor sits in the seat of the Zurichers!" [153] In his last polemical writing, on which he was working at that time and which was to be a commentary on the theses against the Louvain faculty, Luther took no further position on the Communion controversy. The document remained unfinished. His final public word on the subject was a curt and concise renunciation of the blasphemers of the sacrament in Switzerland and the Anabaptists in Holland, uttered parenthetically in a sermon preached in Halle on his last trip, 24 days before his death. [154] Thus he could in fact carry out his intention of taking to his grave the "reputation" that he had in all seriousness and to the last moment condemned and avoided the "enemies of the sacrament." For him the possibilities of further conversation with the Swiss had long been exhausted. It was assertion against assertion, conviction against conviction. The Swiss demanded proof that they should be condemned as heretics, and Luther felt that he had for years supplied more than enough proof.

Turning once more to Melanchthon from this point, specifically the Melanchthon of the *Variata*, we are in a position to see how his reticence and restraint, but inseparably combined with it also his indecisiveness and inconsistency, stand out in clear contrast against the background of Luther's resoluteness. Like Luther, he, too, had to take a stand with respect to the question of condemnations near the end of his life, under far more difficult circumstances, it is true. Luther spoke as one who had only to repeat what he had always said, as everyone knew. From his "Large Confession" of 1528 to his "Short Confession" of 1544 there is a consistent line that was not really disturbed by Luther's apparent yielding at the time of the Wittenberg Concord. But Melanchthon's position was encumbered from the start by his wavering in the doctrine of the Lord's Supper and by his changes in the Augsburg Confession. It is true, the *Variata* had been used for years in church and school without much concern for the alterations. Meanwhile, however, the Lutherans in increasing measure evinced that suspicion to which Eck had already given voice at Worms in 1541. More and more the omission of the condemnatory formula in Article X had developed into a question that called for a decision in interchurch relations. This question became especially acute as a result of the Religious Peace of 1555. This treaty had not specified which edition of the Augsburg Confession should form the legal basis of the Evangelical churches. It had to be clear to all participants how much depended on the settlement of this issue. If the Unaltered Augsburg Confession were legalized, then also the condemnation of the Zwinglians would be valid, and the Calvinists, who since the *Consensus Tigurinus* (1549) had manifestly taken over the Zwinglian heritage, could not share in the provisions of the Religious Peace. If, however, the Altered Augsburg Confession were made official, the base of the Religious Peace would be broadened, but then every strict Lutheran would have to fear for the integrity of the doctrine. Alongside this weighting of the problem of condemnations by church and state politics there was another aspect which after Luther's death made it more difficult to take a stand. For Melanchthon it could no longer be only the clarification of a controversial point in dogmatics and the possible consequences for church fellowship with the Swiss. Rather, in the 11 years since Luther's death the differences with respect to the condemnations had in an essential way helped to establish an ecclesiastical alignment among the Lutherans themselves, an alignment that threatened to lead to a fateful split. Aside from his battle against Rome, Luther had to deal only with the Swiss and with the Enthusiasts. Melanchthon, however, now had to defend himself against the various reproaches coming from his own camp. And it is above all the conflict of Melanchthon and his friends on one side with the groups of Gnesio-Lutherans headed by Flacius on the other side that stands out from among the many dogmatic controversies. This is true because that conflict gave new urgency to the question of condemnations.

Notes to Chapter 9

[112] First printed in Loescher, pp. 199ff.

[113] These and the following proceedings are reported by E. Bizer, *Studien zur Geschichte des Abendmahlstreits im 16. Jahrhundert* (Guetersloh, 1940).

[114] Letter to the convention of the churches at Strasbourg, Loescher, p. 232.

[115] O. Ritschl, I, 280f.

[116] CR 2, 842.

[117] CR 2, 822 (Jan. 10, 1535).

[118] CR 3, 826.

[119] Loescher, II, 44.

[120] WA *Tischreden*, 5, 215, 20.

[121] For the documentation see Melanchthon's edition of the Worms Proceedings (CR 4, 34, 37, 43). See also the German edition: *Alle Handlungen, die Religion belangend, so sich zu Worms u. Regensburg auff gehaltenem Reichstag des MDXLI. jars zu getragen* (Wittenberg 1542), foll. CXXXVb, CXXXVIII, CLXV.

[122] Perhaps reported first in *Gruendliche Wahrhafftige Historia von der Augspurgischen Confession* (Leipzig, 1584), pp. 300f. Also, L. Hutter, *Concordia concors* (Wittenberg, 1614), L. 95, 374b; Loescher, II, 44. References to further repetitions of the report in Chr. A. Salig, *Vollstaendige Historie der Augspurgischen Confession*, I (Halle, 1730), 521, and Vilmar, p. 109.

[123] *Colloquium zu Altenburgk* (Jena, 1569), foll. 463b ff.

[124] G. G. Weber, *Kritische Geschichte der Augspurgischen Confession*, II (Frankfort a/M, 1784), 389ff.

[125] CR 3, 383 (Letter to Veit Dietrich, June 22, 1537).

[126] Cf. WA 30 III, 547ff. (*Open Letter to Duke Albrecht of Prussia*, 1532); Enders 15, 219 (*Letter to Christopher Froschauer in Zurich*, Aug. 31, 1543); 16, 59 (*Letter to Chancellor Gregory Brueck*, beginning of August, 1544); WA 49, 525ff. (Sermon on Rom. 8:12ff., Aug. 3, 1544). Into this context should also be placed the fact that since 1539 Luther promoted the translation into Latin of his earlier polemical works against the "Sacramentarians" (F. Cohrs in WA 54, 124).

[127] WA 54, 142, 20 and 24.

[128] Ibid., 156, 17; 155, 29.

[129] WA 54, 151, 11.

[130] Ibid., 144, 11; 148, 21.

[131] Ibid., 155, 25.

[132] Ibid., 148, 24.

[133] Ibid., 146, 20.

[134] Ibid., 141, 17.

[135] Ibid., 158, 30; 148, 22.

[136] CR 5, 459, 461, 473f. (cf. Cohrs, p. 123).

[137] Enders, 16, 81ff., 83 (cf. Cohrs, ibid.).

[138] *Wahrhaffte Bekanntnuss der dieneren der kirchen zu Zuerych* (Zurich, 1545).

[139] Foll. 135a, 113b.

[140] Foll. 112a, 130b.

[141] Fol. 135a.

[142] Fol. 113.

[143] Fol. 134a.

[144] Foll. 5b, 112a.

[145] Fol. 114b.

[146] Foll. 132a, 138b.

[147] Foll. 62b, 143, 144a.

[148] Fol. 142a.

[149] Fol. 135a.

[150] Fol. 134b.

[151] Enders, 16, 227, 34.

[152] WA 54, 427, 8 *(Against the 32 Articles of the Theologists at Louvain, 1545, Thesis XXVII).*

[153] Enders, 17, 11, 17.

[154] WA 51, 140, 14 (Jan. 26, 1546).

Chapter 10

Condemnation as Practiced by the Gnesio-Lutherans

The controversies between the Melanchthonians and the Gnesio-Lutherans dare not be considered only from the perspective of a discussion between two clearly defined parties in the church. Rather, the conflicts overlap in many ways. In the attack on Osiander's perversion of the doctrine of justification as also the attack on Schwenckfeld the Gnesio-Lutherans made common cause with Melanchthon. And while they regarded with suspicion Melanchthon's approach to the Reformed doctrine of Communion, they themselves came close to the Reformed doctrine of predestination in their opposition to Melanchthon's "synergistic" ideas. I. A. Dorner correctly concludes "that the decisive factor in determining the alignments of the moment was not a conscious partisanship but a concern for the matter itself" and that, in spite of their regrettable attendant circumstances and effects, these battles, too, were of considerable positive significance for the "development of Reformation doctrine." [155] It would therefore be a mistake to interpret matters simply as a struggle for control on the part of two closely integrated groups in the church, or even to present matters from the standpoint of only one of the chief parties (as was done, for example, in the one-sidedly Melanchthonian presentations of G. J. Planck and Heinrich Heppe). The discussions between the leading protagonists, Melanchthon and Flacius, deserve special attention nevertheless because in this context the problem of condemnations was to become particularly acute.

The dogmatic framework had indeed become a different one. The debate did not now revolve around the doctrine of the Lord's Supper and the resulting condemnation, but the proper separation from the Roman Church — on the one hand in the question of ceremonies, which Melanchthon in 1548 had called "adiaphora," and on the other hand in the question of the self-activity of the human will, which Melanchthon in the same fateful year of the Interim had designated as the "ability of applying oneself to grace," just as Major had interpreted the possibilities of the human will in an ambiguous way in his thesis on the necessity of good works for salvation. The latent tension inhering in the Augsburg Confession to the extent that there were no clear rejections of Roman errors corresponding to the antitheses against the Enthusiasts and Zwinglians had become more acute for Melanchthon through unconcealed compromise at least in the Leipzig Interim. The violent opposition which he encountered had clearly shown him that his course had not been the right one, and he had openly regretted his error. Yet Flacius and his supporters now insisted on explicit condemnation of the errors, and through this demand the cleavage between both parties had become so deep that a hopeless split threatened the Lutheran theologians and estates.

The diet announced for Regensburg for March 1, 1556, demanded a unified representation of the Evangelical concerns and made a conciliation of the opposing fronts especially urgent. Early in January 1556 a delegation authorized by Duke Christopher of Wuerttemberg, who was keenly anxious for unificaion, and Elector Frederick of the Palatinate appeared in Weimar, a center of strict Lutheranism, for the purpose of considering the possibilities of a settlement between the warring factions. There a conference of theologians was suggested along with a meeting of the princes. This conference was to put an end to the altercations by simply declaring a fully effective amnesty. It was surely not just theological contentiousness that kept the theologians of ducal Saxony from becoming enthusiastic about the prospects of this proposal. In an opinion requested by their dukes they replied that the Wittenbergers must be required at the very least to pronounce a public rejection of the Zwinglian, Osiandrian, and Schwenckfeldian errors, as well as of synergism, Majorism, and adiaphorism. However, with regard to the last point (which struck Melanchthon himself first of all) they would not insist on public penance.[156] Naturally the princes could not regard this offer as adequate and for the moment gave up their attempts.

Now it was the theologians' turn. The initiative for attempts at mediation rested essentially with Flacius and his friends.[157] In the spring of 1556 he voiced his principles in a series of "gentle proposals," in which he, exactly like his Thuringian partisans, insisted on the condemnation of the various heresies, including the adiaphoristic ones. A new thought was the proposal that these condemnations should be put in writing and signed by representatives of both sides, and that on this basis they should reach agreement. Intermediaries saw to it that these articles were made known in Wittenberg. But the Wittenbergers did not even give Flacius an answer — perhaps in part because they did not trust the peaceful intentions of the zealous Magdeburg warrior, in part because they were bound to see immediately that Flacius was not at all minded to make any concessions and to meet Melanchthon at a dogmatic median line. On the contrary, he demanded nothing less than a complete reorientation of the Philippist front. Nobody in Wittenberg was ready for that.

New attempts at conciliation tried to arrange a personal interview between Melanchthon and Flacius, but after initial wavering Melanchthon declined. Flacius was honestly disappointed. As he wrote to one of the mediators, he wanted nothing more than a rejection of adiaphorism and Majorism,[158] in other words, of those errors from which Melanchthon himself had receded. We may well believe that Flacius was concerned about the issue itself in his refusal to modify his demands. In the accompanying correspondence with Melanchthon much space was given to a tally of the insults and offenses on both sides. Yet the letters of Flacius in particular place constant emphasis on the primacy of the issue itself. Even the condemnation about which he was concerned was to strike not the persons but the teachings. Thus he reminded Melanchthon: "Nowhere is it demanded that you or another participant condemn yourself even with a single stroke of the pen, or that you give in to me, like Hector to Ajax, or admit that you have erred. We only desire to acknowledge and indicate that peace has been reestablished among us on the basis of the submitted articles. And then we will be ready to subscribe our names together with yours without discrimination." [159] The basic considerations, which Flacius had expressed at the beginning of the year in a little paper ("Of the Unity of Those Who in Past Years Have Supported or Opposed the Adiaphora"), were not yet quite so conciliatory but rather insisted only that for the sake of the truth nothing but a rejection of adiaphorism would do as a basis for unification. It must be noted, however, that Flacius did not publish this document until after the negotiations with Melanchthon had broken down.[160]

Melanchthon's letters make perfectly clear that an agreement on the basis of the Flacian proposals was in fact impossible. To some extent Melanchthon could demonstrate that he had not been involved in the Majoristic errors. He may also have felt that he was manifesting a large measure of good will by expressing regret for his errors in the adiaphoristic controversy and by appealing to an impartial church court. Yet he could not bring himself to utter a clear renunciation of his former course, already because basically he viewed the past in a light completely different from that of Flacius. For the latter the so-called "adiaphora" assumed in the hour of confession the dignity of questions decisive for faith; while for Melanchthon they represented nothing more than concessions in the area of indifferent rites, to which he had agreed only because of requests from the prince and in which the integrity of doctrine was never in danger, especially since these ceremonies had never been attacked before.[161]

It is impressive to note that Flacius continued to urge new negotiations in spite of Melanchthon's unconcealed unwillingness. Flacius now approached a number of lower Saxon cities with the plea that they serve as mediators, and as a basis for negotiation he set up the same conditions that he had already formulated in his "gentle proposals." [162] Thus the rejection of adiaphorism was again to be the focal point of the agreement. The proposal of Flacius was accepted by Luebeck, Hamburg (represented by Paul v. Eitzen and Joachim Westphal), Lueneburg and Brunswick (which delegated Moerlin and Chemnitz). On Jan. 17, 1557, the emissaries conferred with the Flacian circle in Magdeburg and then proceeded to Wittenberg, while Flacius and three other Magdeburgers chose to observe the negotiations from the little town of Coswig in Anhalt. After Melanchthon had refused to deal on the basis of the conditions stated by Flacius, the negotiators submitted eight new articles. In addition to a public condemnation of the errors of the Papists, Interimists, Anabaptists, and Sacramentarians, these articles also proposed an unmistakable delimitation against the theses of Major and against adiaphorism. In spite of the caution with which these proposals had been formulated, Melanchthon replied with extreme exasperation and accused the Lower Saxons among other things of trying to force him and many others to "cut their own throat." Nonetheless he was ready to agree to the articles in all essential points, even suggesting the addition of a number of condemnations, for example, against the followers of Servetus, the Antinomians, and others. He also consented to the rejection of the Majorist statements. But the seventh article, which envisioned a joint declaration regarding the adiaphora as well as Majorism, he declined. He regarded such a statement as superfluous since in his earlier writings his views on the adiaphora had been expressed at length. However, it was precisely these earlier utterances of Melanchthon that Flacius and his friends wished to see condemned. They were therefore quite unsatisfied with Melanchthon's explanations and reiterated the old demand: Public repudiation of the adiaphoristic errors, plus a "we condemn" and a "we will condemn" against the Leipzig Interim and all similar formulas. The Lower Saxon negotiators realized that they would make no progress with such demands in Wittenberg, but they were constantly exhorted from Coswig not to make any concessions. But since Melanchthon refused to yield, this attempt at conciliation failed too, just as did a mediating endeavor from Mecklenburg shortly thereafter.[163]

On the whole, the two fronts had not only come no closer to each other but had actually become more firmly entrenched. Again the spirits parted company over the condemnation of the adiaphoristic teachings. Again the rigid, uncompromising objectivity of Flacius, expressed in the demand for condemnations, was opposed by the reluctance of the Wittenbergers, a reluctance that was brought about by a variety of doubts and that was qualified by a wealth of considerations. Melanchthon wanted to be considerate of those—among them some were no longer living—who "preferred to keep the rites that Luther, too, observed, rather than that faithful shepherds and their poor families should be driven out and the parishes should be devastated." Melanchthon also wanted to be considerate of those "most honorable men" who had participated in earlier decisions.[164] By no means did he fight primarily to be vindicated at all costs in everything he had formerly taught and done. Naturally he shrank from "cutting his own throat." Yet even now he was conscious of various wrong decisions and half-way measures and was ready to ask God for forgiveness and to submit to the verdict of the church.[165] Nevertheless, the radical difference in the issue remained decisive. Melanchthon would not and could not condemn what he still did not regard as worthy of condemnation. As long as he was concerned only about inconsequential ceremonies — "rites that Luther also retained!" — he could not comprehend the more profound substantive concern in the Flacian demands for condemnation.

From this point of view it becomes fully plain how much significance must be accorded the discussions of the years 1556 and 1557 for the whole development of the problem of condemnations. The dogmatic environment and occasion for the condemnation had changed; but just as for Luther earlier the truth of the Word itself called for decision and separation in the doctrine of the Lord's Supper, so now Flacius believed that for the sake of the Word he must call for a decided no to the Romanizing tendencies of Melanchthon and his friends. This decision was all the more weighty because it was not directed against false teachers who were separated by boundaries of nationality and country as well as by a differently shaped ecclesiastical past. Now the decision was directed against that man who had inherited Luther's position, the "venerable Teacher" (as the articles of the Lower Saxons addressed him in sincere respect),[166] the man to whom also the Gnesio-Lutherans owed very much. In this point, too, Flacius was aware of the implications of his procedure. However, already in his document on unity he had voiced the conviction that there could here be no personal considerations. Even the great achievements of Melanchthon could not be thrown into the balance because vainglory availed nothing before God, and true honor was to be found only where men were on the side of the truth and of God.[167]

We must ask further whether Flacius was really aware of the possible consequences of his attitude. Did he understand that the ruinous schism in Lutheranism threatened to become even worse? From a one-sided Melanchthonian point of view one would be tempted to answer that with his demands for condemnation Flacius was deliberately working for a split. Such an interpretation would, however, not do justice to the facts. Oral and written utterances of Flacius, as well as his entire behavior, show that he was honestly striving for a settlement with Melanchthon. Untiringly he began new approaches to mediation as often as the previous attempt failed. While waiting at Coswig he fairly trembled at the possibility that the Lower Saxons might break off negotiations prematurely. If it had been his desire merely to play the heresy-judging Lutheran pope, all this would surely have been unnecessary. True, he was not ready to make any kind of substantive concessions to Melanchthon. The "agreement" he wanted would have resulted in a one-sided capitulation on the part of Melanchthon. But did he perhaps wish only to experience the personal triumph of seeing the celebrated teacher of the church come over to his side by an act of penitent recantation? Of this, too, there is no indication. The continued emphasis of his interest in the issues and the explicit repudiation of all purely personal motives may not be brushed aside as hypocrisy and deceit, as the Wittenbergers did. Now as during the Interim, Flacius was manifestly of the sincere conviction "that in an emergency one must for the sake of love pull his teacher out of the water, even if that required pulling his beard." [168]

Thus the conclusion is inescapable that Flacius was entirely serious both in his demands for condemnation and in his will to union. It is evident that he did not regard these two aspects as being mutually exclusive. He sought an understanding on the basis of a joint condemnation, a condemnation which expected of one of the parties a repudiation of a cause he had hitherto espoused, even though, technically, he was not asked to condemn himself. It is quite understandable that Melanchthon could not agree to this proposal. Yet it does remain significant that Flacius could in all seriousness pursue such a goal until the end. If he had merely demanded the conversion of the "heretic" and had declared his willingness thereafter to sit at the same table, this would not yet have been anything unusual. However, his behavior would not be adequately explained in this way. The essential feature is that he simultaneously demanded condemnation and evinced the desire for conciliation. Apparently the condemnation did not imply for him a definitive suspension of fellowship. Rather he strove to go through and beyond the condemnation to reach new accord and fellowship. In this way even the condemnation was given a new and positive accent. It lost none of the rigor that the situation demanded. Yet it did not wish to slam the door for good or to block definitively the way to fellowship, as this was clearly evidenced in Luther's last dealings with the Swiss. On the contrary, the condemnation as Flacius saw it pointed beyond itself to a new fellowship that was to draw its strength from the feeling of joint responsibility for the integrity of the Evangelical teaching.

Was Flacius the man who could dare to attempt the realization of such a fellowship? The outcome has decided against him, and surely not only because the necessary preconditions were lacking on Melanchthon's part, but also because Flacius himself did not come with the proper presuppositions. We dare not question the zeal for pure doctrine as expressed in the demand for condemnations. Yet we may well ask with Preger [169] whether Flacius, who "because of personal irritation, which had developed on both sides in the course of the conflict, had become a partisan himself," was really in a position to assume the exercise of the "judicial verdict" in the name of the whole church. He certainly lacked the necessary "compelling authority," simply because he was anything but the kind of unencumbered umpire that Melanchthon desired. However, we may also ask the counterquestion: In this situation, could there really have been anything like an "impartial ecclesiastical court of arbitration"? Where the integrity of the doctrine, the truth of the Gospel itself was clearly threatened, did not everyone have to take a stand and thus become a "party"? Luther had imposed this responsibility on each Christian and especially on each servant of the Word and, strictly speaking, this responsibility excluded any impartiality or suprapartiality in matters of doctrine. Conscious of this responsibility, Flacius, too, felt obligated to pronounce his condemnations and to make them a condition of reunification with the Wittenbergers. Flacius cannot be faulted for becoming a "party" in this way. But the manner of his taking sides was not beyond criticism. To a considerable degree he shared in the "personal irritation" to which Preger rightly calls attention, which accompanied the whole affair. His unkind contentiousness was not the least of the causes of the failure in the negotiations, though also the Wittenbergers in an uncommon measure came short of personal probity and honorable conduct in the way they carried on the fight.[170] In spite of everything, the unhappy concomitants of the debate must not becloud the fact that Flacius made an important contribution toward a positive development of the question of condemnations.

The political consequences for the church could not fail to appear also in connection with this controversy. As Melanchthon's counsel decisively influenced the church politics of electoral Saxony and Brandenburg, so the attitude of Flacius went far to determine the decisions in ducal Saxony as well as in some of the estates and cities of Lower Saxony. The cleavage of the theologians also split the estates, and this just at a time when unanimity would have been especially necessary. The Resolution of the Diet of Regensburg in March 1557 decreed that the empire should attempt a reunion of the Roman and Evangelical parties. But how could this be done as long as the Evangelicals were so seriously disunited?

A conference of Evangelical princes and theologians, mostly from southern Germany, meeting in Frankfort in June 1557, tried simply to suppress the split (incidentally, under the normative influence of Landgrave Philip of Hesse!).[171] It was asserted that the existing differences were of minor importance. At the forthcoming colloquy with the Romanists they could well proceed on the assumption that the Evangelical estates of the empire were "in principle and in the chief doctrines fully one"[172] — an assumption that had to be wholly unacceptable of course to the Gnesio-Lutherans.

Accordingly, the preconditions for the decisive colloquy that was to be held at Worms [173] were quite unfavorable. In fact there, too, the question of condemnations was to prove to be critical. Duke John Frederick of Weimar assessed the situation accurately when he wrote to Count Palatine Wolfgang of Zweibruecken that as long as "all of our theological delegates are still at odds in the controverted points and are not ready beforehand to recant and to condemn," they will not be able "to stand as one man against the papacy and thus with unanimity carry on the fight with heart and voice on the basis of the Word of God." More likely they would make it possible for their Roman adversaries to defeat the Evangelicals with their own weapons.[174]

Already in the discussion preliminary to the colloquy the

conflict broke into the open. The theologians of Jena had been instructed by their prince, Duke John Frederick, not to participate in any conversations with the Romans before all Evangelical participants had agreed to accept the Unaltered Augsburg Confession and the specific condemnation of the "Sacramentarians," as well as other heretics mentioned by name.[175] Melanchthon had the delegates from Wuerttemberg, the Palatinate, Strasbourg, Hesse, and Brandenburg, a clear majority, on his side when he took a stand against that proposal. The delegates from Thuringia had to report to their duke that with their concern about condemnations they had "made some impression on many persons," but that Melanchthon's position was very strong (some revered him as a sort of deity, Flacius was told);[176] on the other hand, that the people of Wuerttemberg refused to drop Osiander, many others supported Major, and some even "have Zwingli nestling in their bosom."[177] It was agreed that the Thuringians would withdraw their petition temporarily, on condition, however, that in the discussion of the controverted points they "should have the liberty of preserving their conscience and, as the need required, be allowed to make their point in accordance with imperial order and to condemn the dogmas together with their authors."[178]

Melanchthon indeed occupied an awkward position. On the one hand, he apparently considered it worthwhile to uphold the Unaltered Augsburg Confession. On the other hand, he could not share the radical conclusions of the Jena theologians, already because he wanted under no circumstances to abet a split in Evangelical ranks so shortly before the negotiations with the Roman Catholic delegation. He acknowledged the necessity of drawing the line against heresy, if only to avoid an open break with the Thuringians from the outset. Yet he also knew that in Switzerland people were placing great hopes in him and his mediating influence.[179] He himself would much have preferred to stay home at the sick bed of his son.[180] Now, however, he was caught in the middle between the two fronts, especially since the intra-Lutheran conflicts had recently been made public in conversations with the Roman opposition and the Roman Catholic delegates also demanded that the Evangelicals should mark their position by a clear-cut rejection of the heretics.[181] After extended argument Melanchthon sought to salvage what could be salvaged by offering a compromise formula.[182] In this formula of consensus the Anabaptists, Schwenckfeld, and the followers of Osiander were condemned by name, but not the Swiss. Nevertheless, in substance the Zwinglian doctrine of the Eucharist was repudiated together with adiaphorism.

The reaction to this attempt at compromise did not fail to appear. The Flacians, who had been joined by Moerlin of Brunswick, felt that the time for confession had come. They presented their antitheses and finally walked out. The Swiss on their part felt struck by a protestation subsequently made by Melanchthon,[183] because in it among other doctrines also Zwingli's doctrine was suddenly called an "opinion conflicting with our confession." Indignantly Calvin wrote to Bullinger about the "hateful and harmful leniency" of Melanchthon.[184] Of course Melanchthon could not keep the gloating Roman Catholics, under the leadership of Peter Canisius, from taking full advantage of the disunity among the Evangelicals and finding in it a welcome reason for breaking off negotiations. Thus the end result was pitiful enough. Frustrated was not only the attempt to reach agreement with the Roman Catholics (with no prospects of success anyway) but also the desired unification of the Lutherans themselves.

What impelled the Gnesio-Lutherans to be so unyielding, an attitude that was so often bewailed then and later, to insist on their demands for condemnations, and thereby in a manner apparently so irresponsible to sacrifice this never-to-be-repeated opportunity for reaching an accord with the Roman Catholic estates? The protestation which they presented at Worms gives an exhaustive account of their action.[185] They were at pains to demonstrate that they "were not concerned about this or that person" but that "God's Word, the church's need, and their own conscience compelled and urged (them) even at greatest peril to reject the oft-mentioned errors and perversions and regard them as condemned." [186] They were in no way minded to deny that they must "solemnly repudiate the papacy." But must not their own house be set in order first? Only when the Lutherans "had come to agreement and conciliation affirmatively and negatively in all points of doctrine" would they, in their opinion, be prepared to engage in conversations with the Roman counterpart.[187] The protestation asserts that "inescapable necessity" demands that they must defend themselves against both the "sectarians" and the "papacy," so that "no one may entertain the justified suspicion that we had here made concessions to please the colloquy or certain persons in matters that we had formerly built with both hands." [188]

The men from Thuringia stressed furthermore that they could not agree to a merely general condemnation that everyone could interpret as he wished. They were primarily concerned about the "preservation of the pure doctrine of the Gospel and the segregation of the true church from all schismatics and sects," [189] and they saw no reason to drop this point of view for the sake of opportunist church politics. For the same reason they regarded Melanchthon's proposal of a general union on the basis of the Augsburg Confession, the Apology, and the Smalcald Articles as inadequate. They knew Melanchthon's vacillation in matters pertaining to the adiaphora and the Holy Communion, and they could find here no reliable basis for the battle with Rome. Therefore they asked for a specified condemnation of the teaching of Osiander, of all "perverters of the sacrament" from Carlstadt to Calvin, of the theses of Major, of the Interim, in addition to all other "perversions of the Gospel," including the "ungodly decrees of the Synod of Trent." At the same time they stated explicitly that they were willing to have their propositions explored more fully at a future synod.[190]

The warring parties might themselves have had their doubts whether such a synod would be able to settle the differences. The chasm that now not only separated Lutherans and Calvinists but also cut across the ranks of the Lutherans themselves seemed to be too deep. The disagreements which had arisen over the condemnation of third groups had resulted in the condemnation of one Lutheran group by another. While both sides strove for unity, they nevertheless accused each other of untruthfulness and "patchwork" on the one hand and of "paroxysm in condemnation" on the other.[191] Each group claimed to have the true understanding of the Augsburg Confession, and the uncertainty regarding the official status of this confession was not removed but rather increased even more.

The years following the Colloquy of Worms produced on the one hand a mass of new attempts to bridge the rift and on the other a new solidification of the battle lines. Openly or under cover the problem of condemnations is constantly found in the center of decisions. The Frankfort Recess of March 18, 1558,[192] prepared on the basis of an opinion by Melanchthon and adopted by a group of princes favorable to Melanchthon, was to provide a uniform and obligatory doctrinal norm based on the Augsburg Confession as interpreted by Melanchthon and at the same time effectively dispose of doctrinal controversies. Basically this was nothing more than an extract of Melanchthon's theology and already for that reason ill designed to become the instrument of a comprehensive unification. The opponents, again under the leadership of Ducal Saxony, criticized above all that the dogmatic controversies had been reduced to trifles and the false teachings had not been rejected precisely enough. The situation was aggravated in that henceforth the indefinite position of the Melanchthonian party led the Gnesio-Lutherans explicitly to demand the rejection of the false teachers by name — a demand that was to create very considerable difficulties in subsequent discussions of the problem of condemnations. Melanchthon indeed did not want the "condemnation of persons" expressly rejected. It was only that in his opinion this matter did not belong into a statement issued by the princes. "To condemn persons is a task for the scholars who know how to convict by means of their books and who desire to raise accusations not only against false teaching but also against the persons." [193] The strict group could, of course, have no understanding of such restraint. They were not concerned about scholarly polemics as Melanchthon envisioned it, but for the sake of erring consciences they wanted above all to draw the boundary line against the false teachers, unequivocally and publicly.

Duke John Frederick now began on his part to gather the opponents of the Frankfort Recess. First he invited the Lower Saxon estates nearest him to a meeting in Magdeburg. This plan failed, however, because of the hesitancy of the Lower Saxons. Thereupon the duke undertook to accomplish at least for his own territory what he could not get for all of the Evangelical estates, namely a compilation, rejection, and refutation of all "perversions, sects, and errors." This was the Weimar Book of Confutations, which had been prepared by several Thuringian theologians. Flacius evidently participated only with his counsel.[194] Servetus, Schwenckfeld, the Antinomians, the Anabaptists, the old and new Zwinglians, the defenders of free will, Osiander, Stancarus, Major, the Adiaphorists—so ran the roster of the false teachers against whom the individual "Confutations" were directed and whose refutation was by order of the duke to be announced to the congregations in public worship, in the instruction of the young, and in confession.

The manner in which the duke at times tried to compel compliance—the Jena theologians Strigel and Huegel were imprisoned briefly for their objections—led to considerable trouble. Also the signers of the Frankfort Resolution voiced strong protests. In an opinion [195] aged Melanchthon restricted himself to defending himself and the other Wittenbergers vehemently and bitterly even against criticisms that were not leveled at him and his friends at all. Thus he achieved nothing more than talking past the concern of the Thuringians.

A critique of the Book of Confutations offered by Philip of Hesse went essentially farther.[196] While questioning some of the condemnations, he at the same time voiced the general plea "that all who are accused of being heretics should be assembled and cited before a synod, given a fair hearing and then, if they should persist in erroneous and unchristian opinions, be excluded. In this way they will not have the right to say that they had been condemned without a hearing." [197] Philip was further concerned that not all errors should be viewed and treated as on the same level. He did not indicate any specific norms for establishing the differences. Yet he did state that he would not like to have the opinions of the Adiaphorists judged in the same way as, for example, the acknowledged heresies of Servetus and Stancarus. For the latter he demanded condemnation after a hearing before a "Christian synod," but for the former he wished that the discussions be carried on in a "Christian, praiseworthy, and edifying manner." "One side should have patience with the other, they should bear and put up with one another in a friendly and brotherly spirit, they should come together and converse and come to agreement in a Christian way, and not look for prestige and pride or destroy some one's good name." [198] Furthermore, in the "condemnation of those who are called Sacramentarians" special care should be taken lest "the door is opened for the papists to persecute many pious and genuine Christians, to put them to death and mistreat them with extreme cruelty." The experiences of the Huguenots had already very earnestly confirmed this point of view. As for the rest, the landgrave regarded a simple rejection of the "Sacramentarians" as of doubtful value because the victims perhaps "erred in one article" only and could not be "consigned to the chopping block." [199]

In an unprinted essay [200] Flacius responded to the landgrave's criticism, pointing out that in such a relaxation of the practice of condemnation he could see nothing but a senseless attempt as it were "to restore to orthodox status" all sects and schismatics, only to subject them to judgment by a synod. Flacius appealed to the right and the duty every Christian already has to condemn false teachers. Hence the Book of Confutations was not nearly so vulnerable, he contended, as the attempt of a minority of princes to prescribe to the church a form of doctrine that was safeguarded in a wholly inadequate manner.

Nevertheless, it might appear that even Flacius had not closed his mind to the necessity implied in Philip's critique that distinctions must be made among the errors to be condemned. During the Diet of Augsburg in the spring of 1559 Duke Christopher of Wuerttemberg proposed a new convention of Evangelical princes, at which among other items of business the Augsburg Confession was to be resubscribed and the question of condemnations was to be discussed. For this occasion Flacius was asked by his prince to furnish a formal opinion. In it he said that a stand on the Book of Confutations would suffice with reference to teachings already investigated and condemned, such as those of Servetus, the Anabaptists, the Sacramentarians, the Schwenckfeldians, the Antinomians, and the Osiandrians. The treatment of adiaphorism, Majorism, and synergism, however, should be turned over to a synod.[201]

In this sense the plan for a synod was devised that Flacius submitted to the Evangelical estates at the end of 1559 in a petition signed by 51 theologians mostly from central and northern Germany. Since the chief goal of this synod was to be the precise identification and condemnation of all false teachings, Duke Christopher declined the proposal as being contrary to his own plans and pointed to the "Christian amnesty" expressed in the Frankfort Resolution.[202]

Yet even before the men in Jena had received this reply,

the Flacians addressed themselves directly to the duke in a second petition, dated April 21, 1560.[203] This petition contained detailed instructions on the mode of condemnation procedure, which indicated that no serious thought had been given to a distinction among the errors as Philip of Hesse had suggested. First of all, the doctors at the synod were to discuss the errors thoroughly (special attention was again called to the danger of adiaphorism, the Trojan horse of Rome). Then the theologians were to proceed against those "ferments of Satan" orally and in writing, while the princes should promulgate their edicts against them. New doctrinal formulas were not necessary but rather the preservation of existing ones, as well as the "refutation and civil condemnation of errors," as both were being practiced in a model way in Ducal Saxony.

Especially this last reference, however, was bound to cast suspicion on the plan of Flacius, because it pointed to coercive measures which could arouse little sympathy. Furthermore, the opponents of Flacius could scarcely have forgotten that in the first petition the method of voting suggested to the synod had been so arranged that a steady majority was assured the more rigid wing.[204] It was therefore understandable that the plan was generally rejected and that Landgrave Philip reproved the Flacians because "they have such a narrow view of the church and attempt to convince everyone that they alone are the true church." [205] The synod should not merely receive preconceived sentences of condemnation but should be in a position freely to discuss the issues. In addition, true to his old schemes, the landgrave wanted the Swiss to participate. To this Flacius could reply that then it would not be proper to exclude the papists either. Either the estates committed to the Augsburg Confession should settle their differences in private or else create a much broader base for the synod right from the start.[206]

Under such circumstances an Evangelical or even only Lutheran general synod for the moment faced insurmountable obstacles. Still the princes were able to agree on the plan for a new conference of princes. This conference met in Naumburg at the end of January 1561. According to the agenda [207] the Augsburg Confession was to be subscribed anew and representation of the Evangelical estates at a future council could also be considered. The program as circulated by the Saxon Elector

August also specified that "all condemnations in which one side wished to blame the other for the inroads of perversions and sects be entirely omitted." This sentence was left out of the program in the form in which Duke John Frederick distributed it. Already this insignificant difference, which could still be amicably adjusted, pointed up the deeper clashes that ultimately scuttled the conference. In these clashes the question of condemnations played a leading role together with the problem of the Augsburg Confession.

The Flacians made one last effort to have their radical attitude accepted also before this forum of nontheologians by submitting another petition that summarized their point of view once more: [208] They were not interested in strife and argument but in defending the truth. Nor did they wish simply to condemn all who disagreed with them. They were fighting only the protectors of certain perversions, or rather the false teachings themselves. They rejected the charge that they desired a synod while they had their condemnations already prepared in advance and thus wanted to be accuser and judge in one. A Christian must pass judgment on false doctrine at once and without delay. Finally, they had no desire to withdraw from the common fight against Rome. On the contrary, they were waging that fight in a particularly emphatic and conscientious manner by turning their attention first of all to the removal of Romanizing tendencies in their own midst.

The fact that this petition was simply ignored and then turned back did not mean, however, that the Gnesio-Lutheran opposition was excluded from the meeting of the princes. In the circle of the princely participants Duke John Frederick as well as Duke Ulrich of Mecklenburg were determined partisans who soon found occasion to promote their cause. For the moment the princes reached agreement on a proposal to subscribe the German Augsburg Confession in the 1530 Wittenberg and the Latin edition (only slightly altered) of 1531. However, opinions diverged on the question of a new preface they planned to attach to the confession. The majority was in favor of a formulation developed by the electors of Saxony and of the Palatinate — out of consideration for the Frankfort Resolution but especially in view of the Palatinate Elector Frederick's dangerous leaning toward Calvinism. This formula stated that by subscribing the 1530/31 edition they had no intention "to depart in the least" from the *Variata* of 1540 "or to be led away from it, since this edition next to the one of 1542 was now being used by most of the churches and schools." They knew, as they had said earlier, that this edition of 1540/42 merely "repeated a little more fully and in greater detail and was explained and augmented from the Holy Scriptures." [209] The preface explained further that they would tolerate no other doctrine than that of the Holy Scriptures and the Augsburg Confession. All controversies were passed over in silence. No mention was made of the Smalcald Articles (nor of the Frankfort Resolution, although many had wished a reference to it). With regard to the Lord's Supper a formulation mediating in the Melanchthonian sense was adopted. Errors were neither mentioned nor condemned.

Duke John Frederick had said to the two theologians who accompanied him that he would mount his horse and depart with them before he would sign a preface in which the errors were not condemned.[210] Now the hour had come for him to keep his word. He did in fact submit a protest and leave the city. And while the majority of the princes signed the preface in the proposed form, the example of the duke had left its mark. Duke Ulrich of Mecklenburg, too, left the conference early and quite a number of participants, especially from Lower Saxony, also refused to sign. A convention of Lower Saxon theologians at Lueneburg protested against the preface and declared itself in favor of a condemnation of false teachers by name. The Lower Saxon estates, meeting at the same time and in connection with the theologians, approved the decision, yet forbidding all "unseemly scolding and maligning from the pulpit as well as condemnation of people who had not had a hearing and had never been convicted." [211] This mandate was promptly protested by Mecklenburg theologians as well as by Flacius, who had meanwhile been exiled from Jena.

The fragility of the Naumburg agreement became most evident in that even the majority of the principal signers of the preface gradually withdrew from this settlement which really could be no settlement. Above all it was the ambiguous formulation of the doctrine of the Lord's Supper that proved to be untenable. One prince after another declared that he would prefer to have the preface altered in the sense of the Saxon duke or that he wished from the start to have the whole matter interpreted only in a strictly Lutheran manner. Finally Philip of Hesse also capitulated, but the elector of the Palatinate drew his own conclusions and openly shifted to Calvinism.

This unexpected issue of the Naumburg Resolution made clear that the church politics of the Evangelicals had reached dead center, to which again a sort of stagnation of the problem of the condemnation of heretics corresponded. If an attempt is made at this point to strike a tentative balance in this development, one would have to start from the fact that also during the three decades from Augsburg to Naumburg the condemnation of heretics as such had not really become the subject of theological reflection. It had received its fixed place in the basic Lutheran confession and was received and generally acknowledged as a datum, as was done even before 1530. In the domain of the church of Luther no one thought of seriously doubting that the church had to designate and condemn heresy as heresy. The Swiss, too, clung to this principle. The matter became a problem only when the condemnation was applied also to certain deviations within Lutheranism itself. The problem was still preliminary to the question concerning the significance of the condemnation as such. The solution was to be found not so much in discussions about the meaning, scope, and weight of the condemnations as in the debate surrounding the controverted doctrinal points themselves. It is true that these debates also led to placing the validity and method of condemnations in doubt. From this arose a certain relaxation in the practice of condemnations, as will be seen later. For the moment we do not get beyond certain approaches that do not yet provide a basic reconsideration of the essence of condemnations. Melanchthon's desire to confine the condemnation within the narrow limits of a literary polemic among the scholars did not mean to deprive the teaching office of the church of the basic obligation to evaluate and condemn doctrine, an obligation that Melanchthon himself recognized in Augsburg Confession X and elsewhere even against the Zwinglian doctrine of the Lord's Supper.

Yet we cannot fail to notice that between 1530 and 1561 a development has taken place with respect to the scope as well as the weight of the condemnations, even though contemporary theological thought may not have become fully aware of it.

Concerning the extent, a comparison between the Augsburg
Confession and the Weimar Book of Confutations will immediately show the change. The Augsburg Confession had to de-
limit itself—apart from the pre-Reformation heresies—only
against the Anabaptists and the Zwinglians. In 1558, however,
there was a roster of nine different heresies that seemed seriously to threaten the integrity of doctrine. Besides these there
were the specifically Roman errors from which the Lutherans
also had to separate themselves by condemnation. In this way
the imbalance of the Augsburg Confession at this point, as dictated by Melanchthon's practical considerations, was finally
adjusted. Here, too, is to be found one of the reasons why the
strict Lutherans attached particular importance to the Smalcald
Articles, which stated their opposition to Roman "enthusiasm,"
alongside the Augsburg Confession.

As a direct result of this enlarged area of condemnations
the dogmatic antitheses received increasing significance in the
matter of church organization. In 1530 Melanchthon could still
counter the church-political scruples of Philip of Hesse by referring to the obligation of the conscience to be committed to
the true doctrine, as this obligation was expressed in the rejection of the Swiss. The fact that Melanchthon felt compelled at
the same time to suppress the condemnation of Roman errors
in the Augsburg Confession shows how much he himself was
caught up in similar considerations of church politics. Henceforth it was he who in questions of condemnation permitted
himself to be guided more and more by considerations of expediency in matters of church organization. As a result he provoked the opposition of the strict Lutherans. Naturally it could
not remain hidden from the representatives of strict Lutheranism that every condemnation inescapably involved church-
political decisions of far-reaching importance. "'Pure doctrine'
was the legal title for the existence of the young Evangelical
church. It was a determining factor of polity." [212] In this way the
Damnamus had to transcend the area of theoretical discussion
of dogma. It could never again be artificially squeezed back into
the sphere of a polemic that obligated no one. In fact, after Augsburg the *Damnamus* became a moving principle for the whole
Lutheran church organization. This was true also of the Reformed churches, which through their abstention from condem-

nations seemingly appear in a far more favorable light than the strict Lutherans with their "mania for making heretics." It will be shown that this restraint, too, was in large part extorted by church-political considerations.

In addition to the extent of the condemnations their weight, too, experienced a transformation in the course of developments during these three decades. We have to do, first of all, with the question of the authority on which the antitheses rest. There was as yet no problem here for Luther. He assigned to each Christian, each Christian congregation, above all each servant of the Word the obligation of "judging all doctrine," and this included the duty of applying the antithesis. It is true, he experienced having the Swiss, by an appeal to a better understanding of the Word of God, formally deny him the right to pronounce a doctrinal verdict in the name of the church. Thus was posed the question that would henceforth accompany the entire debate concerning condemnations: Where lay the boundary line between a binding condemnation spoken in the name of the whole church and an arbitrary hereticizing in the name of a scholastic pedantry? Here, too, Luther was able to give a clear answer and abide by it: Where the pure doctrine of the Gospel is not correctly presented and where the "chief article" is violated, where God in His Word is willfully and stubbornly "called a liar," there the sign of condemnation must be erected. He did not doubt that this was the case with Rome as well as with the Swiss.

The strength of the later Gnesio-Lutheran protagonists of condemnation lay in their adoption of this strictly objective position as their own. They, too, were concerned that the antithesis dare not be divorced from its immediate substantive reference to the center of doctrinal truth, the Gospel itself. They were confirmed in this stance by the fact that their opponents by and large manifested a dangerous indifference to the central articles of the faith. The Augsburg plan of union sponsored by Philip of Hesse, Bucer's attempts at mediation, the Interim, the Frankfort convention of 1557, the Frankfort Resolution of 1558, and finally the meeting at Naumburg — were not all of these so many stations along the way by which they hoped to achieve a dubious unity by reducing doctrinal differences to insignificant trifles no matter what the motivation? From this vantage point it is easy to understand the assurance with which, for example,

the Flacians defended their position, and with which they
presumably could also ward off the charge that they were speaking only for a small group of fanatics.[213] Where the truth of the
divine Word was endangered, defense was necessary, no matter
how small the number of warriors might be who raised their
voice in the name of the whole church.

It might be well to ask at this point whether the "pure
doctrine" that the Gnesio-Lutherans strove to protect and to
preserve by means of their *Damnamus* was in fact still the faith-
creating "living voice of the Gospel" that was for Luther the
"touchstone and measuring stick" of all doctrinal judgments —
to ask further whether the condemnation still remained subordinated to the principle of the analogy of faith in Luther's sense
or whether behind the facade of orthodox doctrinal formulas
that separation of creed (*fides quae creditur*) and faith (*fides qua
creditur*) was already taking place which changed the "doctrine
of Christ" into a doctrinal deposit and blurred the line of demarcation that existed for Luther's application of the condemnation because of the essential hiddenness of the true church. To
answer this question would require a mass of cross sections in
dogmatics and the history of theology and specific areas of research that would lead far beyond the compass of this study.
Even then it would be very difficult to obtain an intelligible result. This is true, as we know especially from the researches of
H. E. Weber,[214] because just about the middle of the century
and thereafter everything was still in flux. Without a doubt the
decisive shift from a living witness of faith to a "church system"
was already in progress. Attempts have been made to trace this
development particularly in the writings of Melanchthon. In
fact the true doctrine assumed for him more and more the character of the "deposit of the faith" of the "sum total of
religion,"[215] the "teaching church" was made to stand alongside
the self-interpreting Scripture,[216] the high regard for the visible church implied in the "reverence for the ministerial office"
was accented as the third "mark of the church" in a manner that
went clearly beyond Luther.[217] The change manifested itself
also in the understanding of the condemnation: the more acutely
the substantive content of the doctrinal basis is delimited, the
more stringently must retaliation for every departure from the
foundation be demanded. Melanchthon now stressed the execu-

tion of the verdict as something to be required of the civil government (on the other hand, it became all the easier for him to be tolerant in matters he did not regard as fundamental). Unlike Luther, Melanchthon fully approved the burning of Servetus and in general did not shrink from asking the death penalty for heretics.[218]

It must, however, be noted that even the aged Melanchthon was still able to confess the living faith of justification as in the first editions of his *Loci*. Above all, the fateful development cannot be made his responsibility alone. Here, too, the lines that separated the church-political parties were frequently transcended by cross-connections of another kind. In this sense H. E. Weber, basing his conclusions on well-nigh endless materials, has brought the picture drawn by O. Ritschl back into proper focus. The material demonstrates that even those who in opposition to Melanchthon felt that they were the true heirs of the Lutheran heritage were by their very zeal for this their task inevitably led toward the establishment of a "church system." Here we can mention only in passing how Weber demonstrates this development in all areas of dogmatics—yet how, on the other hand, the old approach of the Reformation everywhere still proves itself strong and efficacious, precisely in so consummate a controversialist as Flacius.[219] From this perspective it may truly be said that the Gnesio-Lutherans had one advantage over Melanchthon and his friends: Placed before the decisive alternative of "peace or truth" (as Cruciger aptly paraphrased the situation shortly after the Interim, in a letter to Kegel dated June 19, 1548),[220] the Gnesio-Lutherans believed they could not doubt or vacillate. Though the truth of the Gospel, for which they felt they must take their stand, was no longer grasped in so vital a manner as in the case of Luther and though this truth seemed already to be congealing into a possessed truth, in the fact *that* they made their decision for this truth and permitted themselves to be guided primarily by this principle in their condemnations they remained close to Luther.

It is just this understanding of condemnation that sheds light on the situation from still another angle. Not only the enemies of pure doctrine but also the powers of endurance and restoration in their own camp became a constant source of danger for these epigones of the Reformer. The confession offered the codification and canonization of pure doctrine. What would have been more natural than to be content with that, to let the letter of the doctrinal basis take the place of the living Word, and to become domesticated in this "ecclesiastical system," while permitting the *Damnamus* in the process to become an effective means of safeguarding the status quo? When, for example, at the time of the Frankfort Resolution Amsdorf could say, not without some gratification, "we are sitting still," we have "neither changed nor altered" anything in our heritage, we are staying "with God's Word and with Luther," [221] the danger of mere self-authentication was unmistakable. Yet the same Amsdorf could show that there was another side — that they were not thinking of simply standing guard over the "deposit of the faith" like knights of the holy grail, that they wanted not so much to defend a system of doctrinal truths as rather to be prepared to let the pure doctrine become an event "in the act" of confession. As stated in 1561, it is the function of "the doctrine and confession not only to subscribe and confess the truth in general but also to uncover the seducers and errors and openly reject them." [222] In its essence pure doctrine is always "doctrine against heretics." [223] In applying the condemnation the test is made in each case to show that pure doctrine is not to be kept as a static possession but is constantly to be regrasped in the contrast of thesis and antithesis. It is a matter not only of the authority of the foundation, of the principles as such, but of "the fundamentality that issues in decision." [224] It is significant how also at this point Melanchthon and Flacius diverge: Melanchthon, the teacher who is concerned about "the body of church doctrine as a whole" and who constantly complains that Flacius never addresses himself to "the whole body of doctrine"; [225] Flacius, the tireless polemicist, who seemingly exhausts himself in the little everyday skirmishes dealing with matters of church organization, yet in that way still preserving the "dynamic" character of pure doctrine as it was clearly molded by Luther. Certainly these men had to part company with regard to the Interim, not so much in the "*state* of confession" (here Melanchthon might have been open to discussion) as in the individual "*case* of confession," as Flacius expressed it.[226] By safeguarding this constant reference of pure doctrine to actual confessional situations, the Gnesio-Lutherans in their understanding of condemnation were again and again kept from losing themselves in the nurture and preservation of doctrinal system. To be sure, this did not fully keep them from legalism in their treatment of doctrine and Scripture, a legalism that tried to make its way from the "hiddenness" of the Word and of the church to the "security" consisting of demonstrable outlines of doctrine. Yet they did maintain that the truth of the Word cannot be experienced by means of a spectator attitude, and in this way they retained something of the witness character that Luther had ascribed to pure doctrine.

Although some of Luther's spirit continued to animate the Flacians and their firmness partook of the firmness that enabled Luther to throw the *Damnamus* back at the pope, the voice of the opponents could not be disregarded, and the grief of Melanchthon over the "madness of the theologians" could not be ignored. Were the Gnesio-Lutherans really speaking in the name of the church? Were they not rather one party among others, abusing the condemnation as a weapon in the church-political struggle for power? Was it really proper to pronounce the same verdict of condemnation indiscriminately on Schwenckfeldians and Swiss, Antitrinitarians and Adiaphorists, Roman Pelagianism and Melanchthonian synergism? Was not the cause of the Flacians encumbered by an unspiritual reign of terror, at least in Ducal Saxony? Finally, did not Flacius himself promote a very vulnerable doctrine of sin and a dubious Christology?

For all of these questions the strict Lutheran polemicists had a ready answer. Yet it was evident that here neither merely formal differences in tone and method of condemnation were up for discussion, nor could the objections of the opponents be entered indiscriminately in the ledger of heretical "obstinacy." The weight and the force of the condemnation itself were open to question, and even though the entire problem of condemnations had not yet been reconsidered from this perspective, the strict Lutherans were nevertheless compelled to reexamine their position. The result was an implicit relaxation of the battle lines on both sides of the *Damnamus*, the first symptoms of which became increasingly noticeable since the middle of the century.

These symptoms have contact with that knowledge concerning the boundaries of the condemnation without which Luther refused to pronounce the *Damnamus*. Just as he and Melanchthon had always distinguished between the deceivers and the deceived, between the "leaders" and the "poor people," so also the Flacians aimed in the first place to condemn the authors of error, not simply to damn all who thought otherwise.[227] They understood that the false teaching cannot be separated from the person of the false teacher. Yet, like Melanchthon,[228] even Flacius could emphasize that he was concerned less with the person than with the issue.[229] However, it remained for a later era to clarify the basic principles involved in this problem of person and issue.

A similar situation prevails in the question of treating the errors in different ways. The distinction between "error" and "heresy" was nothing new. Cajetan had once tried to apply this distinction in Luther's favor.[230] Luther himself had observed it and even in his last discussion with the Swiss had left no doubt that he was accusing them of disregard for a central article of Christian doctrine, hence not simply a harmless "mistake," and that for this reason he was dealing so sternly with them.[231] After the extent of the condemnations had been so greatly enlarged since Augsburg, the question of differentiating among the errors was raised anew. We refer only to the reproaches which Philip of Hesse raised against the Weimar Book of Confutations. The presuppositions for a new solution of the problem did not yet exist, and therefore also this question passed into the future without an answer.

A further symptom of the incipient relaxation of the battle lines is seen in the fact that alongside a sharpened emphasis on the things that divided them, both sides, apart from occasional exceptions, continued to leave the door open for further conversation and possible unification. Almost in the same breath Flacius could ask Melanchthon for condemnations (including the rejection of positions that Melanchthon himself had upheld) and offer to negotiate, without letting the one restrict the other. In this way the divisive force of the condemnations was open to question at least as far as the intra-Lutheran area was concerned. It is, of course, a moot point whether Flacius was himself aware of these implications. At any rate the way was opened for new approaches in the direction of a fellowship that was to be attempted, as it were, behind and beyond the separation indicated by the condemnations. Into this context belongs also the fact that especially Flacius and his friends with an astounding tenacity promoted the plan for a general synod, a plan that occupied a prominent place also in the program of the opponents. While the one side might have hoped primarily for a ratification of their antitheses, the other side expected the condemnations and their authors to be discredited. Thus the various conceptions of the function of the synod at first merely reflected the existing battle lines, and the aged Melanchthon knew very well why he rejected the whole idea of a synod as inopportune. Yet even this striving for a synod may be regarded as a symptom that in this era, too, the condemnations were not intended to say the last word on the question of church fellowship.

Finally the latent relaxation of the battle lines is demonstrated also by a gradual realignment of the church-political groups. Toward the end of these three decades since Augsburg a sort of third direction begins to emerge between the promoters and the opponents of the *Damnamus*, a direction that found its support less among the theologians than among the princes. Thus while Duke John Frederick of Saxony fully approved the strict attitude of his Flacian theologians in all questions of doctrine, he could still disagree so strongly with Flacius, the leader, on the question of the church's practice of excommunication that Flacius was finally compelled to leave the country. The majority of the Lower Saxon estates and cities took a similar position. Without conceding anything in their uncompromisingly orthodox orientation especially also in the matter of condemnations, they let it be known in the Lueneburg Mandate of 1561 that they would not tolerate controversy among their theologians simply for the sake of controversy. The men from Wuerttemberg may also be added to this group. They had been particularly zealous in preserving Luther's doctrine of the Lord's Supper and Christology, yet they, too, adopted a more conciliatory attitude toward the errors of the Wittenbergers.

The time was ripe for a new start and a new gathering of forces in the church of Luther. Naumburg represented the bankruptcy of a spirit of compromise that was indifferent to doctrinal questions and was oriented exclusively toward matters of church organization. The battle over condemnations had in many places led to the insight that an Evangelical united front resting solely on organizational concerns could not survive. The successful advance of Calvinism also did its part to create an ever greater sense of need for a Lutheran unification that was based squarely on doctrine. For a while the respective battle lines of the Gnesio-Lutherans and the Philippists continued, but there were indications that the intra-Lutheran differences were beginning to move. The future would have to show whether the strict party would be able to hold the Lutheran forces effectively in line and would thus be equipped for the forthcoming confrontation with the Reformed churches. For this, too, the problem of condemnations had to be of decisive significance.

Notes to Chapter 10

[155] *Geschichte der protestantischen Theologie,* 2d printing (Munich, 1867), p. 335.

[156] Salig, III, 36. Cf. W. Preger, *Matthias Flacius Illyricus und seine Zeit,* II (Erlangen, 1861, 6f.; Heinrich Heppe, *Geschichte des deutschen Protestantismus in den Jahren 1555 — 1581,* I (Marburg, 1852), 114ff.

[157] For the following see especially Preger, pp. 8ff., who on the basis of unpublished sources available to him arranges the various events chronologically in a more correct manner than Heppe, pp. 116ff.

[158] "What in the world are we trying to do, or in what does he resist us, if not in the condemnation of adiaphorism and of Majorism?" *(Letter to Hubert Languet, June 21, 1556,* in Bacmeister, *Acta Philippica* (Tuebingen, 1719), p. 31, also quoted in G. J. Planck, *Geschichte des protestantischen Lehrbegriffes,* VI (Leipzig, 1800), 39, n. 30.

[159] Letter of Sept. 16, 1556 (Preger, pp. 29f.).

[160] Documentation in Preger, p. 22.

[161] Letter to Flacius, Sept. 5, 1556 (CR 8, 841f.).

[162] Cf. the *Acta Cosvicensia* in CR 9, 23ff., also Heppe, I, 126ff.; Preger, pp. 32f.

[163] Bacmeister, pp. 55ff.; Preger, pp. 59ff.; CR 9, 92ff.

[164] CR 9, 63.

[165] "Therefore, if anywhere I have either failed or acted with too little vigor, I beg forgiveness from God and from the churches, and I shall submit to the decisions of the church" (CR 9, 61).

[166] CR 9, 35f.

[167] Preger, p. 12.

[168] Quoted in H. C. v. Hase, *Die Gestalt der Kirche Luthers* (Goettingen, 1940), p. 37.

[169] Pp. 58f.

[170] Examples in Preger, pp. 30f., 49f.

[171] For his role, cf. Heppe, I, 150ff.

[172] *Frankfort Opinion,* cited in Preger, p. 64.

[173] The most detailed of the newer presentations in Heppe, I, 157 — 230.

[174] CR 9, 231f.

[175] Ibid., pp. 213 – 15.

[176] Letter from Monner, Aug. 31, 1557 (CR 9, 246).

[177] CR 9, 237.

[178] From a report of the proceedings prepared by the Electoral Saxon party, cited by Heppe, I, 193.

[179] Cf. the importuning letters of Bullinger and Calvin to Melanchthon, in Carl Schmidt, *Philipp Melanchthon* (Elberfeld, 1861), pp. 603f.

[180] CR 9, 243f.

[181] Cf. Heppe, I, 187.

[182] CR 9, 365 – 72 (there dated too late).

[183] CR 9, 350 – 54.

[184] Letter of Feb. 23, 1558 (CR 45, 61). — *Die Gruendliche Wahrhafftige Historia von der Augspurgischen Confession* (Leipzig, 1584), pp. 395f., contains this report: "At the close of the colloquy at Worms the remaining participants agreed on an explanation of several controverted articles of the time, an explanation written by Philip in his own hand. In it Zwingli and his teaching are mentioned and expressly and explicitly condemned, as also Lavater had acknowledged and noted, and the original is still in existence. However, in the printed copies as in the writings of Philip elsewhere and as later published at Wittenberg in Latin, Zwingli's name and teaching were omitted." Similarly in Theodosius Fabricius, *Historia certaminis sacramentarii* (Magdeburg, 1593), fol. Z ii b; Hutter, fol. 10; Loescher, II, 142. Obviously this report has reference to the above-mentioned protestation of Oct. 21, 1557, which was to demonstrate that the German Lutherans had in no wise accepted the Zwinglian doctrine of the sacrament (cf. Heppe, I, 212). In the version which G. Th. Strobel reprints *ex manuscripto* in his edition of J. Camerarius, *De vita Melanchthonis narratio* (Halle, 1770), we read: "Neither our churches nor we either approve or embrace Zwingli's dogma or any opinions conflicting with our confession, and the existence of our refutations is a known fact." No printed edition of the Protestation in which this passage is omitted could be found (not even in the four-volume edition of the *Opera*, Wittenberg, 1562ff.). However, in two manuscripts that were used for the reprint in CR 9, 350 – 54, the apodosis ("and the existence of our refutations . . .") is missing. How vacillating Melanchthon's attitude actually was in the question of condemning the Swiss is clear from a letter to Bullinger (Oct. 5!), in which he states that he cannot agree to a condemnation of the Swiss (CR 9, 327).

[185] CR 9, 284 – 95.

[186] Ibid., p. 288.

[187] Ibid., pp. 287, 286.

[188] Ibid., p. 287.

[189] Ibid., p. 286.

[190] Ibid., pp. 286, 294.

[191] So even Brenz regarding the Flacians (C. Schmidt, p. 614).

[192] CR 9, 489 – 507.

[193] Ibid., p. 618.

[194] On April 27, 1559, Duke John Frederick wrote to Landgrave Philip of Hesse concerning "our book, which Illyricus did not write" (CR 9, 775).

[195] CR 9, 763 – 75.

[196] Ibid., pp. 753 – 763.

[197] Ibid., p. 756.

[198] Ibid., p. 762.

[199] Ibid., pp. 758f.

[200] Summary in Preger, pp. 81ff.

[201] Ibid., p. 85.

[202] Ibid., p. 89.

[203] Reprinted in Heppe, I, Supplements, pp. 114–126.

[204] Preger, p. 88.

[205] Heppe, I, 360.

[206] Preger, p. 93, note.

[207] Salig, III, pp. 665f.

[208] Ibid., pp. 674f.; Preger, pp. 95f.

[209] Salig, III, 683.

[210] Preger, p. 98.

[211] Salig, III, 767.

[212] R. Seeberg, IV/2, 455.

[213] Petition to the Naumburg·Day of Princes (Heppe, I, 385).

[214] *Reformation, Orthodoxie und Rationalismus,* I/1 (Guetersloh, 1937); I/2 (1940); II (1951).

[215] R. Seeberg, IV/2, 421.

[216] O. Ritschl, I, 301.

[217] Ibid., pp. 316ff.; R. Seeberg, pp. 452f.

[218] O. Ritschl, pp. 283, 321f.

[219] Cf. K. A. v. Schwartz, "Die theologische Hermeneutik des Matthias Flacius Illyricus," *Luther-Jahrbuch, 1933,* 139ff.; G. Moldaenke, loc. cit.

[220] CR 4, 945.

[221] Nikolaus von Amsdorff, *Ausgewaehlte Schriften,* ed. O. Lerche (Guetersloh, 1938), pp. 80f.

[222] Cited in O. H. Nebe, *Reine Lehre* (Goettingen, 1935), p. 12.

[223] Ibid., p. 14.

[224] Weber, I/1, 187.

[225] CR 9, 34, 61, 75; cf. Weber, p. 170, n. 4.

[226] v. Hase, p. 61, n. 64.

[227] See above, p. 139.

[228] See above, pp. 99–100.

[229] See above, p. 125.

[230] See above, p. 25.

[231] See above, p. 114.

Part 4

The Era of Concord
(1565 – 1583)

Chapter 11

The Controversy About Condemnations and the Preliminaries to the Formula of Concord

Events following Melanchthon's death had shown that in spite of some hopeful beginnings there could for the present be no thought of a union of the Evangelical estates, or even of the Lutheran groups, on the basis of a common doctrinal platform. At the religious colloquy of Altenburg in 1568 the gap between the Philippists of Electoral Saxony and the Gnesio-Lutherans of Ducal Saxony was still unbridgeable. For the first the individual territories busied themselves during the sixties with establishing their confessional position by means of their own doctrinal writings. In quick succession a number of such *corpora doctrinae* appeared, and in their contrasting makeup they reflect the divergence of the opposing parties. Yet even now there were attempts at unification, promoted primarily by James Andreae, the chancellor of Tuebingen University. With untiring zeal and by the application of all his arts of diplomacy he supported the peace efforts of his prince, Duke Christopher of Wuerttemberg, and after the latter's death he continued the work under the protectorate of Landgrave William of Hesse and Duke Julius of Brunswick-Wolfenbuettel. During the years 1568 – 1570 he traveled extensively in order to gain princes, cities, and universities for his plans. As a basis for his work he had drawn up five articles [1] in which he sought to establish the most highly controverted points of doctrine in a positive way and through which he hoped "a Christian unity might be achieved in the churches committed to the Augsburg Confession and the scandalous and long-lasting schism might be removed." Viewed as a whole, this hope was not to be realized for some time.

Again it was the problem of condemnations that caused

division of opinion. Doubts were expressed especially in Lower Saxony, where the influence of the Gnesio-Lutherans had increased. In Brunswick the city superintendent, Chemnitz, and his friends expressed the fear that "if a conciliation is undertaken that deals only in generalities, where the existing controversies are either not mentioned at all or not given an adequate affirmative and negative treatment, the situation would not be improved, but rather the malady would only become worse." [2] It should not have surprised Andreae that he met with similar opposition in Saxe-Weimar, the citadel of strict Lutheranism. While each of his five articles contained a general rejection of all divergent teaching, the opponents of the Philippists considered them insufficient. They felt that by continuing to insist on an explicit "personal condemnation" in connection with each controverted point of doctrine they had provided the ultimate safeguard for doctrine, and they could not recede from that position. At the same time they thereby gave expression to their fundamental distrust of Andreae's whole plan. They were convinced that the attitude toward truth as such was decided by one's attitude toward the question of condemnations. As Andreae himself said, his formula aimed at nothing less than "establishing the truth regarding the controverted doctrines briefly and unequivocally," and this "by omitting personal condemnations." [3] It was not intended to be a compromise confession. Yet the question was necessarily raised how Andreae could dare to distill from the opposing opinions what should be regarded positively as true when the truth itself was under fire. Neither the Gnesio-Lutherans nor the Philippists could agree to this all too simple procedure for establishing a common doctrinal basis. Just as Andreae had been rebuffed in Weimar he was also given the cold shoulder in Wittenberg.

On all sides, however, there was appreciation of the church-political value of his plans, and everywhere the willingness to pray for his plans was expressed. For the princes, Andreae's aims might well have proved to be particularly convenient. On the other hand, suspicions were entertained here and there that Andreae had impure motives and was using his peace proposals merely as a cover for spreading the ubiquity doctrine of the Swabians. Hence, in spite of some surface successes Andreae must have come to the realization that this path of "neutralizing the contrasts" [4] would not lead to the goal. In his five articles and the accompanying negotiations Andreae had "laboriously picked his way among the various confessional opinions and parties in order to appear to be standing *above* them. However, precisely by means of this procedure the difference among the tendencies and positions in the church had in a very striking manner come to the fore." [5]

The Andreae who resumed his plan for concord in the year 1573 had become a different person. This is not the place to trace the reasons and backgrounds of his change. In any case he had in the interval come to understand that he could not occupy an Archimedean point beyond the warring parties and drive them together from there, simply because he could not gain such a neutral position. Therefore he aimed first of all at bringing the non-Philippist Lutherans together in order to proceed from this basis and try again to resolve the intra-Lutheran tensions, in case the presuppositions for such an attempt should be more favorable.

Andreae's newly won attitude toward condemnations reflects his transformation. His six sermons in the year 1573 [6] treat thetically and antithetically 10 of the most important teachings that had become controversial among the Lutherans of the Augsburg Confession since 1548. In line with the character of the sermons, there were no express condemnations by name. Yet there should be no doubt for the "simple layman" that the controverted teachings of the Wittenbergers must be avoided as errors, and this applied no less to Flacius' false views of sin. In this way the direction of the succeeding stages of the work of concord is already indicated. In every case the pure teaching is developed in the form of thesis and antithesis, for so Duke Julius of Brunswick had prescribed when he instructed Andreae to transform his six sermons into a set of "Articles," which then became known as the "Swabian Concord." The latter represents a sort of first preliminary draft of the Formula of Concord. [7] From the beginning, therefore, the actual doctrinal articles of the subsequent Formula of Concord are preceded by two sections that give an account of this twofold approach. [8] The one establishes the basis from the Bible and the earlier Lutheran Symbols; the other treats "of controverted articles with respect to the antithesis or opposing doctrine." It also adopts as a basic principle the condemnation of ancient heresies, of those already rejected in the earlier confessions of the Reformation, and of the errors that arose since the Interim.

Recommending his project to the strict Lutheran bishops of East Prussia, Hesshusius and Wigand, three years later, Andreae did not neglect to point out that the just completed "Torgau Book," developed out of the "Swabian-Saxon Concord" and the "Maulbronn Formula," everywhere added the antithesis to the thesis and gave the explicit condemnation of the opposing doctrine its due. No false teachers were mentioned by name, since the plan was to mention only one Reformation teacher in the whole formula, namely Luther.[9] There, for the moment, the problem of condemnations remained. The critiques of the Torgau Book, submitted by the other Lutheran estates and theologians,[10] occasionally gave voice to the wish for a more explicit rejection of individual false teachings and false teachers. Thus, for example, the desire was expressed in Lower Saxony that the Philippist writings published in Electoral Saxony and some of the Flacian documents be rejected in detail.[11] Also mentioned was the request that the false teachers should be compelled to recant at a special synod.[12]

The two East Prussian bishops went farthest in this direction in their critique of the Torgau Book, a critique that was signed at Koenigsberg on Jan. 8, 1577. In this document the arguments of the strict extremists were most emphatically supported.[13] In general the Torgau Book was approved as a "glorious and excellent writing." Yet Hesshusius and Wigand could not forget the mediating theology its chief author formerly promoted, and therefore they demanded that Andreae should publicly apologize for his earlier "grave sin." Furthermore, they fought energetically for the old Gnesio-Lutheran insistence on condemning the false teachers by name. They wanted to know how the common people could be effectively protected against false doctrine if the false doctrines and their originators were not clearly designated. Not only the Bible (Ex. 32:1ff.; Jer. 29:8; Matt. 7:15; 23:13; 2 Tim. 1:15; 2:17, 24; 4:10; and other passages were used) but also the example of the ancient church, as for example, the Fifth Ecumenical Council (II Constantinople, 553) obligated them to follow this procedure. Also for the sake of unity itself this should be done. "What kind of unity will that be, if in Prussia Osiander is condemned by name as a heretic, while in Wittenberg they cannot even mention him by name!" [14] Above all, it was high time to condemn Melanchthon unequivocally to the extent that he was involved as the author of manifestly false teaching. "Should the name of Philip mean more to us than the welfare of the whole church? . . . Should the names of the 'authors and sponsors of perversions' be hushed up in the Formula of Concord, the whole thing will be a sham battle that is not taken seriously. The concord will not amount to anything, for Ezechiel will shout through the window into the council chambers: The prophets are daubing the wall with untempered mortar, but an overflowing shower will soon destroy such daubing. Whoever will not condemn the false teachers by name cannot be serious. He may accommodate himself and sign until the storm has blown over. But just as soon as the wind blows from another direction, he will sing his old refrain: I've never rejected Philipp's opinion." [15]

Such language had hardly been heard even from Flacius and his followers. From the widely acknowledged necessity of the *Damnamus*, conclusions were here drawn that had hitherto been avoided. Condemning persons by name had practically been made into the shibboleth of all genuine Lutheranism. It is not at all surprising that Melanchthon was made the chief target, considering how often he had in fact attempted to tone down the harshness and pointedness of Lutheran teaching, either permanently or in passing. The critique expressly states: "Philipp is not the issue." [16] Hence it would be wrong to dismiss the whole document as an extreme case of anti-Philippist heresy hunting, or even as the excrescence of the impotent vengefulness of the two controversialists who had been driven into exile by the Philippists. Even this exaggeration of the strict Lutheran point of view was still animated by some of that genuine pathos inherent in the battle for the truth. This spirit had ever again manifested itself since Augsburg in the conflict raging around the question of condemnations. The previous attempts at concord had sufficiently demonstrated that in doctrinal decisions halfway measures could not establish an adequate foundation for agreement. They had further proved that such decisions must be secured against the manifold diverging possibilities of interpretation. In view of these experiences it was, therefore, consistent, to say the least. for the Prussian Lutherans to cling tenaciously to their demand for condemning the false teachers by name and to regard this as an important guarantee for the unity and purity of doctrine.

The recipients of this critique were at the same time compelled to face the question whether such a guarantee might not be achieved in a less pointed and wounding manner. All other critiques of the Torgau Book, including those that approved, had been far more restrained in the question of condemnations than the Prussian opinion. The estates that were under Philippist influence and that consistently declined the formula were greatly strengthened in their negative attitude toward the entire effort at concord by the condemnation of Melanchthon's teachings. The Pomeranians admitted that Melanchthon had occasionally been in error. Yet they wished "together with Shem and Japheth to spread their cloak over the nakedness of the aged Noah and earnestly pray that God would graciously forgive him." [17] The theologians of Anhalt spoke in similar vein: Even though Melanchthon had departed from Luther in the doctrine of the Eucharist, they would lay it on his conscience and say with Brenz: "We regret exceedingly the slip of our teacher and friend." [18] In general, they would have considered it proper to draw up nothing but short, affirmative doctrinal articles which, after careful review by ranking theologians, would have suggested the antithesis as a matter of course.[19]

Similarly the Hessian critique, too, objected to the excessively pointed condemnations and especially criticized that the earlier "disapprove" (improbamus) had now everywhere been replaced by "condemn" (damnamus).[20] How this Damnamus was interpreted in this old citadel of "liberal" Lutheranism is clear from a letter of Superintendent Meyer of Cassel to his prince, Landgrave William, in which he complained bitterly about the presumption of Andreae. "It is certainly a great 'temerity and arrogance' to want to condemn so many excellent, pious, and learned men and consign them to the devil, simply because they are unable to endorse and praise every new formulation" (he is thinking of the ubiquity doctrine!), "although there is no disagreement in the main teaching and the old, general, and familiar terminology is retained and defended with less danger." [21] But precisely these premises Andreae could not possibly accept. He could under no circumstances concede that in the doctrine of the Eucharist it was only a matter of substituting new terms for old ones, assuming that there was complete unity in essentials. He could only regard it as a trick of the Sacramentarians that they "did not want to be Calvinists but only opponents of ubiquity," as he had written to Landgrave William earlier.[22] On the other hand, he had said nothing of using the *Damnamus* in all due form in order to "consign to the devil" the false teachers—even though he had made it quite clear that he was convinced it was the devil himself who was at work in Electoral Saxony during the Philippist era and that he was still operating in the false doctrine concerning the Sacrament.

Thus also the critiques of the Torgau Book had on the whole demonstrated that the attitude toward condemnations determined to a large extent, if not exclusively, the attitude toward the entire work of concord. For that reason the question of condemnations required special attention also for the subsequent labors on the settlement. In the spring of 1577 Andreae, Chemnitz, and Selnecker, as well as Musculus, Cornerus, and Chytraeus met in Bergen Abbey in order to evaluate the reactions to the Torgau Book. The six theologians reported to Elector August of Saxony,[23] who since the ouster of the Crypto-Calvinists had made the efforts toward concord his special concern. In their report they stated very plainly that as a matter of principle they took their stand beside the Lower Saxons and Prussians in the question of condemnations. Since for them it was not a matter of "misunderstanding or squabbling about words but of important and big things," they could follow only one course: "Straight ahead and confess fully what is manifest and what can no longer be covered up or denied." On the other hand, they believed to see clearly that a rigorous application of "condemnation of persons" "might create no small hindrance to the whole effort toward concord, which, thank God, was almost completed." This risk seemed unconscionably great to them, nor did the cause itself demand it. Therefore they agreed on a compromise solution: First the attempt should be made to reach unity in the doctrinal articles on the basis of the amended formula. Once this were attained, the prospective general synod (which had been discussed in this connection already in the Torgau

conference in May 1576)[24] might then authorize one general
article regarding the false teachers and all "harmful books."
In it a word should be said about Melanchthon too, but it was
expressly requested that "his profitable writings (should) thereby not be condemned."

It soon became apparent that such a synod of the churches
committed to the Augsburg Confession could probably not be
convened before the signing of the Bergen Book. Such a synod
might all too easily be exploited by the opposition to endanger
the whole effort toward concord. The disastrous example of the
conference at Naumburg, to which the Elector of Brandenburg
expressly called attention,[25] was still too fresh in everyone's
mind. For some future date, however, they were willing to entertain the plan of a synod. Meanwhile it was consistently regarded
as entirely tolerable and proper to permit the publication of the
formula for the purpose of subscription even without condemning the false teachers by name. In all individual articles the
antitheses were so clearly stated as to substance that misunderstanding seemed to be excluded. The rigorous party indeed
raised its objections again. The formula was subscribed in
Prussia, but only with the expressed regret that "the contrary
teachers are not mentioned and refuted by name, as had been
requested." [26] For the same reason three clergymen of Wismar
felt compelled to refuse their signatures.[27] Yet these concerns
receded before the energetic resistance to the formula by the
representatives of the other extreme. The Philippists assailed
the Bergen Book just as they had formerly opposed the Torgau
Book.

In Anhalt it was still impossible to gain Prince Joachim
Ernest and his theologians for the concord. In addition to various
other objections the antipathy to the *Damnamus* again played
a leading role. Here, where the Melanchthonian type of doctrine
was upheld with unflagging determination, the rejection of all
who teach otherwise was regarded as an unacceptable suggestion, besides being unwise. As was stated at the Dessau convention in February 1578, the listing of so many heresies would
achieve nothing but embarrassment for the Evangelicals in the
eyes of the Romans.[28] Likewise it was opposition to the condemnation of Melanchthonian teachings that kept the Bergen
Book from being subscribed in Holstein, Pomerania, Nurem-

berg, and Bremen. Elector Louis of the Palatinate, though attempting to reverse the Calvinistic reorganization of the Palatinate church as introduced by his father, Frederick III, took
offense at the *Damnamus* directed against the Zwinglians and
Calvinists — quite probably out of consideration for his deceased
father and his Reformed brother John Casimir — and demanded
that the *Damnamus* be dropped entirely or at least replaced by
a gentler term such as *improbamus* ("disapprove"). The demands of the Hessians were similar. It was especially Landgrave William who sought to rally all opponents of the Bergen
Book to present a united front against the "ubiquitistic" Lutherans.

In addition to the familiar divergences in specific doctrines
there were new and differently oriented motives that led him
as well as the Palatinate elector to adopt a negative attitude
toward the concord. For the first time it became perfectly clear
that the problem of condemnations had transcended not only
the area of theological controversy but also that of church polity
in the narrow sense and was beginning to become a significant
factor in German politics in general. The impetus for this development had come from England. Already at the meeting of
princes at Naumburg Queen Elizabeth had through a special
emissary expressed interest in a pan-Evangelical union.
Through her conversations with the Roman Church and especially through the influence of Francis Walsingham, her secretary of state and a militant Puritan,[29] her concern had become
even more urgent. It was natural that the queen could only
look upon the increasing separation between Lutherans and
Calvinists with anxiety. As early as the spring of 1577, just when
the Bergen Book was being completed, the queen inserted
herself into the religious and political development within Germany by means of a new diplomatic maneuver and tried through
Walsingham's son-in-law, Philip Sydney, to interest Count Palatine John Casimir, who nurtured the Reformed heritage of Frederick III in his little realm, and Landgrave William of Hesse in
an offensive and defensive alliance of all Evangelical powers.[30]
The landgrave and especially John Casimir, who on his part was
plotting nothing less than a counterconcord against strict Lutheranism as well as a general synod of Evangelicals, were at
first not averse to entertaining this appeal. Immediately after

this first attempt the queen dispatched her special emissary, Dr. Daniel Rogers, on a secret mission to Germany for further conversations. Rogers was instructed not only to promote the plan of a federation and to help settle the fraternal dispute between the two princes of the Palatinate but also to initiate steps toward deleting the Lutheran *Damnamus* against the Calvinists. As Rogers told the landgrave at Bad Ems, it would be impossible to justify the condemnations for the sake of a single doctrinal difference and the inevitably resulting schism among the Evangelicals, particularly in a situation that so urgently required joint action against the common Roman foe. And though at least the landgrave might have been inclined to associate himself with this view of the question of condemnations, before long both he and especially the elector of the Palatinate were induced by a variety of personal and political considerations to respond only with great reserve to the suggestions of the emissary. The queen, however, refused to become discouraged. After only a few weeks she started another maneuver, this time of larger scope. Her confidential secretary, Robert Beale, brother-in-law of Walsingham, visited a great number of the more prominent princely courts of Germany in the interests of a double assignment: On the one hand he was to promote again the firmly formulated plan for a federation; on the other hand he protested in no uncertain terms against the splitting of Evangelical Christianity that was allegedly effected by the new formula of religion. He asked that all controversy should stop until a general synod could be convened. Beale quoted the queen as saying that it was unheard of to condemn in short order and without a hearing the churches in England, Scotland, France, Hungary, Poland, Switzerland, and even the queen herself, and this at a moment when unity among the Evangelical powers was more necessary than ever.

This view of condemnations might have been comprehensible from the queen's perspective, but its questionable character was obvious. Here a matter that could be decided only in responsibility for the truth of the Gospel was in a dangerously one-sided way drawn into a political perspective. In earlier debates about the *Damnamus* political considerations on both sides had perforce played a part. Yet since the days of Philip of Hesse there had hardly been so patent a distortion of perspec-

tives as in the proposals of Queen Elizabeth. She completely
misread the intentions that were originally involved with the
Damnamus in the Lutheran Confessions. For that reason this
attack on the *Damnamus*, by means of which the queen sought
to pave the way for Evangelical unity, was doomed to failure.
In the replies of the German princes the familiar viewpoints
were reflected unchanged. Only John Casimir, slated to become
the English "continental sword," [31] readily acceded to the English arguments. Landgrave William, while approving the protest against condemnations, kept his further plans to himself.
Characteristic of the attitude of those princes who supported
the Lutheran concord is the answer that Robert Beale received
from Duke Julius of Brunswick.[32] The duke told the emissary
that the new formula dare not be regarded as a wholly new
confession. Rather, it aimed only at effectively asserting the
clear teachings of the Augsburg Confession against newly arising
heresies. Contrary to the queen's manifest wish, the difference
in the doctrine of the Lord's Supper could not be overlooked as
of no consequence, since it was in fact of critical significance. The
condemnations were therefore fully legitimate. Moreover, these
had been formulated with great restraint and without mentioning names, besides having the approval of the majority of
princes, so that the charge that the formula did not produce
unity but disunity was completely without foundation. Most of
the other Lutheran princes expressed themselves much like
Julius.

Yet even now Elizabeth refused to be diverted from her
plans. Until the end of 1577 she tried, mostly by letter, to gain
the German princes for her plan of union and federation, always
on the premise that the insignificant doctrinal differences, or
"the slight variation of opinions in one or another point," as
she wrote,[33] could easily be removed and that the offensive
Damnamus must be revoked in any case. But precisely in this
attitude the Lutheran princes felt the queen was grossly misunderstanding them. She was picturing the situation "as if we
intended to expel her from both the Religious Peace and from
the kingdom of heaven," as Elector Louis wrote the Saxon
elector.[34] Evidently the queen did not want to forsake this
premise. There was, then, nothing for the princes to do but to
explain their position and continue to remain faithful to it. This

is the sense of the letter of Duke Louis of Wuerttemberg to the
queen in December 1577, in which he explained how the condemnations should be interpreted: [35] Not as a means of attack
on other churches but as warning signs to keep their own church
from going astray. A consistent support of the truth must necessarily lead to an antithetical delimitation against teaching that
contradicts the truth.

Under such circumstances the English plans had to be
regarded as having come to naught by the end of 1577. A similar
attempt undertaken the following spring also ended in failure.[36]
In the context of the major state and church politics of the 16th
century these attempts remained only an episode. However, in
the development of the problem of condemnations they occupy
an important place in that they furnish the proof that the differences in the understanding of the truth that were impeding
unity could not be bypassed by the "route of diplomacy." [37]
As for the Lutheran princes, their decision showed that for them
the *Damnamus* was not first and foremost a weapon in the
church-political debate, but still primarily a matter of faith and
conscience. This was an attitude that deserves to be approved
even though one might regret that the pan-Evangelical alliance
under English leadership did not materialize. From now on it
becomes clear again and again that an understanding of the
concern of pan-Evangelicalism on the part of German Lutheranism was diminishing in a most fateful way. Certainly the insistence on the *Damnamus* at that time secured the clean lines of
doctrinal decision. But already the uncertain attitude of the
Lutheran estates toward the Huguenots was to demonstrate
that an objective clarity in doctrinal matters could lead to unhappy consequences in other areas.[38]

Meanwhile the opponents of the Lutheran concord, too,
had been seeking clarity in the question of condemnations.
At the Frankfort convention in the fall of 1577,[39] which brought
together for the first time nearly all representatives of Calvinistic churches, the Count Palatine John Casimir had suggested
as the first item on the agenda ways and means of thwarting
the condemnation of foreign churches by the Lutherans. At the
instigation of Daniel Rogers, the English representative, they
soon agreed that the best thing to do was to support the program
of Queen Elizabeth and urgently to warn the Lutheran princes

in the name of the convention against an arbitrary condemnation of foreign churches. The Dutch jurist Knibbius was asked to accompany the English emissary, Beale, with instructions to present a special memorial [40] to the princes expressing the convention's wishes together with the propositions of Queen Elizabeth. In substance this "admonition" brought nothing new. It argued on the basis of the same church-political ideas as those entertained by the queen, except that it did not share the queen's aversion to the Augsburg Confession. On the contrary, the document insisted that the foreign churches were fully committed to this primary Evangelical confession. They might hold differing opinions on some points but only to the extent that they interpreted the confession in the sense of the amended edition published by Luther and Melanchthon at Wittenberg in 1540 and 1542.

It is not surprising that after all that had happened the Lutheran princes could not take these claims too seriously. Hence the Frankfort plans were likewise rejected, together with the English proposals. In addition, the chief project of the Frankfort meeting, the plan of a Calvinistic formula of concord, came to nothing. In contrast to the Lutheran document this writing was to draw the limits of church fellowship as broadly as possible. It was above all the Swiss (who were not represented in Frankfort) who refused to consider this pet project of Count Palatine John Casimir.[41] In some respects their refusal corresponds to the attitude of the Lutherans. They, too, could see no promise in an attempt to create a very broad doctrinal basis through the use of compromise and ambiguous formulas and to blur all differences as much as possible.[42] Since a Reformed concord could not seriously be considered apart from the Swiss, there could be no thought of realizing the scheme of John Casimir.

Naturally the Frankfort convention and the English approaches as well as the negative and critical reviews of the Bergen Book did not fail to make an impression on the princes promoting the Lutheran concord. They saw themselves compelled to reexamine their own position and continually to reassess the question of condemnations in addition to the strongly controverted doctrine of ubiquity, the validity of the *Variata*, as well as the authority of Luther and other points at issue. As the chief promoter of this undertaking, Elector August had to bear the brunt of the attacks. It is true, he and his partners had rejected the English proposals as a dangerous temptation and had retained the *Damnamus* of the Bergen Book. Yet they could by no means remain indifferent to the conclusions that could be drawn from the condemnations elsewhere. To clarify these and other problems, the elector first of all instructed Andreae to prepare an opinion [43] that would once more thoroughly explain the Lutheran position in all debated questions.

In this opinion every weakening of the *Damnamus* is emphatically discouraged. Andreae stated that in this way they would not only expose themselves to the justified charge of inconsistency but also proceed in an improper manner to wipe out the alternative between true and false doctrine as set forth in the doctrine of the Eucharist and thus they would fail to heed the unequivocal words of Christ's testament: Moreover, they had consistently practiced the virtue of "modesty" in that they had "not condemned the persons or the churches, but had rather committed to the judgment of God those persons who might still experience some change of heart." They need not attach too much importance to the English courtship since here "nothing but human ideas, suggested by flesh and blood and reason, were being proposed, while there was no argument based on the Word of God, but rather everything was designed to draw us away from the plain Word of God and our faith for the sake of temporal advantage or to cast doubts on our faith." [44] The attacks which were seemingly directed only against the word "condemn" were in reality meant to serve the establishment of Zwinglian and Calvinistic errors. Furthermore, those attacks operated with false arguments throughout. In fact "every Christian (is) a judge of the whole world in matters of faith," and he must not wait to be sure of his cause until "the deniers of the truth had all been given a hearing and had been condemned by an orderly process of law and understanding of their teaching," as the opposition demanded. When did "Christ or his apostle conduct such a trial?" It must also be remembered that the Sacramentarians had been given the opportunity at many colloquies to defend their opinion and to come to their senses, but they "became all the worse and subsequently derided the pure doctrine of our churches more than ever." [45] But if the opponents should cite the law of love in opposition to the *Damnamus*, they should be reminded of the word of Luther: "Cursed be that love which is observed to the detriment and loss of the truth of the faith, before which everything must retreat, be it love, apostle, or even an angel from heaven." [46] Finally Andreae also took up the point raised by Queen Elizabeth that many of those Christians who had been condemned by the Lutherans were now witnessing to their faith at the risk of their life. According to Andreae the martyrdom of the French Protestants, who were chiefly concerned in this discussion, did not alter the fact that their faith was not the right one. Whoever drew the sword against the government contrary to the command of Christ must reckon with the possibility that he may perish by the sword.

In spite, or perhaps because of, the comprehensiveness and thoroughness of Andreae's opinion, the scruples of the Saxon elector had not been overcome. At his wish a special convention was to be held at Tangermuende for the purpose of giving thorough consideration to the possibility of making it easier for the opponents of the Bergen Book to join the project after all. The instructions of the elector to his counselors [47] are a most revealing document, demonstrating on the one hand the church-political anxieties of the elector and on the other hand the earnestness and sense of responsibility with which he treated the question of condemnations. The elector's chief concern was that "all reasons for writing against this effort at concord and for arguing against it should be removed and cut off" for everyone. For that reason all formulations attacked by the critics of the concord should be examined once more to see whether the formulations might not be altered in conformity with the criticisms to the extent that this "is possible without injury to and distortion of the true meaning of the doctrine." Thus there was provided a final opportunity to revise the condemnations. The elector's instructions strongly hint that this opportunity should be exploited. They ought to be considerate of the elector Palatine whose respect for his Reformed father would not let him agree to a condemnation of the Reformed. They should also bear in mind that the word "condemn" (*condemnare*) "was not used in that sense in the Augsburg Confession, the Apology, or in Luther's time generally." The words "condemn" (*damnare*) and "disapprove" *(improbare)* might be essentially synonymous, "yet the proper significance of the word 'condemn' connoted for the world a due process of law in which the accused is summoned, given a hearing, and then condemned if he is found to be in the wrong." [48] Finally, Christian charity should be made the norm in all conversations to avoid offense and going off on a tangent, of course only "without injury to the foundation of the truth." All changes in the formula presupposed as a matter of principle "that there is full agreement in the substance of the doctrine and that there is mutual understanding." [49]

After reading these instructions the seven theologians, among them Andreae, Chemnitz, and Selnecker, went to work on March 11, 1578. After four days the results were given in a "unanimous report," [50] which comes to the same conclusions with regard to the question of condemnations as Andreae's personal opinion. The theologians felt that there was no longer any leeway to permit the application of watered-down formulas without harm to the issue itself, especially since the formula had already been subscribed in many localities. The theologians emphasized that they had not the slightest desire to condemn. But the matter itself permitted them no concessions whatsoever. The situation had now become so pointed that "the fanaticism of the Sacramentarians (was) no longer a simple mistake, an error of good and teachable men, (but) a stiff-necked and evil blasphemy and the source of many horrible heresies," against which mere expressions of disapproval that obligated no one were no longer adequate.[51] There was all the less reason to complain about the condemnations since these were not, as in the Augsburg Confession, directed against persons but explicitly only against "false teaching." Therefore they were not condemning entire churches, "much less entire kingdoms." In Article X of the Augsburg Confession the "disapprove" sufficed because at that time the "wretched controversy had not yet progressed so far and there was still good reason to hope that the opponents, or Sacramentarians, would not further promote their heresy." Now, however, a moderation of the condemnations could only achieve the result that the false teachers would "construe it not only to the disparagement and disregard of our confession but to their own advantage." [52] Also their agreeing to consider the English proposals of union would only result in the spread of Calvinism. In this connection they expressly noted that the "foreign churches had openly and repeatedly and harshly condemned" the Lutherans and their teachings and had "never consulted with them about it." They could therefore not blame the Lutherans if they on their part sought to protect themselves and their churches by means of condemnations against the dangers of false doctrine.[53]

Neither the Saxon counselors nor the elector would or could offer objections to these statements made with such notable unanimity. Thus both the necessity of condemnations and the factualness and relevance of the formulations were acknowledged. The *Damnamus* was not intended to express a premature and unalterable separation from dissenting Lutheran estates, especially Hesse and Anhalt. This is demonstrated by the fact that the conversations with these people were continued right along. It soon became evident that one conviction was pitted against the other and no party was willing to give in. For this reason the question of condemnations receded more and more in these conversations. Landgrave William of Hesse tried to have all pending questions reserved for a general convention of the Evangelical estates. This plan was actively supported also by Queen Elizabeth because she believed this might be a new point of contact for her politics of union. However, the project failed, and the vacillating attitude of Elector Louis of the Palatinate was not the least reason for the failure. Andreae had to oppose it altogether, for it was easy to see that this plan could represent a grave danger to the effort toward concord if the plan would be realized before the Bergen Book had been subscribed. On the margin of a letter written by Andreae the Count Palatine John Casimir noted laconically and not without justification, "This is where the dog lies buried." [54]

Elector Louis was the prince whose cooperation in the concord seemed indispensable, and indeed inwardly he was already committed to it. Yet the *Damnamus* continued to be a serious obstacle to signing the formula. Not only did he consider the naming and condemnation of the "Synergists" a violation of the principle of declining to name names, but he continued to request that in the article on the Lord's Supper "the harsh word 'condemn' in the antithesis be either dropped altogether or at least toned down." [55] How were they to meet him halfway, since they could no longer permit doubts about the substantive propriety of the *Damnamus?* Again it was the versatile Andreae who knew what to do: At the Smalcald convention in October 1578, his suggestion was adopted that the doubts of the elector be given consideration in a preface to the formula and dispelled as much as possible. As for the *Damnamus,* the preface should make perfectly clear once again that it was directed against teachings, not against persons. The report of the Smalcald meeting referred also to the difficult problem of the Huguenots: "The proposed preface should especially and publicly testify that we take no pleasure in the butchery and brutal persecution of the poor Christians who observe such teachings, and we should clearly manifest our Christian love toward those poor persecuted Christians" — at the same time seeing to it that false teaching is condemned "with due seriousness," since they did not wish "to become responsible for any soul's damnation." [56] This sentence shows an unmistakable advance over the opinion Andreae had prepared for Elector August at the beginning of the year. While at that time he at least created the impression that the doctrinal differences excluded every intervention on behalf of the Huguenots, considerably more leeway was now permitted for joint action in common Evangelical concerns. At least there was more understanding of the fact that in France the whole Evangelical cause was endangered. To what extent Andreae was influenced exclusively by consideration for the elector of the Palatinate or in fact by a better insight need not be decided at this place. In any case it remains significant for the understanding of the *Damnamus* that Lutherans were now consciously counteracting the oversimplified alternative of the *Damnamus* on one side and the law of love on the other. They were now ready to be receptive simultaneously to the demands of love that were valid even apart from the doctrinal differences. It is ultimately due to the stubborn objections of Elector Louis that this question was treated in the preface of the Formula of Concord in a manner that sought to do justice to all criticisms of the *Damnamus* based on fact.

Notes to Chapter 11

[1] Hutter, foll. 29–31; Heppe, II, 250–54.

[2] Heppe, II, 274.

[3] Letter to the Wittenbergers, May 1569 (Hutter, fol. 27).

[4] Wagemann-Kolde, Article: "J. Andreae," RE, I, 503.

[5] Heppe, II, 342.

[6] Heppe, III, Supplements, pp. 3–75.

[7] Letter to Andreae, Oct. 4, 1573 *(Bekenntnisschriften,* XXXV).

[8] Cf. *Book of Concord,* pp. 503–508.

[9] Letter of July 14, 1576 (Heppe, III, 114).

[10] Cf. the summary in *Bekenntnisschriften,* XXXVIIIf.

[11] Convention of Moelln, Nov. 2, 1576 (Heppe, III, 132).

[12] Convention of Riddagshausen, Aug. 9, 1576 (Hutter, fol. 112; Heppe, III, 127).

[13] Excerpts in Heppe, III, 140–143, and *Bekenntnisschriften,* p. 841, n. 1.

[14] Heppe, III, 141f.

[15] Ibid., pp. 142f.

[16] Ibid., p. 142.

[17] Ibid., p. 148.

[18] Ibid., p. 185.

[19] Ibid., p. 183.

[20] Ibid., p. 154; cf. p. 178.

[21] Ibid., p. 158, n. 1.

[22] Letter of Feb. 13, 1577 (Heppe, III, Supplements, p. 402).

[23] Hutter, foll. 118–21.

[24] *Bekenntnisschriften,* p. 841, n. 1.

[25] Heppe, III, 215.

[26] Ibid., p. 261.

[27] Ibid., p. 256; *Bekenntnisschriften,* p. 841, n. 1.

[28] Heppe, III, 297.

[29] Milton Waldman *(Elizabeth, Queen of England* [London, 1933], p. 251) regards him as the real promoter of the plans of federation. "His political dream was a vast Protestant league embracing France, Germany, the Netherlands, and Scotland, to be organized by English diplomacy and supported by English money, with the utter extermination of papistry north of the Pyrenees and the Alps as the ultimate object."

[30] For this and the following cf. Heppe, IV, 5ff.; H. Leube, *Calvinismus und Luthertum im Zeitalter der Orthodoxie,* I (Leipzig, 1928), 23f.; above all, mention must be made of the great work by Conyers Read, *Mr. Secretary Walsingham and the Policy of Queen Elizabeth,* I (Oxford, 1925), 298ff., a work not used by Leube.

[31] In support of his plans Elizabeth had made 20,000 pounds sterling available and only the changed situation in France (peace between the Huguenots and the king) induced her not to forward this sum (Read, pp. 303f.).

[32] Heppe, IV, 15.

[33] Letter to King Frederick of Denmark, Oct. 29, 1577 (Hutter, fol. 141).

[34] K. F. Goeschel, *Die Concordienformel* (Leipzig, 1858), p. 238.

[35] Ibid., p. 239.

[36] Heppe, IV, 72ff.

[37] Thus there were repeated here the causes of the collapse of attempts at unification between England and the Smalcald League as early as the years 1535 – 40: The members of the Smalcald League placed unity in confession into the foreground, while in England political concerns predominated (cf. Fr. Prueser, *England und die Schmalkaldener, 1535 – 1540*, Leipzig, 1929).

[38] Leube, pp. 24f.

[39] Rud. Hospinian, *Concordia discors* (Geneva, 1678), pp. 143 – 46; Heppe, IV, 16ff.

[40] Hospinian, pp. 150 – 52.

[41] Leube, p. 27.

[42] From the letter of the Zurichers, June 24, 1579 (Hospinian, p. 146): ". . . they were afraid that this confession could hardly be approved by all the churches, unless in some places some things were deleted, added, changed, or at least explained more clearly: Lest those who hitherto had set forth clearly and simply their opinion on all articles of the Christian faith now seemed to be speaking more obscurely and yielding something to the opponents. Daily examples teach that obstinacy can be overcome with no moderation."

[43] Dated Feb. 13, 1578, Hutter, foll. 143 – 52.

[44] Ibid., fol. 150b.

[45] Ibid., foll. 150b f.

[46] Ibid., fol. 151b. The quotation from Luther is not from his Galatians commentary, 1531 – 35, on Gal. 6, as Andreae says. The nearest equivalent in meaning is a passage on Gal. 5:10 (WA 40 II, 51, 13).

[47] Hutter, foll. 165 – 67b.

[48] Ibid., fol. 167a.

[49] Ibid., fol. 167b.

[50] Ibid., foll. 168b – 73b.

[51] Ibid., fol. 171b.

[52] Ibid., fol. 172a.

[53] Ibid., fol. 173a.

[54] Heppe, IV, 75, n. 3.

[55] Letter to the Electors of Saxony and Brandenburg, Oct. 17, 1578 (Heppe, IV, 91, n. 1).

[56] Hutter, fol. 181b.

Chapter 12

The Controversy over Condemnations in Strasbourg

To one who reviews the entire epoch of the Formula of Concord it may seem strange that the discussions regarding condemnations are all of a church-political character. What was to be observed already for the period before 1561 becomes even more strongly apparent: The *Damnamus* extends into the sphere of the great religious and political decisions, yes, even beyond them into the area of world politics. Even where the contracting parties made conscious efforts to go behind the areas of church-political struggles for power and to keep the question of condemnations within the context of actual theological differences, the church-political encumbrance of the whole complex could no longer be excluded and in fact became a contributing factor in all decisions. This is quite true even of the statements in the Formula of Concord itself. There was, however, one place, though somewhat on the periphery of the main events, where a dialog regarding the *Damnamus* was held, in which the condemnation was consciously treated as a dogmatic problem. Though this contest, too, flared up because of church-political conflicts and was in part carried along by church-political aims and though it has been largely overlooked in the shadow of the work of concord, it occupies a unique place and dare not be slighted in evaluating the development of the problem of condemnations during this entire period.

The arena of this dispute was Strasbourg, where, following the era of Bucer's efforts at mediation, the pendulum had swung under the leadership of John Marbach toward a strict, militant Lutheranism. The disputants were John Sturm and John Pappus. The latter,[57] a compatriot of Marbach's from Lindau, had been called as professor of Hebrew to the Stras-

bourg academy in 1570 at the age of 21. Both at the school and
in his office as preacher-at-large he labored in the spirit of
Marbach. He had also received powerful impressions from
Flacius, who had found refuge in Strasbourg at that time.
Sturm,[58] who was more than 40 years older, embodied a segment
of old humanistic tradition. Born in the year of Luther's ordination (1507), he subsequently studied the classical authors of
antiquity as well as dialectics in Paris. Through contacts with the
circle of Margaret of Navarre and under the influence of Bucer's
writings he had become Evangelical. From that time he also
inclined toward Calvinism. This inclination manifestly had yet
another background, as the Lutheran polemics diligently
pointed out. By virtue of various diplomatic services Sturm
had amassed a considerable fortune and had placed it as a loan
at the disposal of the war chest of the Huguenot leader Condé.[59]
An open break between Strasbourg and the Reformed would
surely have endangered this investment. Moreover, the founding
and the modern organization of the Strasbourg academy, which
had numbered also Bucer, Capito, and Calvin among its teachers, had made Sturm famous throughout Europe and secured
him a prominent place in the history of education.

The prelude to the dispute was a controversy over the
Lutheran concord. In August 1577, Duke Louis of Wuerttemberg sent a copy of the Bergen Book to Strasbourg and soon
thereafter delegated his court preacher, Lucas Osiander,
to invite the Strasbourgers to sign the formula. While the
city's clergy soon decided in favor of the formula, the city
government delayed its answer. Finally, under date of May
23, 1578, a letter was sent to the duke. The letter's involved
presentation amounted to a rejection of the effort at concord.[60]
It is significant that the aversion to the *Damnamus* played
a leading role in the rejection of the formula. It is true that
they claimed to be in substantial agreement with the aim of
the new formula and for that reason regarded a special subscription as superfluous. At the same time, the men of Strasbourg must have realized that this position was hardly convincing. Therefore they formulated in even greater detail
what they regarded as an impossible request, namely the
idea that "by our opinion and our subscription we should cut
off all those churches and their members who are not ready to

see eye to eye with us in all points and by such isolation to throw them as booty to the dreadful tyranny of the true hereditary enemy of the most holy merit of Christ." Interpreting the *Damnamus* in this way, the city government acted quite consistently in also appealing to church history in support of its rejection: They were aware of the fact "that in the churches, as history reports, there frequently arose differences among the old fathers in matters of religion that could not always be resolved, but nevertheless they tolerated and loved one another in a Christian way and did not at once condemn one another as unfruitful members." They contended furthermore that approval of the Formula of Concord would place the city into an embarrassing situation over against the Huguenots.

The theologians of Strasbourg were not minded to accept this attitude of their government. With a sure touch Pappus had pointed up the critical area of the differences in a series of 68 theses for debate "on the subject of Christian love," which he published as early as March 1578, even before the city's letter to the duke. These theses became the starting point of embittered arguments between Sturm and Pappus, in which the most disparate motives were intertwined—all the way from purely personal animosity, in which the difference in age may have played a part, through concerns about jurisdiction, which had already previously led to serious friction, to purely church-political interests.[61] Finally a literary feud developed which had hardly an equal in extent and intensity, even in an age that already had more than its share of polemics. At least 30 polemical writings appeared during the short period from 1578 to 1581, roughly 15 from each side, among them at least 11 written by Sturm himself and 7 by Pappus.[62] Their supporters claimed responsibility for the remainder. Today it is impossible, even for external reasons, to trace the highly tangled course of these disputations in all stages. Since the problem of condemnations was soon overshadowed and pushed aside by other issues, not much could be gained for this area of study from an analysis of all the polemical writings.

The 68 theses of Pappus that started the battle may be regarded as the most significant piece of the whole argument.[63] They deserve special attention because they draw the *Damnamus* explicitly into the light of "Christian charity." This was a definition of the issue that had hitherto appeared only in the form that on the one hand the opponents of condemnations exploited the law of love in a one-sided way against the *Damnamus*, while on the other hand the defenders of the *Damnamus* either were content to demonstrate that the two were compatible or that in matters of faith charity could not be the most important consideration. Now Pappus went a step farther, not only in recognizing the tension between condemnation and brotherly love as a problem at all, but especially in following the course he did. He was interested in transcending the tensions between the two aspects and in placing them in a positive relation to each other. The two chief questions around which the theses revolved give evidence of this special concern at once: "(1) Whether it is contrary to Christian charity to fight such false teachings as conflict with the Word of God and (2) Whether it is contrary to charity publicly to renounce those churches which stubbornly defend such false teachings." [64] The first question takes the *Damnamus* in its basic significance, as delimitation against false doctrine (in the definition the "foundation of faith" plays a role here too: "To condemn false doctrines is nothing else than to segregate the true position from the false position, which undermines the ground of faith").[65] The second question aims at the application and at the church-political conclusions.

That the *Damnamus* does not violate the law of love is, first, demonstrated indirectly. According to the Scriptures the church has the task of reproving the gainsayers. Love, however, nowhere abrogates an office and hence cannot be in opposition to the church's office of reproof. Furthermore, the condemnation is necessary for the sake of the certainty of faith, for thesis and antithesis must "illumine" each other. But neither does love suspend the certainty of faith and for this reason, too, it is compatible with condemnation. Pappus was not content with that. He also attempted to demonstrate the positive relationship between the law of love and the *Damnamus*. Christian love is a "disciplined" love *(ordinata)*. Hence all depends on *how* love is practiced. That is to say, the love to the brother must never supersede the love to God and His truth, which determines the proper application of the condemnation of false teachings. In case there is a conflict, it will be "safer to permit an offense than that the truth is not defended or the false teachings are not refuted." [66] Beyond this it must be seen that the condemnation — to the extent that it is really based on the Word of God — is the highest service of love to the erring themselves. One must, of course, distinguish sharply between carnal passion and a genuine zeal for the truth. For the sake of love the true servants of the church must both earnestly condemn the false teachers and have sympathy for those whose false teachings they condemn. This double obligation rests on all servants of the Word everywhere and at all times. Whoever says that only God may condemn is not taking the ministry seriously as the office of the Word of God. Whoever promises peace to the church without condemning false doctrine is asking the sheep to turn the dogs over to the wolves, because the dogs are the authors of the disunity between the sheep and the wolves.[67]

The second part of the theses deals with the necessity of the "public confession" against the false teachers. It begins by asserting that the condemnation is not merely a concern of the theologians but a function of the whole church. For the sake of the present and future members of the church, but no less for the sake of the false teachers themselves, i. e., so as not to strengthen them in their delusions, all doubts concerning doctrine must be excluded. But this can be done only by distinguishing clearly in the public confession between truth and error — from which it follows, incidentally, that the church's confessions may be expanded and may require expansion.[68] For the question of the public confession, too, the primary point of view is a positive one, namely the glory of God. "The public confession proclaims the glory of God and places it — according to the First Commandment — above the neighbor and even above itself."[69]

If we attempt to survey the situation in an orderly way and to comprehend the countertheses produced by Sturm, first in private negotiation and then in printed polemical writings, we get the following picture: [70] For the first, Sturm insisted that in his opinion Pappus had violated the academic statutes. Sturm's critique of the theses of Pappus proceeded in the first instance from formal, Scholastic points of view. Without much trouble Pappus could refute such objections.[71] In the discussion of the issue itself Sturm devoted the most space to church-political and historical arguments. It is clear what he was after: At all costs he would like to keep the two dissenting parties in Strasbourg — the government and the college on one side and the clergy on the other — from reaching an agreement in favor of the Bergen Book. He felt that the *Damnamus* must be dropped, not so much for theological reasons as for the sake of the church-political implications (as he saw them!). He was still living in the age of Bucer and the *Tetrapolitana* and would have liked to see the Strasbourg church structure permanently oriented, as formerly, toward Switzerland rather than toward the Lutheran North and East. At the same time he mourned the failure of the great plans of a pan-Evangelical federation, in the promotion of which he had once cooperated.[72] He therefore saw in the theses of Pappus an unbearable affront to those imperial estates that resented the *Damnamus* of the Bergen Book. He even discovered that Pappus had done injury to the honor of the Augsburg Confession — of course he had the *Variata* in mind.[73] Above all he tried to establish the *Tetrapolitana,* which contained no specific condemnations, as the permanently valid primary confession of Strasbourg, though he could hardly have failed to realize that he was fighting for a lost cause. Too much had happened between the Lutherans and the Reformed since 1530 to make a continued adherence to the old party symbol possible. Besides, as an opinion of the Strasbourg theologians noted,[74] the Zwinglians had meanwhile adopted the *Tetrapolitana* as a legitimate expression of their faith. Sturm's frank admission that he had not even read the Bergen Book could likewise do nothing to enhance his position.[75]

Much the same is true of the historical proof that Sturm adduced and that lay fully in the area of Reformed polemics. All his proof attempted to demonstrate that the differences between the Lutherans and the Reformed were not founded in the historical development but were rather provoked by Lutheran fanaticism. Luther, Melanchthon, Bucer, and Calvin were all interpreted at the level of the Wittenberg Concord as understood by the Swiss. This was not too difficult in the case of Bucer and Melanchthon in view of their uncertainty in the doctrine of the Lord's Supper. Pappus on his part, attempting to cite those two as star witnesses for his views,[76] could do so with no less and no more propriety than Sturm. Furthermore, like the later Lutheran polemicists, Pappus fell into the danger of reconstructing history in his way no less one-sidedly than

Sturm and the Reformed were doing. Still, he was fully justified in appealing to the fact that the Melanchthon of the Augsburg Confession had made no dogmatic concessions whatever
to the Reformed, though he may have changed his opinion
later.[77]

From this debate one may already gain the impression
that Sturm was evading a substantive-theological discussion of
the theses of Pappus — perhaps in the knowledge, though not
admitted, that the issue about which Pappus was concerned
must in its deepest dimensions remain foreign to his thinking.
Sturm did concede that the condemnation of false teaching
cannot be entirely avoided in the church, but he strove all the
more zealously to assign the application of this truth as far as
possible to an unreal place far away. He held that in principle
only God Himself may pronounce a *Damnamus*. How could men
presume to make decisions concerning the eternal welfare of
false teachers, how could they sit in judgment on the conscience
of others before such a judgment had become manifest to the
Holy Spirit? [78] In reply Pappus could point out that this was
imputing a significance to the *Damnamus* that it did not have at
all (this leads to a definition of which more will be said later).
No less dubious would be another of Sturm's objections by
means of which he likewise hoped to make every practical
application of the *Damnamus* by its users illusory, namely, that
the court of jurisdiction which pronounced the *Damnamus* could
in no respect lay itself open to criticism and rebuke. This was
easily answered by pointing out that heretics, just because they
are heretics, would always find something to criticize in the
church and its teachings. They were simply like that criminal
in the fable who considered no tree good enough for his hanging.

Lastly, Sturm felt he must set up another condition for the
users of the condemnation, namely the well-known demand
that they could not be accusers and judges at the same time, and
this demand, too, was obviously designed to make the *Damnamus* impossible in practice.[79] However, this call for impartial
objectivity, born of a genuinely humanistic spirit and once
urged by Erasmus in defense of Luther, must at once raise the
counterquestion: In the central issues of doctrine is there such
a thing as standing above parties? Is not neutrality in the battle
for truth already equivalent to treason?

Also with regard to the method of condemnations Sturm

was out to undermine their practical application by inserting numerous retarding features. He would prefer to see the time of condemnation postponed to Judgment Day. At the very least the *Damnamus* against the Reformed should be deferred to that much-discussed general council of Evangelicals — something that Pappus, like his partisans, could regard as "useful," but neither as feasible at the time nor as absolutely necessary, judging by examples from the Scriptures and the practice of the ancient church.[80] For Pappus, too, it was self-evident that condemnations could not be uttered frivolously and without due deliberation but only, as Sturm had demanded, "for proper cause, in a good manner, not arbitrarily at any time, not against anybody, and not prematurely." Pappus established the good Lutheran rule that the "condemnation" itself must be preceded by the "examination, refutation, and admonition." Sturm had simply extended the same procedure by calling for seven distinct steps: "Prayer" for purity of heart; "grasp of the entire controversy"; an "evaluation" of both lines of argument; a "distinction" between true and false, true and half-true (Pappus subsumes these four points under "examination"); further, "refutation" from the testimony of Scripture and the fathers (Pappus will admit the latter only to the extent that they conform to Scripture); "admonition on the part of the churches"; "synod" and "condemnation." [81] Here, too, Sturm's real concern is unmistakable: Not only a cautious application of the *Damnamus* is to be guaranteed, but also the detailed apparatus of preliminary steps and presuppositions is to serve as the instrument of a well-planned delaying tactic and as such is to hamstring the *Damnamus* itself.

A similar situation obtains in the distinctions demanded by Sturm with regard to the recipients of the *Damnamus*. Pappus, too, did not intend the *Damnamus* to strike all who think otherwise indiscriminately and routinely. Again and again he had to defend himself against the charge that he was after a "condemnation of persons," i. e., branding all who believe otherwise as "children of the devil," and hence the French Christians as "martyrs of the devil." [82] As a matter of fact, so he himself said, he was moving the "judgment of doctrines" very clearly into the foreground.[83] Also the attitude of the Strasbourg church toward the persecuted French Protestants had sufficiently demonstrated that it was possible to condemn the teachings and manifest all love and kindness to the erring at the same time.[84] Thus Pappus, too, decisively favored consideration for the persons, just so the *Damnamus* against false teachings was not surrendered in the process. He well knew that even consideration for the persons may have its limits, namely when the false teachers behaved "impenitently" and "stubbornly." "Errors must be condemned, that is, refuted and rejected," as he explained his concept of condemnation (he explicitly declared *damnare* and *improbare* "synonymous"); [85] "the erring must not be condemned, that is, given over to the devil, but as long as they live, we must hope the best for them, unless they show open signs of impenitence and stubbornness. When they are dead, they must be left to the judgment of God." [86] In this connection Sturm quite naturally cited the parable of the tares, especially Matt. 13:30. Pappus countered by offering a different explanation. The "weeds" that should be permitted to grow do not refer to the protagonists of "false doctrines" but to people of "bad habits." And even though the "weeds" were to be construed with reference to "false doctrine," this did not yet prove that the servants were to be equated with the "ministers of the church." [87]

We may pass over other charges that were commonly raised in the polemics of the time and that Sturm also raised against Pappus. That the Lutherans, for example, desired to consign whole churches with all their members to the devil, or that the *Damnamus* aimed solely at the surrender of false teachers to the civil courts or even at the bloody persecution of Christian brethren, such charges were no more convincing here than elsewhere. More significant is a last objection of Sturm's, which shows more than others how deeply his opposition to the *Damnamus* was rooted in humanistic ways of thinking and how ill-equipped he was basically to speak to the point. He believed that one might think objectively as he wished about the *Damnamus*, but in any case the present threatening situation of the church as a whole did not permit speaking about it as Pappus was doing in his theses.[88] Pappus in turn could hear in this objection nothing but the voice of an extremely dangerous "political shrewdness." [89] Had not the church found herself in even greater peril at Augsburg? Yet there was no hesitation at that time to condemn false doctrine. Moreover, it was now not only a question whether the Reformed errors should be condemned or not, but in principle whether for the sake of "public tranquility" everybody could be free to believe as he chose.[90] It was no accident that this area of inquiry called to mind how Luther had once brought the *Damnamus* into relationship with the church's "teaching authority" in opposition to the Strasbourgers. Only now there might be more danger than in 1525 that the doctrine of the church was no longer understood as the "living voice of the Gospel" but rather as a rigid law of teaching, especially since at this point Pappus was already in danger of moving away from Luther's distinction between erring faith and erroneous teaching.[91]

Yet even this reservation changes nothing in the impression that Sturm was really not the man capable of grasping fully the theological concerns of Pappus. Sturm indeed wished to be regarded as a Lutheran (it is a peculiarity of this dialog in Strasbourg regarding condemnations that as an intra-Lutheran debate it unveils the full dimensions of the problem). He could emphasize that he wanted to assert nothing contrary to the Augsburg Confession.[92] Even though he believed that the Reformed mistakes did not basically involve "true errors, conflicting truly with the true foundation of faith," he certainly did not wish to be counted among the Reformed. What drove him into the argument was not a firmly founded conviction regarding the material rightness of those against whom the Lutheran *Damnamus* was directed, but on the contrary it was an "indifferentism" to which, for example, the "oral reception" could appear as irrelevant for the essence of the Lord's Supper as two hairs plucked from the tail of a horse would be for the beauty of the animal.[93] The Lutherans could hardly be blamed for recalling certain items to memory: Was it not precisely from Strasbourg that they had heard similar voices years ago? Bucer had once asserted that "the dispute was only a matter of words."[94] From Strasbourg, too, Calvin had brought along his conviction, expressed in his brief essay on the Lord's Supper, that the differences in the doctrine of the Lord's Supper were not very grave.[95] And finally, if it was really true, as Sturm had allegedly testified himself, that for more than 20 years he had neither heard a sermon nor received the Holy Communion,[96] the Lutheran embitterment

against this "Lucianic wrangler" and "atheologist" is quite
understandable.

The real nub of these accusations is clearly the fact that
Sturm's "Lutheranism" was domiciled less with Luther than
with Erasmus. Not without reason Sturm had expressed the
opinion to Pappus that Erasmus with his conciliatory manner
had weakened the authority of the pope far more effectively
than Luther.[97] It is in fact quite patently the spirit of Erasmus
that asserts itself in the whole fight with Pappus. The suspicion
of all "positive statements," fear of "unrest" and the high value
placed on "tranquility," the tendency to pass over certain points
of doctrine for reasons of expediency, and finally the exploita-
tion of the law of love in opposition to the obligation to doctrinal
truth — everything that Luther had already criticized in Erasmus
also characterized Sturm in his attitude toward the *Damnamus*.
On the basis of such premises the concern that moved his opponents to defend the *Damnamus* must indeed have remained
foreign to his thinking. Their battle for the truth and purity
of doctrine could only look to him like inane squabbling that
probably served merely as a front for church-political maneu-
vering. In the course of the discussion he therefore did everything he could to draw the debate into the area of church politics
(and to a large degree he was successful). It apparently bothered
him very little that the unrestrained, apodictic manner of his
polemics could hardly promote his goals. In this respect there
was left in him scarcely a trace of the Erasmian spirit of moderation. The lack of all restraint in his polemics finally became a
cause for his dismissal in December 1581 and thus for the victory
of the opposition. It should not be surprising that in this era of
militant theology the opponents on their part were not sparing
with their use of invective. The fact remains that through later
researches about Pappus it was established that he fought "undoubtedly with far greater circumspection" than the "rector
who was old in years but young in impetuosity." [98]

The ecclesiastical victory of the strict Lutheran party in
Strasbourg did not mean that the new approach to the question
of condemnations had led to an exhaustive treatment of all the
issues raised or even to valid decisions. There were too many
overtones and interfering noises to permit the clear keynote of
the 68 theses to assert itself permanently. In any case Pappus,

as perhaps no one else since Luther, had recognized the tension between truth and love as a focal point of the question of condemnations and, more important, he had resisted the temptation to resolve this tension one-sidedly in one direction or the other. He was closer to the New Testament concept of "speaking the truth in love" than his opponents who pleaded for a pragmatic tolerance. Probably Pappus was also closer to this concept than most of his cohorts. From this point of view it may be regretted that his attempted correlation of Christian charity and of condemnation could not be made productive any more for the formulations of the Formula of Concord. Yet in Strasbourg it had been made plain once again that a "tolerance" achieved at the price of indifference toward the central questions of the faith could hold no promise in the church, however enticing the possibilities suggested by such a course might be. In the direction of this insight must be sought the abiding significance of the formulations with which the Formula of Concord brought this half century of the controversy regarding the *Damnamus* to a close.

Notes to Chapter 12

[57] K. Hackenschmidt, "Joh. Pappus," RE, XIV, 654–57; W. Horning, *Dr. Johann Pappus*, Strasbourg, 1891; J. Adam, *Evangelische Kirchengeschichte der Stadt Strassburg* (Strasbourg, 1922), pp. 339f.

[58] C. Schmidt and J. Ficker, "Joh. Sturm " RE, XIX, 109–13; Hackenschmidt, pp. 655f.; Adam, pp. 221ff.

[59] Hackenschmidt, p. 655. See also the report of the Strasbourg clerical ministerium concerning the dismissal of Sturm from office, Hutter, fol. 271b.

[60] Reprinted in Heppe, III, 316ff.

[61] The various phases of the controversy are presented by Horning, pp. 38–78, Hackenschmidt, pp. 655f., and Adam, pp. 343–50. Some details also in Hospinian, pp. 230ff., 315f., 366ff.

[62] Overviews in Salig, I, 453ff., and Feuerlin-Riederer, *Bibliotheca Symbolica Evangelica Lutherana* (Nuremberg, 1768), pp. 199ff., supplement each other in some points.

[63] German text in Horning, pp. 42–47. The Latin text was not available.

[64] Horning, pp. 42f.

[65] Ibid., p. 43.

[66] Ibid., p. 44.

[67] Ibid., p. 45.

[68] Ibid., p. 47.

[69] Ibid., p. 46.

[70] Sturm's *Antipappi* were not available. However, his objections are reproduced and treated extensively in the *Defensio secunda* of Pappus *(de caritate et condemnatione Christiana)* (in: *Defensiones duae, quibus D. Joannis*

Sturmii Rectoris Antipappis duobus respondetur [Tuebingen, 1580], pp. 9–80); also in the anonymous writing *Spongia Laonici Antisturmii* (Tuebingen, 1580). I have also made use of the excerpts from Sturm's writings as published in Schluesselburg *(Theologiae Calvinistarum libri tres* [Frankfort a/M, 1594]), III, foll. 15ff., and Hutter, foll. 122b, 203bff.; Hospinian, pp. 230ff.; Horning, pp. 48ff.

71 *Defensio,* pp. 3–8.

72 He had corresponded with Walsingham concerning the English plans (Read, 1, 299, n. 2).

73 Horning, p. 53.

74 Adam, p. 346.

75 Horning, p. 53.

76 *Defensio,* pp. 20–54; cf. also *Spongia,* pp. 51ff.

77 *Defensio,* p. 43.

78 Ibid., p. 66.

79 *Spongia,* pp. 37–39.

80 *Defensio,* pp. 65f., 119ff.; *Spongia,* pp. 39–45.

81 *Defensio,* pp. 63f.

82 Ibid., p. 68.

83 Ibid., p. 67.

84 Ibid., p. 68 ("it is possible to condemn teachings while at the same time showing every kindness and gentleness and love to the erring").

85 Ibid., p. 69.

86 Ibid., pp. 53f. Similarly and in conjunction with a delimitation against the anathema: "Condemnation with anathema pertains to the erring, something about which I do not argue. Condemnation in a simple sense, that is, as disapproval and rejection, pertains to errors, to genuine errors which actually, not seemingly, conflict with the Word of God and undermine the foundation of faith" (p. 62).

87 Ibid., pp. 68f.

88 *Spongia,* pp. 47–51.

89 *Defensio,* p. 55.

90 Ibid., p. 54 ("Many even demand this that no error whatever, even one that they themselves might regard as an error, even if it actually conflicts with the Word of God, even if it undermines the foundation of faith,—no error whatever, I say, should be condemned. But for the sake of public peace each one should be free to believe what he wants without the reproof of any one, even of the minister of the church).

91 See above, pp. 69–70.

92 Schluesselburg, III, fol. 17b.

93 Ibid., fol. 20a. The comparison probably stems from Beza. Cf. the allusion in FC, SD, VII, 67, Book of Concord, pp. 582f.

94 Sasse, pp. 155f. W. Koehler, *Religionsgespraech zu Marburg,* remarks, p. 22: "Bucer averred that the difference regarding the Lord's Supper did not touch 'the summary of faith,' which is, 'that we are all nothing and that God desires to make us holy and blessed through Christ alone'—Erasmus of Rotterdam and the Stoa suggested this relativization."

95 *Petit traicte de la saincte cene* (1541), CR 33, 460.

96 Hutter, fol. 203b; Schluesselburg, III, fol. 15a; Gustav Frank, *Geschichte der protestantischen Theologie,* I (1862), 267.

97 Schuesselburg, III, fol. 19.

98 Hackenschmidt, p. 656.—The fact that Heppe shows no understanding of the "Lutheran agitators" can bear no weight (III, 321).

Chapter 13

The Formula of Concord and the Damnamus

The preparation of the preface of the Formula of Concord afforded the fathers of the concord the last opportunity for a thorough clarification of the pro and con of condemnations. The work began with two drafts by Andreae in December 1578 and extended through a variety of complicated discussions into the summer of the following year.[99] Even at the concluding deliberations in Heidelberg (end of July 1579) it was still very difficult to reach final agreement with Elector Louis. Some of these difficulties are reflected in Andreae's report to Elector August: "The devil was not easily driven out of this place. For that reason we feel Christian sympathy for the pious elector who has the Christian and proper spirit, but, alas, experiences many, many obstacles and truly can prevail only by the power of God."[100] When the elector finally signed the preface, he had nevertheless succeeded in having several changes made, among them the deletion of a lengthy paragraph in the section on condemnations, which had been designed to prove that a general council of Evangelicals was both unnecessary and impossible. But he was unable to change the basic thrust of the entire section.

Duke Julius of Brunswick-Wolfenbuettel was more successful with his proposed corrections, which were incorporated at least in part even after the first publication of the preface. The duke, who had hitherto been a zealous promoter and the chief financial supporter of the concord, was not able to participate in the preliminaries of the preface because just at this time he had permitted one son to be consecrated as bishop of Halberstadt and another son to receive the tonsure. This step created consternation among all the Lutheran estates and led to a break with Chemnitz as well as to the duke's temporary isolation from the work of the concord. Not until the fall of 1579 could Julius get back into the undertaking, and now he came forward with proposals for changes in which once again the rigorous attitude in the question of condemnations that had become well-nigh traditional in Lower Saxony was given expression. The duke had let himself be inspired by Hesshusius, who had meanwhile exchanged his episcopal office in Prussia for a professor's chair in Helmstedt. And now, as radical as ever, he expressed the view that according to Christ's command in Matt. 7 God's threat applied not only to the "stiff-necked deceivers" but also to the "ingenuous" deceived.[101] Accordingly the duke expressed, along with several other suggested changes, his doubts about the treatment that had been given the question of condemnations in the preface. Unless there would be a condemnation also of those who erred from simplicity or ignorance, neither he nor other districts of Lower Saxony would sign the concord.[102] Upon Elector August's comment that they had never intended to exculpate the ingenuous completely, Hesshusius rejoined that love to "misled people" was always "inopportune" in matters of faith.[103] Finally the duke signed the preface anyway, after he had personally conferred with Andreae. He did, however, hold fast to two additions of which the one in the section on condemnations was included in the final form of the preface. Here the theologians are obligated "to remind even those who err ingenuously and ignorantly of the danger to their souls and warn them against it (Andreae substituted *warnen* for the stronger *verwarnen*), lest one blind person let himself be misled by another." [104] In this way the concern of the Lower Saxons was expressed with such restraint that even Elector Louis could be expected to approve the addition. Before he could bring himself to do so, further extended negotiations were required, which could not be brought to a successful conclusion by Andreae until early summer 1580. On June 25, 1580, exactly 50 years after the presentation of the Augsburg Confession, the completed Book of Concord could finally be made public.

As for the condemnations, the preface had changed nothing in the basic thrust already established in the Bergen Book. Yet the numerous discussions with the opponents and critics of the *Damnamus* had driven the fathers of the concord to rethink their position even more profoundly and thoroughly. Thus also this section in which the preface deals at length with the "condemnations" [105] adds several new features to the total picture (in the summary below, note points 6 and 7 of the first series and points 4 and 5 of the second series!) or underscores them where necessary. In the total development this clearly marks a further step forward both in the internal clarification of the problems surrounding the condemnations as well as in the external defense against misunderstanding. Together with the explanations of the antitheses, contained already in the Torgau Book and the Bergen Book,[106] this section affords an impressive testimony to the efforts of the Formula of Concord to steer a middle course between the "extremes of an unrestrained laxity and an egotistical rigor." [107] Clearly noticeable is the endeavor to steer clear of a dangerous one-sidedness and to do justice to both demands — on the one hand the firmness needed for the sake of the issue and on the other hand the moderation and caution required for the sake of love.

If we now attempt to coordinate the aspects subserving the first demand, we arrive at the following series:

The condemnation of false teaching is demanded:

1. By the Scriptures (Titus 1:9; Jer. 15:19; John 10: 12-16, 27); [108]
2. By the confessions of the ancient church and of the Reformation; [109]
3. For the sake of preserving "concord within the church"; [110] and here the errors that have arisen since the Interim are in principle on the same level with those condemned in the earlier confessions; [111]
4. For the sake of clearly establishing the positive doctrinal truth, which must be witnessed to the "contemporaries" and to "posterity"; [112]
5. For the purpose of preserving our own church from errors; [113]
6. For the purpose of warning "pious, innocent people" in the dissenting churches; [114]
7. As a witness against "stiff-necked proponents and blasphemers," where the condemnation is explicitly to strike not only the teachings but also the persons.[115]

The following points give expression to the necessary limits of condemnation:

1. The thesis must have priority over the antithesis in every case; the latter must serve the former. Already the structure of the individual articles indicates this. See also point 4 of the first series!

2. The distinction between "needless and unprofitable contentions" and "necessary controversy (dissension concerning articles of the Creed or the chief parts of our Christian doctrine)" is presupposed in all condemnations.[116] Here belongs also the statement that no church should condemn the other for the sake of "ceremonies not commanded by God." [117]

3. In the condemnations of the Formula of Concord there are no names of persons and no titles of books.[118]

4. The condemnation is not directed against "those persons who err ingenuously and who do not blaspheme the truth of the divine Word." [119]

5. Nor is it directed against "entire churches inside or outside the Holy Empire of the German Nation," [120] in which "one can find many pious, innocent people" whom the writers are still hoping to win.[121]

6. The condemnations are not to give occasion for any "persecution of poor, oppressed Christians" with whom "Christian charity causes us to have especial sympathy." [122]

Surveying all these statements in their double orientation, we are justified in saying that a high degree of clarity has been reached here. An evaluation of this fact in the framework of the total development of the question of condemnations will be discussed later. For the moment the two series are merely to illustrate the state of affairs that was created with regard to the problem of condemnations by the publication of the Book of Concord. How did the opponents of the condemnation come to grips with this state of affairs? They showed little interest in discovering the basic significance and intention of the *Damnamus* as it had been established or in doing justice to it. Rather, they saw in it — quite understandably — above all a church-political weapon aimed at them, the pregnant mark of the "egotistical harshness" characterizing the new Lutheran denomination. Their reaction corresponded in large measure to this assessment. Not all of them handled the matter as conveniently as King Frederick of Denmark, who was violently opposed to the concord. He simply banned the Book of Concord from his whole country and underscored this prohibition by means of a gesture about which he himself reported to Landgrave William of Hesse: "Because it is proper that the government should itself not lag behind its own laws, when our dear sister, the electress of Saxony, sent us two printed copies, so beautifully bound, we took them, as soon as we laid eyes on them, to a good fire in the fireplace and burned them." [123]

The German opponents of the Formula of Concord took the matter more seriously and engaged in a literary campaign. Neustadt on the Hardt, the intellectual metropolis of the Reformed Palatinate, became the headquarters of this opposition. Three of the four major Calvinistic or Crypto-Calvinistic writings against the Lutheran Book of Concord which were circulated in 1580 and 1581 were published in Neustadt. The most significant one, the so-called Neustadt Admonition,[124] written by Palatinate theologians, probably especially by Zacharias Ursinus, devotes a special chapter to the "unjust condemnation of our doctrine in the Book of Concord." [125] Two main arguments are advanced against the Lutheran *Damnamus:*

1. The Calvinistic doctrine, especially that of the Eucharist, is not heresy but is in harmony with the Scriptures, the ancient Creeds, and the Altered Augsburg Confession.
2. The condemnation does not rest, as it properly should, on an authoritative doctrinal decision of the church, which in turn would require confirmation obtained from a thorough and official examination of the alleged Calvinistic heresy. Instead of this, the Calvinists are being condemned without a hearing.

The preceding chapters of the Admonition served as proof for the first thesis. In them the writers believed they had demonstrated that the Calvinists were not "heretics" and hence not "worthy of the anathema." Not all who err in Christian doctrine are "heretics" — so the argument runs — but only those who entertain an error that militates against the "foundation of religion," that is, against the Decalog or the "articles of the Creed," or errors from which the destruction of a part of this "foundation" would follow.[126] All members of the church could err, "brothers" as well as real "heretics." They could also err in the same points—but not "in the same manner." Already in the earliest days of Christianity there were Christians who erred out of weakness (Rom. 14:4), yet they were judged to have "preserved the foundation" (1 Cor. 3:15) and not to have "disrupted the church" (Phil. 3:15). Even the twelve disciples erred in this sense at some points without having to be condemned as heretics because of their error.

Furthermore, with reference to the second thesis, the condemnation of heretics must include admonition of those concerned and a refutation of their error from the Scriptures, not only in private but also "in the public judgment and name of the church." The real heretics would then identify themselves by clinging stubbornly to the error even after repeated admonition and by disturbing the church through schism.[127] The "Bergen fathers" might rejoin that they were only repeating previously uttered condemnations. But the Calvinists did not feel themselves struck by these condemnations. They acknowledged the anathemas of the ancient church since these were based on a "completely just verdict of the church." But such a "legitimate and certain recognition and decision" had never been directed against Calvinistic teaching. Certainly the Lutherans could not qualify as "judges" since they were only one party to this dispute.[128] The Lutherans have good reason to fear a public and churchly treatment of the Calvinistic teachings because they know very well that the growing influence of the Calvinists throughout Europe could only hurt their cause. For that very reason the Calvinists preferred to rely on the Scripturally based increasing approval of their doctrine, rather than to acknowledge the antiscriptural condemnation pronounced by the Lutherans.

It is true, the Lutherans pointed to earlier religious colloquies and conventions at which the Calvinistic doctrine had been sufficiently aired. However, it was never a matter of "official and public judgments of the church," or of "being given a hearing for the purpose of investigating and deciding the issue." Also the negotiations ordered by the princes did not constitute "public assemblies of the church" but merely attempts at settling the controversies. At those conventions there had been neither genuine "doctrinal debates" nor genuine "condemnations." The Romanists and others indeed pressed for condemnation of the Calvinistic teaching. But the princes possessed enough "piety and wisdom" manfully to resist such attempts.

It is clear that the course of this Calvinistic defense coincides in large measure with the counterpolemics which the Zurichers once opposed to Luther's attacks. In both instances the real split was kindled not so much by the concept of the *Damnamus* as rather at the point where the individual doctrines—above all the doctrine of the Lord's Supper—diverged. In both instances those struck by the condemnation sought primarily to deny the substantive justification for the condemnation, and from this it follows as a matter of course that the authorization of the authors of the condemnation and their method of applying it were likewise questioned. The necessity and propriety of condemning false doctrine and its authors are questioned in principle neither in Zurich nor in Neustadt. The concept of heresy was in both cases so defined that the Lutherans, too, could approve it. Yet just at this point a further development is unmistakable: It is nothing new to derive the definition of heresy from the concept of the "foundation of religion." Luther had already indicated this relationship,[129] and the Formula of Concord had taken it over.[130] But it is striking that the foundation is now precisely circumscribed as to content and extent ("Decalog" and the "articles of the Creed"). This at once provides the possibility of developing more clearly than before the distinction between "heresy" and "error." At the same time there is the danger of a quantitative schematization.

On the whole the Lutherans had to assess the situation in basically the same way as a half century earlier. Just because they claimed to see in the Calvinistic as well as in the Zwinglian doctrine of the Lord's Supper an attack on the "foundation of the faith," they had to view it as providing the obligation for condemnation. What the men of Neustadt were able to say about the possibility of erring out of weakness the Lutherans could fully accept. They themselves had taken this possibility into account in the Formula of Concord. But they were unable to see how the proponents of the Zwinglian or Calvinistic doctrine of the Eucharist, with their massive and insulting polemics against the Lutheran "cannibalism" *(Sarkophagie)*, could be numbered among those who erred from weakness and simplicity.

The Calvinistic objections that revolve around the second main argument of the Admonition and above all concern the procedure of condemnation factually lose much weight over against the central difference in doctrine. Viewed purely in an external way, they do occupy a great deal of space in the Admonition, but it is probable that the determining factor was less a consideration of the theological issues than a very definite evaluation of the church-political situation, about which there will be more to say presently. The Lutheran counterpolemics had no great difficulties with this point. The Apology of the Formula of Concord, 1584, summarized what needed to be said: [131] They knew since the time of Luther that a valid condemnation of false teachings by no means always required the official decisions of a council. The Calvinists had implicitly acknowledged this to the extent that they themselves had condemned the errors of Rome, of the Anabaptists, the Schwenckfelders, and others. There was no dearth of documentation from the ancient church. Later on Hutter could also point out that in this connection Melanchthon had appealed to Gregory of Nazianzus in resisting the Flacians who were demanding a synod.[132] Thus according to the Lutheran view the principle must be upheld that false doctrine must be condemned wherever and whenever it arises. If the Calvinists thought they were being condemned without a hearing, the Lutherans reminded them of a whole series of religious colloquies, beginning at Marburg, 1529, in which particularly the opponents' doctrine of the Lord's Supper had been amply treated and shown to be false. Lastly, they might also remember that many Reformed theologians were not stingy with their condemnation of the Lutherans.

Conrad Schluesselburg, militant defender of orthodoxy in Rostock at the time of Flacius, who while superintendent in the diocese of Ratzeburg was the author of an apologetic manual, 1594, for discussions with the Reformed,[133] gave an entire chapter of his collection of sources the heading: "The Calvinists regard us as brothers, whom they nevertheless condemn as heretics, and they desire to enter into fellowship with us whom they are rabidly persecuting." [134] He adduced the example of the Frenchman Daneau (Danaeus), who appealed expressly to the model of combating heresy in the ancient church for his condemnation of the Lutherans and even defended the "condemnation of persons." [135] The manner in which Theodore Beza waged war on Lutheran "cannibalism" *(sarcophagia)* seemed to warrant the conclusion that he was condemning the Lutheran doctrine of the Eucharist. [136] The fact that at Montbéliard in 1586 Beza had refused the "right hand of fellowship and humanity" proffered by the Lutherans in spite of the doctrinal dissent could only strengthen this impression later on. [137] Lastly, the "warnings" which the Zurichers had included in their reply to Luther's "Brief Confession" of 1544 were not too far removed from a public *Damnamus*. [138] Hence we can well understand Schluesselburg's question: How does all of this make sense in view of the fact that the Calvinists elsewhere make so much of their desire to seek a fraternal relationship with the Lutherans?

It is true, the Calvinistic "condemning" that the Lutherans deplored — in distinction from the Lutheran *Damnamus* — moved entirely within the framework of theological polemics and therefore in an area where the warring parties conceded nothing to each other in embittered harshness and were hardly in a position to reproach each other. In the Reformed confessions there is no confessionally anchored *Damnamus* against the Lutheran teachings, although both the Zwinglian and the Calvinistic confessions do not otherwise hesitate to draw clear-cut limits against heresies. [139] The fact that the differences with the Lutherans, particularly in the doctrine of the Holy Communion, were regarded by the Reformed largely as less serious and less "fundamental" than was the case with the Lutherans may count as a first inner cause for the absence of a Reformed *Damnamus*. In this connection it is permissible also to think of that "pious and liberal relativism" which — alongside "a strictly factual dogmatic attitude that fears no consequences" — has been pointed out by Karl Barth as a characteristic of the early Reformed formulation of confessions. [140]

Thus on the part of the Reformed it was possible, where it seemed opportune and feasible, to be willing in all good conscience to travel farther on the same road with the Lutherans than the latter felt they could justify. The Reformed could also remain more open to irenic and unionistic endeavors than was possible for the Lutherans. But on the other hand this constantly led to the danger of an indifferentism that did not scruple to risk doctrinal truth for the sake of church-political and political considerations. That this danger was occasionally recognized as such also by the Reformed is demonstrated by the reserve of the Swiss over against the Frankfort convention of 1577 and their criticism of the far-reaching union plans of the Count Palatine John Casimir.[141]

Beyond this it was chiefly an exterior reason, namely the religio-political situation of the German Reformed, that did not permit them to isolate themselves from the Lutherans by means of a public *Damnamus*. As long as there had been no clarification of the question whether the Augsburg Confession mentioned in the Religious Peace of 1555 referred to the unaltered or the altered edition, they could still hope for a legal guarantee of their existence. The decisive question was whether they could succeed in disarming the condemnation expressed in 1530 in Article X. All hope of achieving this desired goal would have been destroyed if in this situation the Reformed had openly condemned the Lutheran churches. At the same time they would have seriously endangered their penetration of Lutheran territories, in which up to this time they had made considerable progress, openly or under cover. Their situation had become even more acute through the fact that the Formula of Concord made the explicit claim that the Lutherans were according exclusive recognition to the Augsburg Confession of 1530 with its condemnation of the Reformed doctrine of Communion, and that an acceptance of the Formula of Concord was completely out of the question for the Reformed. More than ever it must now be their strategy to claim and to demonstrate their basic doctrinal unity with the Lutherans — a task to which the Reformed irenic has since the end of the 16th century addressed itself with increasing vigor. A condemnation of Lutheran teachings would have been completely incompatible with these plans.

In view of this church-political dilemma of the Reformed it is understandable that their polemic must to a large extent talk past the actual concern that controlled the Lutheran *Damnamus*. More and more the accent shifted to the demonstration that the Lutheran *Damnamus* did them an injustice not only theologically but also church-politically and historically. Against this background we must also view the objections that were raised against the *Damnamus* in the Neustadt Admonition, as well as all other attempts to interpret the events of the past five decades in a sense that was tactically more favorable for the Calvinists, particularly with reference to the authenticity of the *Variata*. The history of the split between the Lutherans and the Zwinglians/Calvinists moves into the foreground of the polemical concern, and in the process violence is done to history again and again by both Reformed and Lutherans. "One is almost tempted to say that the historical polemic has outlasted the dogmatic polemic." [142] It is revealing that the first Calvinistic attack on the Formula of Concord, published as early as 1580 in Neustadt by the Nuremberg jurist Christopher Hardesheim under the pseudonym of Ambrosius Wolfius, did not concern itself so much with the theological points of difference as rather with the historical picture, not indeed without considerable distortion of historical truth. [143]

Here too, in the area of historical polemic, the Lutherans were not at a loss for answers. They could in any case point out that the Unaltered Augsburg Confession had never been repealed or replaced by the *Variata* and that the condemnation of the Zwinglian doctrine of the Lord's Supper retained its firm place in the confession of the Lutherans. Also the discussions about the authority of the original confession could be interpreted by the Lutherans in their own favor at least as much as the Calvinists tried to do.

For the consideration of these and all other apologetic questions that had become acute through the attacks on the Formula of Concord, the Saxon and Palatinate electors called together a commission of three men in 1581, consisting of Chemnitz, Selnecker, and Professor Timothy Kirchner of Heidelberg. The draft of an apology of the Formula of Concord, prepared by this commission, had already received very favorable reviews when the whole project was seriously jeopardized by a new eruption of the old intra-Lutheran tensions. Once again it was the radical group, represented by Lower Saxony, that raised its voice. Once again it was the question of condemnations that stood in the center of the debate. Other aspects were also involved, such as the personal animosity which Duke Julius of

Brunswick bore Chemnitz since the affair of the tonsure and which had brought him completely under the influence of the radical Helmstedt controversialist Hesshusius; furthermore, the desire of the duke for a general convention of all estates committed to the concord and also aversion to the doctrine of ubiquity allegedly supported in the apology. The differences became so rigid that a convention had to be assembled at Quedlinburg (January 1583) for the purpose of reaching a settlement. Besides the demand for a condemnation of the false teachers by name, the so-called hypothesis, the representatives of Brunswick even advanced the claim that "the formula of condemnation in the preface of the Book of Concord had been weakened," and had been interpreted "in the apology . . . directly contrary to the Word of God," since a distinction had been made between the "misled hearers" and the "false teachers." [144] This raised the question in all due form whether the Formula of Concord had proceeded too gently in its interpretation of the condemnation. The representatives of the elector energetically defended the position of the Formula of Concord: "Why should we without further ado and without any distinction condemn the poor hearers in the Zwinglian church who err ingenuously, are no blasphemers, and have not yet been instructed?" [145] They were determined to maintain the interpretation offered in the apology. "Heretic and heresy belong together and are conjoined, but not heresy and a sheep that has been led astray." [146] Manifestly the representatives of Brunswick could not prevail against this decisive affirmation of a thesis that had already been supported with all clarity by Luther. In any case the whole question was no longer mentioned in the final report of the convention.

The representatives of Brunswick were more successful with regard to the hypothesis. The final report of the convention at Quedlinburg established that "in addition to the theologians already mentioned in the hypothesis of the apology others should also be mentioned by name who had taught impure doctrine such as had been exposed in articles of the Christian Book of Concord that were in controversy." But one qualification should be made: "The hypothesis should not be treated in the schools or in the pulpit without necessity, but only when the extreme need and edification of the church and people of God demands it and when the wolf would presume to enter God's sheepfold and introduce false doctrine or when the books that contained such incorrect points had to be explained in the schools." [147] In this reservation the electoral theologians sought to preserve something of the restrained spirit of the preface of the Book of Concord. Yet the unconvincing character of the compromise could hardly be concealed in this way, and above all, it was and remained embarrassing that even after the publication of the Concordia a rigorism that could hardly be justified on the basis of the issues should lead to a renewed discord in the question of condemnations. However, we must not assign too much weight to these events. They ran their course in the train of decisions that had already been made and could no longer change anything in the principles established in the Formula of Concord.

Incidentally, it is noteworthy that the attitude of the Brunswick theologians made no headway in northern Germany either. A decade after the Quedlinburg debates the strict Lutheran Schluesselburg expressed himself as definitely opposed to every "condemnation of persons." He conceded that there were "pedantic and contentious disturbers of the peace" *(quidam ecclesiarum morosi et contentiosi turbatores)* who called the condemnation without "condemnation of persons" mere shadow-boxing *(skiomachia)*. They should be told that the condemnation of persons could in some cases help clarify the issue, but it was very questionable whether this ever promoted the welfare of the church. It would therefore be better to choose a procedure in which people were not needlessly offended, without, however, subtracting from the glory of God. In the final analysis one would have to be content with committing the persons to the judgment of God.[148]

Looking back on the long and tension-filled history of this conflict, we note that the statements of the definitive confession carry a special weight, and we should not try to dispose of them by regarding them as dictated by a church-political group that had gained control or by a theological school. Especially the last stage of the way, the period since the collapse of the church-politically based union endeavors, had called for the gravest kind of decisions. The intra-Lutheran differences, which were to a considerable extent differences in the question of condemnations, could indeed be bridged by the concord but only at the cost of having a part of the dissenting estates go over to Calvinism. At the same time the extension of the problem of condemnations into the area of international politics had given rise to new questions that subjected the work of unification to a severe test. Even in strict Lutheran circles it could not for a moment be overlooked that great dangers continued to threaten from Rome and that this threat had become worse because of the intra-Evangelical rifts. Events in France spoke an unmistakable language. It could be no easy matter for any of the princes and theologians committed to the concord to reject the advantages of a mighty Evangelical coalition because of theological differences — however dear their own territorial church organization may have been to them — and, instead of heeding the "call of the hour," continue to impede the seeming political necessities by means of their inconvenient *Damnamus.* Yet this is what they did, but certainly not for the sake of inconsequential theological speculations.

It will be quite helpful to point back to the time of the first tensions between Zurich and Wittenberg. The ways were parting already around 1524—25. The way of the Swiss led quite self-evidently in the direction of the alliance entered into with the South German cities and later with other partners, and this for the sake of the Gospel. No less consistently Luther's way led to the "self-confirmation" of the faith in the act of confessing and excluded an alliance "as long as this was encumbered by difference in the faith." [149] But was "the obedience of the subject to the imperial government," which paralyzed "political mobility," really the only impelling and obligating force here? [150] Or does not already the development of the next years and decades prove that Luther and his followers were not so far wrong — even against Philip of Hesse — when they saw, lurking behind this kind of Evangelical politics of alliance, the danger that the "faith must pay the costs"? [151] It is on account of this fear that the *Damnamus,* its symbol, is so hotly contested again and again, in Augsburg as in Naumburg, and fully in the battle for the concord. That is to say: It is matters of faith, it is the pure doctrine, which people see at stake and for the sake of which they cling to the *Damnamus,* quite apart from the fact that often enough an unchristian censoriousness and theological dogmatism make the verdict of condemnation serve their own ends.

It is all the more significant that in the Formula of Concord they sought consciously to avoid *both* dangers. They had experienced that the *Damnamus* could all too easily be wielded as a powerful weapon in the arena of church-political struggles for power. Against this, too, they had to secure themselves, though the battle for the "condemnation of persons" and then for the "hypothesis" may not have been as important as the battle for the validity of condemnations in general. To do justice to the decisions made by the Formula of Concord in the question of condemnations this second front must certainly be kept in view also, against whose "egotistical harshness" the confession is directed as much as against the "unrestrained laxity" of the other side.

But even in the era of the Formula of Concord the chief emphasis rested on the debates with the indifferentist front, which now extended from a part of the German Philippists to the queen of England and to Reformed groups. Again this opposition to the *Damnamus* was spurred on especially by church-political motives, motives that were individually of quite disparate orientation. Before the interests of dynastic and territorial power politics Zwingli's old idea of an alliance for the sake of the Gospel undoubtedly was dominant. His plan constantly received new nourishment from the danger threatening from Rome. In this perspective the *Damnamus* had to appear as the instrument of a disastrous intensification of the intra-Evangelical schism, a fact which threatened more and more to block the vision for the great concerns of Evangelical Christendom as a whole. Nevertheless, the defenders of the Lutheran concord were compelled to reject these arguments. They could not concede that a receptive attitude toward the far-ranging objectives of Evangelical church politics should be purchased at the price of half measures in questions of doctrine, and that meant for them disloyalty to the Gospel itself. Andreae himself, the originator of the concord, had at first come to grief through an attempt at "conciliation by means of generalities." He knew all the better that a forced "neutralizing of the contrasts" could produce no blessings. It was significant enough that even the Swiss had adopted a similar position over against the high-flying schemes of Count Palatine John Casimir.[152] The Lutherans could readily acknowledge the weight of the political considerations entertained by the opposing party. But they could not acknowledge that these considerations should weigh more heavily than the doctrinal differences that called for a *Damnamus*. They were not, like the English queen, debating about a "trivial variety of opinions in one point or another," but they were fighting for the very foundation of the faith. The example of a man like Sturm in a very impressive way confirmed how fatefully great political ideas and blindness for the essentials of the faith could affect each other. It was this kind of indifferentism that made the Lutherans suspicious of all church politics reaching beyond the Lutheran area itself, politics that could even lead to the alternative of either alliance or confession, and against which they felt they must defend the *Damnamus* above all. On this line their situation had remained unchanged since 1561, except that now the concord had given them firmer ground to stand on. What could still appear as church-political partisan opinion 20 years before was now supported by the consensus of the overwhelming majority of Lutherans who were anchored in the confession.

This fact deserves to be noted also with regard to the inner history of the problem of condemnations. The condemnations had been pronounced already in the Augsburg Confession, and the Formula of Concord would not and could not change or even make superfluous the old primary Evangelical confession in this point any more than in the others. The significance of the Formula of Concord lies, however, in this that it does not simply repeat the *Damnamus* but also clarifies and interprets it. Thus not only the bare *Damnamus* but also its interpretation as now provided became a part of the confessional content. And this is an interpretation that takes up and utilizes the whole essential progress made in the debates surrounding the *Damnamus*. The separate stages of the way that led to this goal have shown what obstacles had to be overcome and what dangers had to be encountered. The result does credit to the fathers of the concord who, without evading the questions raised by the critiques, sought and found a way between the extremes and succeeded in large measure to preserve unabridged the firmness that was demanded for the sake of the cause, without, however, losing the clear vision for the limits of the *Damnamus*. In this bipolarity of firmness and caution they were able to preserve for the Lutheran Church an essential result of Luther's thinking about the condemnation, a result that in the meantime had been endangered by the "indifferent" opponents of the *Damnamus* as well as by the promoters of a "condemnation of persons."

It must, however, not be overlooked that the statements regarding the *Damnamus* — like the entire confession — are not designed to serve the cause of systematic theology, but bear an "historico-thetical" character.[153] It is not their intention exhaustively to clarify the theological problem of the condemnation. Rather, in the battle for the integrity of doctrine they have become and have grown to be, as it were, a function of the church's self-protection, and it should not be surprising that they still bear in themselves the traces of this becoming and this growing. In the genetic history of the problem of condemnations they represent only one stage, a stage in which a significant end product is obtained from a long and stirring prehistory. The problems involved in the condemnation are seen more clearly and handled more circumspectly than ever before. Yet the Formula of Concord did not desire and was not able to make the claim that it had solved all the problems of the *Damnamus*. Questions remained unanswered that had arisen already during the years of controversy. Yes, the very decisions the confession formulated gave rise to questions with which posterity must deal — questions whose thorough treatment would lead beyond the framework of an historical investigation and can here be indicated only by way of conclusion.

First of all, there is the question of authority. Both in the Formula of Concord and in the Augsburg Confession it is the churches, that is to say, it is the church that is claimed as the subject of the *Damnamus*. As stated above, it was a superiority that distinguished the Formula of Concord and placed it above many opinions, memoranda, and private confessions of the past years of conflict — not only a church-political and tactical advantage — namely, that its condemnations as well as the accompanying explanation did not depend on the word of two or three theological witnesses but were supported by the consensus of the majority in the Lutheran Church. The rather unconvincing objection of the opponents that in fact only the six authors of the Bergen Book had imposed their theological opinions on the churches may here be disregarded. But what about Luther's old principle that every one by virtue of his "power" as a baptized Christian was permitted to judge all doctrine and also pronounce the *Damnamus*, a principle to which the Lutherans appealed again and again when they were called upon to resist the Calvinistic pressure for a synod? How, for example, should the simple Christian see through the difficult backgrounds of the controversy over Communion? Does not the *Damnamus* after all now threaten to become the business of a few militant theologians? Here indisputably lay an element of danger that threatened the credibility of the *Damnamus*, a danger that had asserted itself already in the days of Flacius and that was to result three quarters of a century later in having orthodox theologians develop an entire system of theological censorship.[154]

Also with respect to those against whom the *Damnamus* was directed some questions remain unanswered. On the whole the fathers of the concord had successfully resisted the insistence on "condemnation of persons." It may even be said that in the Formula of Concord the whole problem of the condemnation of false teachings and false teachers was treated in a way that is a model of clarity and restraint. They took the position in principle that doctrines were to be condemned but neither "persons who err ingenuously" nor entire churches. However, they also knew just as well that the really "stiff-necked teachers and blasphemers" could not remain unaffected by the condemnation even as persons. Rather, the *Damnamus* was pronounced over them as a sign that by virtue of their own decision they are on the wrong way (though the exact definition of "stubbornness" must always remain an uncertain factor).[155] It is noteworthy that Andreae was convinced he had moved a step forward in this point even as compared with the Augsburg Confession.[156] Luther's distinction between erring faith and erroneous teaching was not explicitly adopted but was preserved as to its sense when the confession declared that it did not want the "stiff-necked teachers" placed on the same level with the "simple sheep." Also the distinction between "unnecessary wrangling" and "necessary controversy" could be very useful in this connection. This very distinction, however, contains a new question: If "necessary controversy" refers to what "concerns the articles of the Creed or the most important chief parts of the Christian doctrine," then the whole problem of the "foundation of faith" and of the fundamental doctrines was posed in all due form, a problem that had been connected already with the problem of condemnations by Luther, although they had since then not yet succeeded in clearly circumscribing the concept of the "foundation." Here lay difficulties that were to cause a great deal of trouble especially for Orthodoxy.[157]

One more facet of the problem of condemnations must be mentioned, a facet which is frequently touched in the Formula of Concord but not fully clarified. This is at the same time a facet of the issue that places the decisions of the Formula of Concord directly into the large context of the problem of condemnations as it has evolved since the days of primitive Christianity: What might be called the operation or the function of the *Damnamus?* It seems that on this point we may properly expect special solutions from the Formula of Concord since in distinction from the earlier symbols it makes statements *about* the *Damnamus,* its meaning and its validity, for the first time. We may properly leave out of consideration the possibility of the curse or the imprecation by means of which a person could *de facto* be told to "go to the devil," as well as the intention constantly imputed to the Lutherans by the opposition of using the *Damnamus* as a device to surrender a troublesome opponent to the police. It is beyond question that under certain circumstances a verdict of condemnation could set the inquisitorial penal apparatus of the government in motion. However, this secondary executive power has no direct connection whatever with the *Damnamus* as such. Furthermore, in the Lutheran *Damnamus* there is hardly a trace of the disciplinary significance that constituted the essence of the medieval anathema. Doctrinal discipline and church discipline, *Damnamus* and excommunication have no immediate relationship to each other. But what about the "church-divisive" effect of the *Damnamus?*

It is striking that the Formula of Concord evidently did not reflect on this question especially. For the Luther of 1544 it could follow from the condemnation that the one struck by it could be denied intercession or be certified as one to be completely avoided and "left to his own devices." Such language is not used in the Formula of Concord. In the Apology Melanchthon had stated that those who believed otherwise and to whom the condemnations of the ancient creeds applied were "outside the church of Christ." There is no reason to assume that the Formula of Concord took a different position. In principle it, too, put the heresies of the ancient church on the same level with those of the Reformation century. Yet a certain restraint is unmistakable. The Lutheran princes stated that they were "not at all (minded) to tolerate" the "stiff-necked teachers and blasphemers" in their "lands, churches, and schools." [158] Otherwise, as already stated, they did not intend definitively to deny the individual false teacher his soul's salvation nor to condemn entire churches. Apparently no effort was made to clarify the rupture of fellowship in individual cases or even knowingly and intentionally to widen the gulf as much as possible. They knew that in the fellowship of the Lutheran faith they had *the* church, in accordance with Augsburg Confession VII. But they did not forget that the boundaries of the church of Christ do not coincide with those who are in the Lutheran fellowship of faith. Just as Luther was always conscious of the fact that true believers were to be found also under the dominion of the Roman Antichrist, so the Formula of Concord emphasized that outside the Lutheran Church there are "many pious, innocent people" who most certainly belong to the church of Christ. And in spite of the *Damnamus* the conversation with those of another confession was allowed to continue, even and especially in the Eucharistic controversy, though an attentive listening to the other side was often enough made impossible because of the noise of the polemics. Doubtless the conviction remained unbroken that the heretic, who "stubbornly" undermines the "foundation of the faith," according to Titus 3:11 has his punishment. Unshaken, too, remained the obligation for the church and her servants to attest this condition to the heretic and to all Christians by means of the *Damnamus* and to "convict the gainsayer." Yet it may be said that the center of gravity lay less in this punitive function than in the teaching office that is to serve one's own church; less in the witness against the false teacher than in the warning signal for Christians who have not yet been captured by false teaching but are perhaps threatened by it.

At this point that strict adherence to the issues, that has been characteristic of the condemnation since Luther, comes into its own once more. By virtue of it the condemnation was lifted above the sphere of private scholarly polemics and beyond the circle of the church-political struggle for power. Unmistakably the Formula of Concord understood once again that the

Damnamus did not exist for its own sake, that it did not establish limits for the sake of the limitation. The *Damnamus* stands and falls with the doctrinal difference to the extent that this difference is of a kind to affect the "foundation of the faith." This much had become clear as a result of the debates concerning the condemnation: Where the seemingly peripheral *Damnamus* was attacked, the suspicion at once suggested itself that behind the criticism, though frequently justified in some detail, there lay concealed an uncertainty in the central points of evangelical truth. Against this background the *Damnamus* as understood by the Formula of Concord is seen in its proper light: It bears the character of a sign, a warning signal, and as such it must above all be evaluated positively—as pointing to the issue, its seriousness and its importance. The antithesis exists in fact only for the sake of the thesis and must be used in its service. This means that it serves to warn, instruct, and guide the members of one's own church. In this sense F. H. R. Frank, the interpreter of the Formula of Concord, has undoubtedly hit the mark in defining the condemnations of the Formula of Concord as "the negative expressions of the conscience that is bound by the Word of God in the first place with reference to one's own position toward the articles of faith as fundamental." [159]

Here, too, one should again raise the question that had cropped up already when the Gnesio-Lutherans treated the problem of condemnation: Is the line of demarcation between pure doctrine and false doctrine still determined so strictly and exclusively by the witness to the Gospel that creates faith as it was in the case of Luther? Must not the way that leads from the salvation grasped by faith as the "foundation of faith" to the establishment of fundamental *articles* of faith have had fateful consequences also for one's understanding of the condemnation? In fact there can be no doubt that since Luther a retrograde movement has set in—not indeed, as in the Middle Ages, in the direction of becoming frozen in forms of church discipline and canon law, but in the direction of becoming objectified in a different way and of being characterized by a linking of the *Damnamus* with a quantitatively determined concept of "pure doctrine." Certainly the *Damnamus* receives its rightful place in the area of the church's teaching office and not in an area where an individual must make decisions in matters of faith. Invoking the *Damnamus*, as Pappus did, against one who had the intention of "believing what he wished," constituted a serious distortion of the problem, a distortion that threatened to lose sight of the necessary distinction between erring faith and erroneous teaching. The duty of the church's teaching office to watch over doctrine — and that means, first of all, the proper preaching of the Word — and the duty to distinguish between true and false doctrine and to reject false doctrine was something that could not and might not be doubted in the Lutheran Church. Luther himself never thought of making any concessions here. But now everything depended on the manner of defining the concept of doctrine. Luther could speak of the "proper doctrine that a Christian must know" only in living confession of the Lord, who is Himself the Word. However, the list of "things to be believed," or the variously ranked "fundamental articles of faith" as arranged by the epigones,[160] lie on a different level insofar as in them that "doctrinaire attitude" is precipitated that was to become the destiny of the later Orthodoxy — not, indeed, only in the Lutheran Church.[161] The Word as event, as God's speaking and acting, recedes into the background. "What is intended to be a ministry through which doctrine assists the hearer to appropriate the Word turns into a captivity, a process that progressively turns the Word into doctrine."[162] This indicates the decisive departure from Luther that becomes increasingly noticeable in all areas of preaching and of theology in the 16th century and that necessarily affects the *Damnamus* also. The Word is no longer heard and grasped primarily as the "living voice of the Gospel," but in the form of doctrine it becomes something that can be used to render theological judgments. In this way the path is opened for the progressive development of a theory of fundamental doctrines, and this development in turn offers enlarged possibilities for the identification of heretical aberrations in doctrine and thus for the application of the *Damnamus*. The intensified study of the authority and the limits of the *Damnamus* as deposited in the statements of the Formula of Concord is unable to call a halt to this development.

This, in conclusion, permits us to see the point at which today's reflection on the *Damnamus* ought to start. It is certain that the *Damnamus* of the 16th century, through its association with the position regarding fundamental doctrines, belongs into the context of that fateful development toward a "doctrinaire attitude." Yet it is equally certain that the *Damnamus*, rightly understood, must continue to stand as the mark of an antithesis that reaches down to the very "foundation of the faith," remembering that this foundation is not to be defined on the basis of quantitative, objectivized concepts of doctrine but has its place in an encounter with the living Lord who attests Himself in the Word. Wherever a divergence appears that is "fundamental" in this sense, the church's teaching office cannot evade the responsibility of drawing boundary lines. To give expression to this task of drawing boundary lines the Lutheran Symbols offer the services of the *Damnamus*.

The condemnations expressed in the theological declaration of Barmen in 1934 show in an ecclesiastically legitimate way that such boundaries in repelling new heresies can still be drawn today. These declarations also demonstrate how this can be accomplished. Whether and to what extent the boundary lines of the Reformation century as drawn by the *Damnamus* of the Lutheran Symbols can still be maintained today can be decided only on the basis of rethinking the inherited doctrinal differences. In any case the Lutheran Church would contradict her own confessions if she were not constantly receptive to, and ready for, a revision of the earlier condemnations. Precisely in this sense the *Damnamus* is a question that is addressed to the Lutheran Church and that demands an answer.

Notes to Chapter 13

[99] For the most complete overview of these events see Ernst Wolf's historical introduction to the Formula of Concord (*Bekenntnisschriften*, p. XLIf.).

[100] Reprinted in Th. Pressel, "Churfuerst Ludwig von der Pfalz und die Konkordienformel," *Zeitschrift fuer die historische Theologie*, 1867, pp. 464f. See also the letter of Elector August to Chemnitz, in Ph. J. Rehtmeyer, *Der beruehmten Stadt Braunschweig Kirchen-Historie*, III (Brunswick, 1710), Supplements, p. 313.

[101] *Bekenntnisschriften*, p. 756, n. 1.

[102] Pressel, pp. 537f.

[103] *Bekenntnisschriften*, p. 756, n. 1.

[104] Pressel, pp. 542f.; *Bekenntnisschriften*, p. 757 (Apparatus to line 1).

[105] *Book of Concord*, pp. 11–13.

[106] Antitheses in the Controverted Articles, ibid., 506–508; see above pp. 155–156.

[107] F. H. R. Frank, *Die Theologie der Concordienformel*, I (Erlangen, 1858), 23.

[108] *Book of Concord*, pp. 506f.

[109] **Ibid., p. 507.**

[110] Ibid., p. 506.

[111] Ibid., p. 507.

[112] Ibid., p. 507.

[113] Ibid., pp. 11, 12, 506.

[114] Ibid., p. 11; also "Duke Julius' Addition" (see above, p. 190, n. 104).

[115] *Book of Concord*, p. 11.

[116] Ibid., pp. 506f.

[117] Ibid., p. 493.

[118] Ibid., p. 507.

[119] Ibid., p. 11.

[120] Ibid.

[121] Ibid.

[122] Ibid., p. 12.

[123] Letter of Feb. 8, 1581, reproduced in part in Heppe, IV, 276. Cf. Hospinian, p. 307.

[124] *De libro concordiae, quem vocant, a quibusdam theologis, nomine quorundam ordinum Augustanae Confessionis, edito, Admonitio Christiana, scripta a theologis et ministris ecclesiarum in ditione illustrissimi principis Johannis Casimiri Palatini ad Rhenum* (Neustadt, 1581).

[125] Pp. 244–49.

[126] Ibid., p. 244.

[127] Ibid.

[128] "One part has condemend and still condemns the other part; but no one is judge of both" (p. 247).

[129] See above, p. 49.

[130] See above, pp. 191–192, point 2.

[131] *Apologia oder Verantwortung dess Christlichen Concordien Buchs*, Dresden, 1854), chapter 11: "*Bestendiger Bericht vnd Antwort auff die Klage, das des Gegentheils Lehre zur Vnbilligkeit solte verworffen vnd ausgesetzt werden*" (pp. 193–95). Quite similar also Hutter, *Praefatio apologetica*, foll. f 4b – g 3a.

[132] Hutter, *Praef. apol.*, fol. g 2b.

[133] For the title see pp. 179–180, n. 70.

[134] Part III, foll. 48ff.

[135] Part II, fol. 15; III, fol. 16a.

[136] Hutter, fol. 23b.

[137] Leube, p. 116.

[138] See above, p. 117.

[139] Cf. *Die Bekenntnisschriften der reformierten Kirche*, edited by E. F. Karl Mueller (Leipzig, 1903), pp. 49, 39; 73, 18; 108, 19, and others. – For the Calvinistic treatment of heretics see W. Koehler, *Reformation und Ketzerprozess* (Tuebingen, 1901), where the comment is made on the burning of Servetus (p. 3): "Calvin and his friends did not experience pangs of conscience. For them the burning of heretics was good Protestantism (and still is for the strict Refromed)." Koehler refers to H. H. Kuyper, *Het gereformeerde beginsel en de kerkgeschiedenis* (Leyden, 1900), p. 53. n. 99.

[140] Wuenschbarkeit und Moeglichkeit eines allgemeinen reformierten Glaubensbekenntnisses," *Die Theologie und die Kirche* (Munich, 1928), p. 79.

[141] See above, pp. 166 – 167.

[142] Leube, p. 34.

[143] *Historia der Augspuergischen Confession, wie vnd in welchem verstandt sie vorlaengst von dero genossen vnnd verwandten im Artickel des Heiligen Abendmahls nach der Wittenbergischen Concordiformul Anno 36 ist angenommen, auch wie sie seidhero sonst etlich mal in offentlichen Religionshandlungen ist gemehrt vnd erklaert worden.*

[144] Hutter, fol. 284. The presentation of Heppe (IV, 301ff.) one-sidedly hostile to the concord, has strangely permitted this point to escape him.

[145] Hutter, fol. 286.

[146] Ibid., fol. 285b.

[147] Ibid., fol. 312.

[148] Schluesselburg, III, fol. 662.

[149] W. Koehler, *Religionsgespraech zu Marburg*, p. 25, with reference to v. Schubert, *Bekenntnisbildung und Religionspolitik*, pp. 21ff.

[150] Koehler, p. 25.

[151] Ibid., p. 24.

[152] See above, p. 167.

[153] F. H. R. Frank, I, 3.

[154] Significant is the title of a book published in Danzig, 1648, directed against Latermann of Koenigsberg, a pupil of Calixtus: "Judgments of Orthodox Theologians, in Which the Errors of Dr. John Latermann Are Examined and Condemned."

[155] Cf. G. Hoffmann, *Lehrzucht und Glaubensduldung*, pp. 194f.

[156] See above, p. 170.

[157] Cf. O. Ritschl, I, 300ff.; IV (Goettingen, 1927), 231ff.; M. Keller-Hueschemenger, *Das Problem der Fundamentalartikel bei Johannes Huelsemann in seinem theologiegeschichtlichen Zusammenhang* (Guetersloh, 1939), pp. 37ff.

[158] *Book of Concord*, p. 11.

[159] I, 27.

[160] *Hutterus Redivivus*, 9th ed. (Leipzig, 1858), pp. 23f.

[161] G. Hoffmann, *Lehrzucht und Glaubensduldung*, p. 197.

[162] H. E. Weber, I/2, p. 256.